GW01458159

Blackstone's
POLICE MANUAL

# ROAD TRAFFIC

Blackstone's
POLICE MANUAL

# ROAD TRAFFIC

2000 edition

Fraser Sampson, LLB, LLM, MBA

BLACKSTONE
PRESS LIMITED

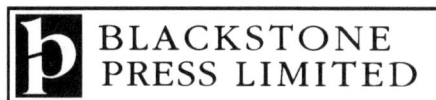

First edition published in Great Britain 1998 by Blackstone Press Limited,
Aldine Place, London W12 8AA. Telephone (020) 8740 2277
www.blackstonepress.com



First edition 1998
Second edition, 1999

ISBN: 1 85431 912 4

British Library Cataloguing in Publication Data
A CIP catalogue record for this book is available from the British Library.

Typeset by Style Photosetting Ltd, Mayfield, East Sussex
Printed by Ashford Colour Press, Gosport, Hampshire

# CONTENTS

CONTENTS

CONTENTS

## CONTENTS

# PREFACE

There is a widely held public view that police officers are the guardians of the law. The assumption is that officers know the law. It is therefore surprising that, given this view, the average police officer is ill equipped when it comes to law books. Many police officers will remember with affection the old *Consolidated Guide*. Some will even remember the much loved works of Moriarty and Baker & Wilkie. Interestingly, none of these books were official books but they became the *vade-mecum* of many police officers.

Police officers have not only to know the law, they have to understand it. In the past police officers and support staff have had to choose between books written for lawyers which have too much law on too many pages and books supposedly written for police officers which have too little law on too many pages.

*Blackstone's Police Manuals* are designed for all police officers. They have been written by police officers who understand the problems that confront officers on a daily basis. They are designed to be read by probationers, sergeants and inspectors, and it is assumed that even more senior police officers will find them useful.

The Manuals are fully indexed and cross-referenced and are published each year to keep them up to date, thus doing away with the need for inserts or supplements. More importantly for OSPRE candidates, if the law isn't in the latest edition of the Manual, it won't be in the exam. This edition contains a number of paragraphs — all in chapter 1 — that appear with a vertical rule in the margin. This is to signify that the material has only been included for completeness and will NOT be tested in the promotion examination syllabus.

The legal regulation of road traffic is a highly specialised subject. Much of it is contained in subordinate legislation which is frequently amended, extended or appended.

Covering the key principles and the content of the various syllabuses, this Manual is intended to help readers navigate their way through that legal regulation, rather than drown them in its volume and complexity.

Tackling any subject which ranges from the breaking of speed limits by police drivers to the specifications of brake lights on steam-powered road-rollers calls for some judicious pruning. As with even the best prepared speeches, it will be felt by some that I have mentioned things which don't deserve to be included and left out things which don't deserve to be excluded. In keeping with such speeches, I apologise to both groups in advance. I know that they say you can't please all the people all of the time, but then 'they' didn't have my Editor!

While every care has been taken to ensure the accuracy of the contents of this manual, neither the author nor the publishers can accept any responsibility for any actions taken, or not taken, on the basis of the information contained in this manual.

# ACKNOWLEDGEMENTS

Writing the first edition of this book to meet the needs of the varied readership was a challenge in itself; to have done it within the many other constraints and pressures that surrounded the project in its first year made the task a little more challenging than I would have liked. The many and varied contributions from police officers, Force Training Managers, trainers, lawyers and others have helped shape this second edition.

It would be difficult here to thank everyone individually but I would like to thank the following people for their helpful suggestions: Tim Batten (Leicestershire); Mark Bird (Essex); Jeremy Parkhurst (North Wales); Mark Redpath (Surrey); John Willet (Sussex)

I would particularly like to thank: Stuart Fairclough of No 1 Area Training Unit, Metropolitan Police; Paul Murphy of Greater Manchester Police; George Cooper from Northamptonshire Police and David Anson for their painstaking work and (relatively) painless feedback. I would also like to thank the Crown Prosecution Service for permission to include the CPS National Casework Guidelines: Driving Offences Charging Standard.

Thanks also to Alistair, Heather, Mandy and Richard at Blackstone and, of course, to CC, TA, TJL and now AC for their patience and support in this as in all things.

# TABLE OF CASES

## TABLE OF CASES

## TABLE OF CASES

## TABLE OF CASES

## TABLE OF CASES

# TABLE OF STATUTES

# TABLE OF STATUTORY INSTRUMENTS

## TABLE OF STATUTORY INSTRUMENTS

## TABLE OF STATUTORY INSTRUMENTS

# CHAPTER ONE

# CLASSIFICATIONS AND CONCEPTS

## 1.1 Introduction

The majority of the most common road traffic definitions can be found in ss. 185 and 192 of the Road Traffic Act 1988. However, there are some other definitions which are specifically set out in the relevant piece of legislation, the most obvious examples being those relating to the construction and use of road vehicles (**see chapter 9**) and driving licences (**see chapter 11**).

The definition of a particular vehicle will generally be determined by its size, weight and construction; on occasions (as with recovery vehicles — **see para. 1.2.6**), it will also be determined by the way in which the vehicle is used.

In approaching any situation involving road traffic legislation it is critical to establish the exact definition *as it applies to that particular piece of legislation.*

This chapter sets out the more commonly-encountered definitions which are referred to, where appropriate, throughout the rest of this book. Where different definitions apply, they are included in the relevant chapter. For instance, 'large goods vehicles' and passenger carrying vehicles' as defined under s. 121 of the Road Traffic Act 1988 are dealt with in **chapter 13**.

## 1.2 The Definitions

Most of the more commonly-used definitions can be found in the Road Traffic Act 1988 but many are duplicated in other legislation (e.g. the Road Vehicles (Construction and Use) Regulations 1986, as amended).

### 1.2.1 Motor Vehicles and Mechanically Propelled Vehicles

The definition of a 'motor vehicle' which will apply in most cases can be found in s. 185 of the Road Traffic Act 1988. Section 185(1) defines a motor vehicle as a mechanically propelled vehicle intended or adapted for use on roads. (Similar definitions of motor vehicles, motor cars etc. can be found under the Road Traffic Regulation Act 1984, s. 136 and the Road Vehicles (Construction and Use) Regulations 1986, reg. 3.)

If a vehicle is not intended or adapted for use on a road it will not be a motor vehicle for these purposes. Whether a vehicle is so intended or adapted is a question of fact to be decided in each case.

A mechanically propelled vehicle is, quite simply, a vehicle that is constructed so that it can be propelled mechanically. If the vehicle is so constructed, it does not cease to be 'mechanically propelled' just because the mechanism is not being used to propel it at the relevant time. Therefore a motor-assisted pedal cycle (but not an *electrically* assisted one; see below) has been held to be a mechanically propelled vehicle even when it is being pedalled (*Floyd* v *Bush* [1953] 1 WLR 242). So the test as to whether a vehicle is 'mechanically propelled' is one of construction rather than use (see *McEachran* v *Hurst* [1978] RTR 462). The prosecution bears the burden of showing that a vehicle meets the requirements of being 'mechanically propelled' (*Reader* v *Bunyard* [1987] RTR 406).

The test will be an objective one which looks at the *raison d'être* of the vehicle's design; it does not look at the intention of the owner (*Chief Constable of Avon and Somerset* v *F (A Juvenile)* [1987] RTR 378).

Note that a motor vehicle continues to be such if it is towed by another vehicle (*Cobb* v *Whorton* [1971] RTR 392), and a car which is rebuilt for off road racing continues to be 'intended' for use on a road even though those rebuilding it never intended to use it so again (*Nichol* v *Leach* [1972] RTR 476).

Dumper trucks intended for use solely on construction sites will probably not be 'motor vehicles' but, if you are able to adduce evidence that they *are suitable* for use on a road, they may be held to be motor vehicles (*Daley* v *Hargreaves* [1961] 1 All ER 552).

'Mechanically propelled' generally includes steam and electrically powered vehicles (*Elieson* v *Parker* (1917) 81 JP 265). It does not include electrically assisted *pedal cycles* (**see chapter 15**). However, in a Scottish case, 'mechanically propelled' has been held to include a van powered by an electric motor with onboard storage batteries (*McMorrow* v *Vannet* 1998 SLT 1171).

Removing an engine from a vehicle does not stop it from being 'mechanically propelled' if you can show that the engine could easily be replaced (*Newberry* v *Simmonds* [1961] 2 All ER 318) or, in a case like *McMorrow* above, by taking the batteries out. A car with a flat battery is still a mechanically propelled vehicle (*R* v *Paul* [1952] NI 61).

Section 189 specifies which vehicles will *not* be treated as motor vehicles; they include pedestrian controlled vehicles and some implements for cutting grass.

### 1.2.2 Passenger Vehicles

A 'passenger vehicle' is defined under reg. 3(2) of the Road Vehicles (Construction and Use) Regulations 1986 (SI 1986 No. 1078) as being a vehicle 'constructed solely for the carriage of passengers and their effects'.

The test to be applied to a vehicle in order to see if it falls within the definition of a 'passenger vehicle' is by asking whether or not at the material time the vehicle was of a type that would ordinarily be used for the carriage of passengers and their effects (*Flower Freight Co. Ltd* v *Hammond* [1963] 1 QB 275). The inclusion of the word 'solely' in the definition means that vehicles ordinarily used for the carriage of passengers and their effects *or* the carriage of goods will not be 'passenger vehicles' (*Flower Freight Co. Ltd*).

If a passenger vehicle is constructed or adapted to carry more than 8 but no more than 16 passengers it will be a 'mini-bus', and if more than 16 seated passengers it will be a 'large bus' (reg. 3(2)).

References to passengers do not include the driver for this definition.

A large bus as defined above which has a maximum gross weight of 7.5 tonnes and having a maximum speed exceeding 60mph is a 'coach'. (For large passenger carrying vehicles, **see chapter 13.)**

### 1.2.3 Goods Vehicles

Although some goods vehicles will also fall under the categories above (e.g. motor cars), 'goods vehicles' are themselves defined under s. 192(1) of the Road Traffic Act 1988 as motor vehicles constructed or adapted for use for the carriage of goods or a trailer so constructed or adapted. 'Goods' for these purposes includes goods or burden of any description. Goods vehicles are further categorised into 'large' goods vehicles and 'medium-sized' goods vehicles. For large goods vehicles **see chapter 13**. Medium-sized goods vehicles are defined under s. 108(1) of the 1988 Act as motor vehicles constructed or adapted to carry or haul goods, which are not adapted to carry more than nine persons including the driver and the permissible maximum weight of which exceeds 3.5 tonnes but not 7.5 tonnes (including a combination of such a motor vehicle and a trailer where the relevant maximum weight of the trailer does not exceed 750 kg).

### 1.2.4 Motor Cycles, Motor Bicycles and Mopeds

Confusingly there are differences in definition between motor cycles, motor bicycles, large motor bicycles and mopeds. In practice, the same machine may fall into a number of these definitions. Again, it is important to identify in what context the definition is used.

#### Motor Cycle

The general definition of a *motor cycle* can be found — alongside most of the other important general definitions — under s. 185(1) of the Road Traffic Act 1988. Section 185(1) defines a motor cycle as 'a mechanically propelled vehicle, not being an invalid carriage, with less than four wheels and the weight of which unladen does not exceed 410 kilograms'. This definition would include some three-wheeler cars and pedestrian controlled vehicles.

For the purposes of Part III of the 1988 Act — the part that deals with licensing (**see chapter 11**) — s. 108 creates further definitions of:

- A motor bicycle.
- A moped

#### Motor Bicycle

Under s. 108(1) a motor bicycle is defined as:

> *. . . a motor vehicle which—*
> *(a) has two wheels, and*
> *(b) has a maximum design speed exceeding 45 kilometres per hour and, if powered by an internal combustion engine, has a cylinder capacity exceeding 50 cubic centimetres, and includes a combination of such a motor vehicle and a side-car, . . .*

## Moped

Also under s. 108(1), a moped is defined as:

> *. . . a motor vehicle which has fewer than four wheels and—*
> *(a) in the case of a vehicle the first use (as defined in regulations made for the purpose of section 97(3)(d) of this Act) of which occurred before 1st August 1977, has a cylinder capacity not exceeding 50 cubic centimetres and is equipped with pedals by means of which the vehicle is capable of being propelled, and*
> *(b) in any other case, has a maximum design speed not exceeding 50 kilometres per hour and, if propelled by an internal combustion engine, has a cylinder capacity not exceeding 50 cubic centimetres,*

These definitions are really sub-divisions of motor cycles and are relevant for the purposes of driver licensing.

### Learner Motor Bicycle

Section 97 of the Road Traffic Act 1988 deals with the granting of driving licences (as to which **see chapter 11**). In particular, s. 97 sets out the requirements for, and restrictions on, provisional licences and, in that context, makes reference to *learner* motor bicycles, introducing yet another sub-division of motor cycles. A learner motor bicycle is defined at s. 97(5) as a motor bicycle which is either:

- propelled by electric power; or
- the cylinder capacity of its engine does not exceed 125 cc and the maximum net power output of its engine does not exceed 11Kw.

### Large Motor Bicycles and Standard Motor Bicycles

As if all this were not confusing enough, the Motor Vehicles (Driving Licences) Regulations 1996 (as to which **see chapter 11**) create another sub-division; that of 'large' and 'standard' motor cycles.

Large motor bicycles are defined (under reg. 3) as being:

- in the case of a motor bicycle without a sidecar, a bicycle the engine of which has a maximum net power output exceeding 25Kw or which has a power to weight ratio exceeding 0.16Kw per kilogram; or
- in the case of a motor bicycle and sidecar combination, a combination having a power to weight ratio exceeding 0.16Kw per kilogram.

For the purposes of reg. 3, a 'standard' motor bicycle is a motor bicycle that does not fit into the above category (i.e. it is the opposite of a 'large' motor bicycle).

### Minimum Ages

The table of minimum ages for holding or obtaining licences in respect of certain vehicles is set out at s. 101 of the Road Traffic Act 1988 (**see appendix 1**). Regulation 7 of the 1996 Regulations increases the minimum age for motor bicycles if the vehicle is a 'large motor bicycle' (except, as you might have guessed, in certain circumstances). The definition of a 'large' motor bicycle is also relevant for the purposes of a full licence being used as a provisional entitlement to drive some other vehicles (**see chapter 11**).

**Summary**

So, to summarise, the definition of a motor cycle, which will be of general application, can be found under the Road Traffic Act 1988, s. 185.

In relation to the *licensing of drivers of vehicles under Part III of that Act*, there are further classifications of motor bicycles and mopeds. These are defined at s. 108 of the 1988 Act.

In relation to the *licensing of learner drivers generally*, s. 97 of the 1988 Act refers to a further classification, namely a learner motor bicycle.

And finally, in relation to the *minimum ages for holding and obtaining a driving licence*, and *the provisional entitlements of other licences*, the 1996 Regulations make reference to 'large' motor bicycles and their opposites, 'standard' motor bicycles.

Having considered all these, it is difficult to look at a motor bike in the same way again!

### 1.2.5 Trailer

A 'trailer' is defined, for most purposes, under s. 185(1) of the Road Traffic Act 1988 as a vehicle drawn by a motor vehicle (however, a different definition applies under Regulation EEC 3820/85 in relation to drivers' hours).

When a motor vehicle is towed by another motor vehicle, the latter still falls within the category of motor vehicle but can also be regarded as a 'trailer' (*Milstead* v *Sexton* [1964] Crim LR 474).

As 'vehicle' is not defined in the Road Traffic Act 1988 virtually anything would appear to be capable of amounting to a vehicle under the right circumstances, even a chicken shed on wheels (see *Garner* v *Burr* [1951] 1 KB 31) or a hut (*Horn* v *Dobson* 1933 JC 1).

Where a 'heavy motor car' or 'motor car' (not being an articulated bus) draws a trailer with at least 20 per cent of the trailer's load being borne by the drawing vehicle, the combination will be regarded as an 'articulated vehicle' (Road Vehicles (Construction and Use) Regulations 1986, reg. 3(2)).

### 1.2.6 Other Definitions

**Motor Car**

Section 185(1) of the Road Traffic Act 1988 also defines a 'motor car':

> . . .
> *'motor car' means a mechanically propelled vehicle, not being a motor cycle or an invalid carriage, which is constructed itself to carry a load or passengers and the weight of which unladen—*
> *(a) if it is constructed solely for the carriage of passengers and their effects, is adapted to carry not more than seven passengers exclusive of the driver and is fitted with tyres of such type as may be specified in regulations made by the Secretary of State, does not exceed 3050 kilograms,*

*(b) if it is constructed or adapted for use for the conveyance of goods or burden of any description, does not exceed 3050 kilograms, or 3500 kilograms if the vehicle carries a container or containers for holding for the purposes of its propulsion any fuel which is wholly gaseous at 17.5 degrees Celsius under a pressure of 1.013 bar or plant and materials for producing such fuel,*

*(c) does not exceed 2540 kilograms in a case not falling within sub-paragraph (a) or (b) above, . . .*

However, in relation to the law regulating driving instruction (Part V of the Road Traffic Act 1988) there is a further definition of a 'motor car'. This definition is a motor vehicle other than an invalid carriage or motor cycle which is not constructed or adapted to carry more than nine persons including the driver and which has a maximum gross weight not exceeding 3.5 tonnes (s. 141A).

### Heavy Motor Car

Section 185(1) defines a heavy motor car as:

*. . . a mechanically propelled vehicle, not being a motor car, which is constructed itself to carry a load or passengers and the weight of which unladen exceeds 2540 kilograms, . . .*

### Small Vehicle

For the purposes of driver licensing (Part III of the Road Traffic Act 1988), a small vehicle is defined as a motor vehicle other than an invalid carriage, motor bicycle or moped, which is not constructed/adapted to carry more than nine persons including the driver and which has a maximum gross weight not exceeding 3.5 tonnes (and including a combination of such a vehicle and a trailer) (s. 108(1)).

### Locomotives

Section 185(1) also defines locomotives as:

*'heavy locomotive' means a mechanically propelled vehicle which is not constructed itself to carry a load other than any of the excepted articles and the weight of which unladen exceeds 11690 kilograms, . . .*

*'light locomotive' means a mechanically propelled vehicle which is not constructed itself to carry a load other than any of the excepted articles and the weight of which unladen does not exceed 11690 kilograms but does exceed 7370 kilograms, . . .*

The 'excepted articles' referred to in s. 185(1) are water, fuel, accumulators and other equipment used for the purpose of propulsion, loose tools and loose equipment (s. 185(2)).

### Motor Tractor

The definition of a motor tractor can be found, unsurprisingly, in s. 185(1), which states:

*. . . 'motor tractor' means a mechanically propelled vehicle which is not constructed itself to carry a load, other than the excepted articles, and the weight of which unladen does not exceed 7370 kilograms, . . .*

The 'excepted articles' are those listed above.

### Invalid Carriage

An invalid carriage is defined (under s. 185(1)) as being:

*. . . a mechanically propelled vehicle the weight of which unladen does not exceed 254 kilograms and which is specially designed and constructed, and not merely adapted, for the use of a person suffering from some physical defect or disability and is used solely by such a person, . . .*

An invalid carriage complying with the regulations under the Chronically Sick and Disabled Persons Act 1970 will not be treated as a motor vehicle under the Road Traffic Act 1988.

### Heavy Commercial Vehicle

A 'heavy commercial vehicle' is defined under s. 138 of the Road Traffic Regulation Act 1984 (and also under s. 20 of the Road Traffic Act 1988) as any goods vehicle with an operating weight exceeding 7.5 tonnes.

### Recovery Vehicle

A recovery vehicle' is defined under the Vehicle Excise and Registration Act 1994, sch. 1:

. . .

*'recovery vehicle' means a vehicle which is constructed or permanently adapted primarily for any one or more of the purposes of lifting, towing and transporting a disabled vehicle.*

*(3) A vehicle is not a recovery vehicle if at any time it is used for a purpose other than—*

*(a) the recovery of a disabled vehicle,*

*(b) the removal of a disabled vehicle from the place where it became disabled to premises at which it is to be repaired or scrapped,*

*(c) the removal of a disabled vehicle from premises to which it was taken for repair to other premises at which it is to be repaired or scrapped,*

*(d) carrying fuel and other liquids required for its propulsion and tools and other articles required for the operation of, or in connection with, apparatus designed to lift, tow or transport a disabled vehicle, and*

*(e) any purpose prescribed for the purposes of this sub-paragraph by regulations made by the Secretary of State.*

The equipment or apparatus for lifting, towing or transporting disabled vehicles must be permanently mounted or form an integral part of the vehicle. Therefore, a vehicle, which was in effect a mobile workshop that had towing and lifting capabilities, was not a recovery vehicle as defined above (*Vehicle Inspectorate* v *Richard Read Transport Ltd*, 25 November 1996, unreported).

## 1.2.7 Key Concepts

### Weights

The weight of a vehicle will often determine its classification and the use to which it may be put, together with the licensing conditions of those who drive it.

Reference will usually be made to the *laden* weight or the *gross* weight of a vehicle in offences involving its construction and use, while offences concerning the speed and excise duty of larger vehicles will usually be concerned with *laden* and *unladen* weight.

Calculation of a vehicle's *unladen* weight for most purposes is contained under s. 190 of the Road Traffic Act 1988.

Most locomotives, motor tractors and heavy motor cars are required to show their *unladen* weight, either on their nearside or on the relevant plating certificate(s) (see Road Vehicles (Construction and Use) Regulations 1986, regs 66 and 71).

For construction and use purposes, the *gross* weight under reg. 3(2) of the 1986 Regulations will be:

- for motor vehicles – the sum of the weights transmitted to the road surface by all its wheels.
- for trailers – the sum of the weights transmitted to the road surface by all its wheels *and* of any weight of the trailer which is imposed on the drawing vehicle.

*Axle* weights are, generally, the sum of the weights transmitted to the road surface by all the wheels of that axle.

### Accident

'Accidents' are relevant in a number of road traffic offences (e.g. drink driving (**see chapter 5**) and notices of intended prosecution (**see chapter 3**)).

Apart from 'reportable' accidents (**see chapter 4**), there is no single definition of what an accident is. Rather, the courts have warned against creating any hard and fast rule as to what will amount to an 'accident' (*Chief Constable of West Midlands Police* v *Billingham* [1979] RTR 446).

The general test which courts will apply is whether an ordinary person would say that there had been an accident in all the circumstances.

Such an approach will include, not only an unintended occurrence or an inadvertent act, but also a deliberate act by a driver such as ramming a gate (*Chief Constable of Staffordshire* v *Lees* [1981] RTR 506).

There is no need for the involvement of another vehicle in an 'accident' (*R* v *Pico* [1971] RTR 500).

### Driver

It is possible for more than one person to be the 'driver' of a vehicle: s. 192(1) of the Road Traffic Act 1988 makes provision for the 'steersman' of a motor vehicle also to be included in the definition of 'driver' (except for the offence of causing death by dangerous driving under s. 1). Where one person sits in the driving seat while another reaches across them and operates the steering wheel, both can be 'drivers' of the vehicle (*Tyler* v *Whatmore* [1976] RTR 83). Similarly, a learner driver and his or her instructor may be the drivers of a vehicle (*Langman* v *Valentine* [1952] 2 All ER 803).

The only situation where the above will not apply is in cases of causing death by dangerous driving under s. 1 of the Road Traffic Act 1988 (**see chapter 2**).

Whether a person was actually *the* driver of a vehicle at a particular time cannot be inferred from the fact that they are also the owner; more evidence of their actual involvement in the driving of the vehicle will be required (*R* v *Collins (George)* [1994] RTR 216).

### Driving

Although s. 192 of the Road Traffic Act 1988 provides that a 'steersman' can be a driver of a vehicle under certain circumstances, it does not define what, or who, the driver of a vehicle is.

There are a number of different situations where a person can be said to be 'driving' a vehicle even though they do not conjure up a picture of conventional driving.

Whether they are 'driving' or not will be a question of fact. This question will be decided by considering the extent to which the person has control of both the direction and movement of the vehicle.

In addition, what the person is actually doing must fall within the ordinary meaning of the word 'driving' (see *McQuaid* v *Anderton* [1980] 3 All ER 540 – defendant steering car which was being towed; held to be driving while disqualified).

Other factors which will be considered by the courts will be:

- How long the defendant had control of the movement and direction of the vehicle (*Jones* v *Pratt* [1983] RTR 54 — the defendant was a passenger who grabbed the wheel to prevent the driver hitting an animal — held not to be 'driving').
- Whether the defendant set the vehicle in motion deliberately (*Rowan* v *Chief Constable of Merseyside, The Times,* 10 December 1985).
- Whether the defendant used the vehicle's controls in order to direct its movement (*Burgoyne* v *Phillips* [1983] RTR 49).

Applying these principles, pushing a car along while steering it has been held not to be driving so far as the law in England and Wales is concerned (*R* v *MacDonagh* [1974] RTR 372) although in Scotland such behaviour would amount to driving (*Ames* v *MacLeod* 1969 JC 1).

For the purposes of road traffic law, motor cycles are 'driven' as opposed to being 'ridden'.

Straddling a motorcycle and 'pedalling' it along with the feet can amount to driving (*Gunnel* v *DPP* [1993] RTR 619).

Kneeling up on the driver's seat of a car and releasing the handbrake briefly has been held to be 'driving' (see *Rowan* above). For the situation relating to what will amount to 'taking' a motor vehicle under the Theft Act 1968 (**see Crime, chapter 12**).

### Attempting to Drive

Whether a person is 'attempting to drive' is also a question of fact and will usually be determined by the principles applying to attempts generally (**see Crime, chapter 3**).

Simply put, these will include acts which are more than merely preparatory to the act of driving (such as opening a car door). The fact that the vehicle is incapable of being driven (say, because the engine is faulty), will not prevent a charge involving an 'attempt' to drive (*R* v *Farrance* [1978] RTR 225).

If a defendant sits in the driver's seat of a car and, being drunk, tries to put their house keys in the ignition, that behaviour may be enough to prove a charge of 'attempting to drive' while unfit (*Kelly* v *Hogan* [1982] RTR 352 *obiter*). **See also chapter 5.**

## In Charge

The principles to be applied when considering whether a person is 'in charge' of a vehicle are set out in *DPP* v *Watkins* [1989] 2 WLR 966. Two different situations might arise:

- Where the defendant is the owner of the vehicle or where they have recently driven it. In these cases it would be for the defendant to show that they were no longer in charge of it and that there was no likelihood of their resuming control at the relevant time (e.g. while they were drunk).

- Where the defendant is not the owner or has not recently driven the vehicle. In these cases the prosecution must show that the defendant was in voluntary control of the vehicle or intended to become so in the immediate future.

In arriving at their decision, courts should consider:

- whether the defendant had the keys for the vehicle

- where the defendant was in relation to the vehicle at the time

- what evidence there is of the defendant's intention to take control of the vehicle.

Note that the supervisor of a learner driver can be 'in charge' of the vehicle and can therefore commit an offence if unfit through drink or drugs at the time (*Langman* v *Valentine* [1952] 2 All ER 803) (**see chapter 5**).

## Owner

'Owner' in relation to a vehicle subject to a hire purchase agreement is defined under the Road Traffic Act 1988, s. 192. Section 192 provides that the 'owner' in such circumstances means the person in possession of the vehicle under that agreement. Whether a person is the owner of a vehicle in any other case is a question of fact to be determined by the court in each case. Facts including the way in which the alleged owner treats and uses the vehicle, whether they have spent any money on its purchase or upkeep and whether they have taken out insurance in relation to it may all be evidence of 'ownership'.

A 'keeper' is different from an owner but again the question will be one of fact for a court. In any enactment relating to the keeping of vehicles on public roads (e.g. vehicle excise offences, **see chapter 12**), a person so 'keeps' a vehicle if he/she causes it to be on such a road for any period, however short, when it is not in use there (Vehicle Excise and Registration Act 1994, s. 62(2)).

Somewhat confusingly, for the purposes of Part II of the Road Traffic Act 1991 (which regulates parking in London), 'the owner of a vehicle shall be taken to be the person by whom the vehicle is kept' (s. 82(2)).

Whereas an owner probably remains as such until they dispose of the vehicle or pass ownership to someone else, a keeper can cease to be so if they temporarily part with the vehicle (e.g. by leaving it with a garage for repairs) (*R* v *Parking Adjudicator, ex parte the Mayor and Burgesses of the London Borough Council of Wandsworth,* 10 July 1996, unreported).

## Automatism

Where a person's movements are beyond his/her control or his/her actions are brought about involuntarily, he/she will not generally be liable at criminal law as the element of *actus reus* is not present (**see Crime, chapter 2**).

A notable example of this is *automatism*. Automatism occurs where the defendant is temporarily deprived of his/her ability to control his/her movements. When this happens to the driver of a vehicle, it may remove his/her liability for certain offences such as driving without due care. This is because there is no willed action or omission by the defendant. It is also highly unlikely that he/she would have the required state of mind (**see chapter 2**).

Such a situation might be brought about by a swarm of bees flying in through the open window of a moving car (*Hill* v *Baxter* [1958] 1 All ER 193) or the driver lapsing into a coma.

If a defendant is suffering from a particular medical condition or is prone to effects which are likely to impair his/her driving ability (such as dizziness – *R* v *Sibbles* [1959] Crim LR 660), he/she has a duty to take reasonable steps to avoid driving when the symptoms are likely to arise. If a diabetic continues to drive while experiencing the start of a hypoglycaemic episode, it is unlikely that the defence of automatism would be available to a charge of careless driving; the diabetic should have stopped driving until the episode had passed (see *Moss* v *Winder* [1981] RTR 37).

Similarly, where the loss of voluntary movement or control is brought about by self-induced measures (such as taking/failing to take medication or by drinking), automatism is not generally available as a defence (*R* v *Quick* [1973] QB 910).

Driving in a state of reduced awareness brought on by the continuous focusing on a long, featureless road (sometimes called 'motorway hypnosis' is not enough to raise the defence of automatism (*Attorney-General's Reference (No. 2 of 1992)* [1993] RTR 337).

For a more detailed examination of this and other general defences, **see Crime, chapter 4**. For the defence of 'mechanical defect', **see chapter 2**.

## Road

A road is defined under s. 192(1) of the Road Traffic Act 1988 as:

> . . . *any highway and any other road to which the public has access, and includes bridges over which a road passes* . . .

This definition (or one very similar to it, e.g. under s. 142(1) of the Road Traffic Regulation Act 1984) is applicable to most occasions where the expression 'road' is used in statutes.

Whether the public has access is a question of fact. If only a restricted section of the public (such as members of a club) has access to a road, that is not enough to make it a 'road' (*Blackmore* v *Chief Constable of Devon and Cornwall, The Times*, 6 December 1984).

Any access enjoyed by the public must be with the agreement of the landowner. As Lord Sands put it in *Blackmore*, the members of the public must not have obtained access 'either by overcoming a physical obstruction or in defiance of prohibition, express or implied'. Therefore roads are capable of being closed or cordoned off in a way that alters their status as such.

In two recent cases, both involving car parks, the Court of Appeal took a very broad approach to the construction of the definition of a 'road' in relation to the requirements for compulsory insurance (**see chapter 6**). The first case, *Clarke* v *Kato*, *The Times*, 29 November 1996, involved a person being struck by an uninsured driver while in the car park behind a parade of shops. The second case, *Cutter* v *Eagle Star Insurance Co. Ltd*, *The Times*, 22 November 1996, involved a passenger being injured while in a vehicle in a multi-storey car park. On appeal to the House of Lords, the plaintiffs in both cases argued that the Road Traffic Act 1988 already made provision for the distinction between roads and car parks and that there was no justification for extending the meaning of the definition of a road beyond its normal meaning. In each of the cases before the House, the car parks were provided solely for the parking of vehicles. The House of Lords accepted the plaintiffs' arguments and overturned the earlier decisions of the Court of Appeal. Whether a particular location falls within the definition under s. 192 of the Road Traffic Act 1988 will ultimately be one of fact for the court to decide, having reference to the character and function of the land in question. Their lordships held that, on that construction, it would only be exceptional circumstances that a car park would be deemed to fall within the definition of a road. Their lordships held that, in the first case, the mere presence of an alleyway which joined onto the car park did not change the ultimate character or purpose of the land while, in the second case, the parking bays within a multi-storey car park could not be regarded as an integral part of the carriageway which led into the car park itself (*Clarke* v *Kato*; *Cutter* v *Eagle Star Insurance Co. Ltd* [1998] 4 All ER 417).

In practical terms, the effect of these decisions will be limited to offences and regulations which are confined to 'roads' (e.g. the requirement for compulsory insurance under s. 143(1)(a) of the Road Traffic Act 1988: **see chapter 6**). Many of the more common or more serious road traffic provisions relate to roads *or* 'public places' (**see below**) and may still be committed in the sorts of places considered by the House of Lords in the above cases.

Car parks and forecourts may, in exceptional cases, be shown to be roads (see *Baxter* v *Middlesex County Council* [1956] Crim LR 561) but the prosecution would need to show that they fell squarely within the definition under s. 192 in the light of *Clarke* v *Kato* above. As well as showing them to be roads, you can also show some pub car parks to be 'public places' — at least during licensing hours — for the purposes of drink/drive offences (*Sandy* v *Martin* [1974] Crim LR 258).

Generally a road stretches to the boundary fences or grass verges adjacent to it, including any pavements (*Worth* v *Brooks* [1959] Crim LR 855).

If a vehicle is partly on a road and partly on some other privately owned land it can be treated as being 'on a road' for the purposes of road traffic legislation (*Randall* v *Motor Insurers' Bureau* [1969] 1 All ER 21).

'Public roads' which are referred to in the Vehicle Excise and Registration Act 1994 are those roads which are repairable at the public expense. Clearly this is a much more restrictive definition than that under the Road Traffic Act 1988.

## Public Place

In order to prove that a place is in fact a 'public place' for the purposes of road traffic offences, it must be shown by the prosecution that:

- those people who are admitted to the place in question are members of the public and are admitted as such, not as members of some special or particular *class* of the public (e.g. people belonging to an exclusive club) or as a result of some special characteristic that is not shared by the public at large; *and*
- those people are so admitted with the permission, express or implied, of the owner of the land in question

(*DPP* v *Vivier* [1991] RTR 205).

Whether a place is in fact a 'public place' will be a question of fact for the court. This means that different magistrates' courts can arrive at different decisions when presented with the same facts. Some examples of places which have been held to qualify as 'public places' are:

- a privately-owned caravan site open to campers (*DPP* v *Vivier* above);
- a school playground used outside school hours as a leisure park by members of the public (*Rodger* v *Normand* 1994 SCCR 861);
- the 'Inward Freight Immigration Lanes' at Dover Eastern Docks (*DPP* v *Coulman* [1993] RTR 230);
- a field used in connection with an agricultural show (*Paterson* v *Ogilvey* 1957 SLT 354);
- a multi-storey car park (*Bowman* v *DPP* [1991] RTR 263).

These requirements should not be confused with the test for whether a piece of land amounts to 'a road' (**see above**).

For a place which is ostensibly *public* in its nature to become a *private* place, either permanently or temporarily, there needs to be some form of physical obstruction to be overcome in order to enter that place (*R* v *Waters* (1963) 107 SJ 275). Therefore a pub landlord, by ordering people to leave the car park of his pub, had not done enough to turn what was a public place (the car park during opening hours) into a private place.

In deciding whether or not a place is in fact a 'public place', magistrates may use their own local knowledge, but must be circumspect in doing so (*Clift* v *Long* [1961] Crim LR 121).

## Highway

A 'highway' is a way over which the public has a right to pass and re-pass by foot, horse or vehicle, or with animals (*Lang* v *Hindhaugh* [1986] RTR 271).

For a highway to exist, there must be some form of 'dedication' of the relevant land to the public and, once so dedicated, it is unlikely that the public status of a highway can be changed.

Unlike a road, a highway does not cease to be such when it is temporarily roped off or closed (*McCrone* v *Rigby (Wigan) Ltd* (1950) 50 LGR 115).

Highways will include public bridleways and footways; they also include public bridges over which they pass.

### Use, Cause or Permit?

The concepts of using, causing or permitting are central to many road traffic offences, particularly in relation to construction and use (**see chapter 9**). They are also relevant in the fixed penalty system which is not available for offences of 'causing or permitting' (**see chapter 14**).

### Use

'Using' has been held to involve an element of 'controlling, managing or operating the vehicle as a vehicle' (*Thomas* v *Hooper* [1986] RTR 1).

The 'using' of a vehicle is generally, though not exclusively, restricted to:

- the driver
- the driver's employer (when the driver is driving the vehicle on the employer's business).

If a person driving a vehicle is doing so in the ordinary course of his/her employer's business, the employer is *using* the vehicle (see e.g. *West Yorkshire Trading Standards Service* v *Lex Vehicle Leasing Ltd* [1996] RTR 170). In such a case you must prove that:

- the defendant (employer) actually owned the vehicle;
- at the relevant time, the driver was employed by the defendant; and
- the driver was driving the vehicle in the ordinary course of his/her employment

(*Jones* v *DPP*, *The Times*, 23 April 1998).

It is immaterial that the employer has not specifically authorised the employee to use the vehicle in such a way — *Richardson* v *Baker* [1976] RTR 56.

If the driver is not an employee then the employer is not using the vehicle, even if that driver is a partner of the firm or has been asked to drive the vehicle by the employer (*Crawford* v *Haughton* [1972] 1 WLR 572). The employer may, however, be shown to be 'causing' or 'permitting' (see below).

If a garage lends one of its vehicles to a customer and the customer then uses the vehicle on his/her own business, the garage cannot be said to be 'using' the vehicle (see *L.F. Dove* v *Tarvin* (1964) 108 SJ 404).

If a vehicle is shown to be a 'motor vehicle' (**see para. 1.2.1**) and on a 'road' (**see para. 1.2.7**), it may be said to be in 'use' even if it is in such a state that it cannot be driven (*Pumbien* v *Vines* [1996] RTR 37). There is now no longer a need to show some element of control or operation of the vehicle by the owner in order to prove 'use'.

The *intention* of the owner is irrelevant in determining whether or not a vehicle was being 'used' at the time of an offence; what matters is that the defendant can be shown to have 'had the use of' that vehicle (*Eden* v *Mitchell* [1975] RTR 425).

Therefore, if a vehicle is not in a roadworthy condition it can still be available for the owner's use even though the owner has no intention of utilising it while it remains in that state.

For the owner of a vehicle to be convicted of 'using' a vehicle without insurance when it is being driven by someone else, you must prove that the defendant was in fact the owner *and* that the driver was his/her employee acting in the course of their employment (*Jones* v *DPP*, *The Times*, 23 April 1998).

It should be noted that the Divisional Court has applied a broader interpretation to the meaning of 'use' when considering offences involving *trailers*. The court held that the owner of a defective trailer who is responsible for putting it on a road should not be able to escape liability for its condition simply by arguing that it was being drawn — and therefore 'used' — by someone else (*N.F.C. Forwarding Ltd* v *DPP* [1989] RTR 239).

A pillion passenger on a motor cycle or a passenger in a car does not generally 'use' the vehicle (see e.g. *Hatton* v *Hall* [1997] RTR 212). However, if a passenger arranges to travel in or on the vehicle for his/her own benefit, he/she will 'use' the vehicle (*Cobb* v *Williams* [1973] RTR 113). A passenger can also 'use' the vehicle if there is an element of 'joint enterprise' (*O'Mahoney* v *Joliffe*, *The Times*, 24 February 1999; see also **Crime, chapter 2**).

### Cause

'Causing' will involve some degree of 'control' or 'dominance' by, or some express mandate from, the *causer*.

Causing requires both positive action and knowledge by the defendant (*Price* v *Cromack* [1975] 1 WLR 988). If the owner of a vehicle is to be shown to have 'caused' an offence to be committed, he/she must be shown to have done something to contribute to it (e.g. by instructing another to drive it) *and also* to have known of any relevant facts (e.g. that it was overloaded) (*Ross Hillman Ltd* v *Bond* [1974] QB 435).

In cases involving employers' vehicles it may be easier to prove 'use' of the vehicle (see above).

Wilful blindness by employers to their employees' unlawful actions (e.g. not completing drivers' records) is not enough to amount to 'causing' the offence (*Redhead Freight Ltd* v *Shulman* [1989] RTR 1).

### Permit

Permitting is less direct or explicit than causing. Permitting involves giving leave or license to do something (see *Houston* v *Buchanan* [1940] 2 All ER 179). The relevant permission (e.g. to use a vehicle in a certain way or subject to some proviso) can be express or it can be inferred by the relevant person (such as where someone is given the use of a friend's car without any conditions being stipulated by the friend).

Generally, in order to prove an offence of 'permitting', you will need to show knowledge by the defendant of the vehicle's *use,* and the *unlawful nature* of that use. However, it is necessary to consider the relevant piece of legislation in each case, together with its intended purpose. (For the situation regarding insurance, **see chapter 6**.)

You cannot 'permit' yourself to do something (*Keene* v *Muncaster* [1980] RTR 377).

If there is any doubt as to which offence is appropriate it is acceptable to charge 'using' *or* 'causing' *or* 'permitting' as alternatives (see *Ross Hillman Ltd* above) but the advice of the local Crown Prosecution Service should be sought.

# CHAPTER TWO

# OFFENCES INVOLVING STANDARDS OF DRIVING

## 2.1 Introduction

This chapter deals with the main offences involving driving below the required standard or in a way which presents a danger to others.

Those offences which involve drink or drugs are covered in **chapter 5**, although the offence of causing death by careless driving while over the prescribed limit is dealt with here.

Reference should also be made, where appropriate, to the CPS charging standards, **see appendix 4**.

When considering the various definitions within the offences (e.g. 'drive', 'motor vehicle'), you should refer to **chapter 1**.

## 2.2 Causing Death by Dangerous Driving

**Offence — Causing Death by Dangerous Driving — Road Traffic Act 1988, s. 1**

*Triable on indictment. Ten years' imprisonment. Obligatory disqualification – minimum two years. Compulsory re-test.*

***(Serious arrestable offence)***

The Road Traffic Act 1988, s. 1 states:

> *A person who causes the death of another person by driving a mechanically propelled vehicle dangerously on a road or other public place is guilty of an offence.*

**Keynote**

This offence applies to a 'mechanically propelled vehicle' — a wider term than 'motor vehicle' (**see chapter 1**) and one which includes dumper trucks, cranes, trials and quad bikes.

It can be committed on a road or in other public places which again give it a wider effect.

Provided the basic elements (mechanically propelled vehicle on a road/public place) are met, you must prove that:

- the defendant caused the death of another person
- the defendant drove dangerously.

### 2.2.1 Causing Death of Another

The death must be that of a person other than the defendant. This has been held (in a Scottish case) to include a foetus which was later born alive but which subsequently died (*McCluskey* v *HM Advocate* [1989] RTR 182).

Note that the offence under s. 1 also amounts to manslaughter (*R* v *Governor of Holloway Prison, ex parte Jennings* [1983] 1 AC 624 and **see Crime, chapter 5**) but it will rarely be charged as such.

The driving by the defendant must be shown to have been *a* cause of the death; it is not necessary to show that it was the sole or even a substantial cause of death (*R* v *Hennigan* [1971] 3 All ER 133). Therefore it is irrelevant whether or not the person killed contributed to the incident which resulted in his/her death.

### 2.2.2 Dangerous Driving

Section 2A of the Road Traffic Act 1988 provides that:

*(1) For the purposes of sections 1 and 2 above a person is to be regarded as driving dangerously if (and, subject to subsection (2) below, only if)—*
*(a) the way he drives falls far below what would be expected of a competent and careful driver, and*
*(b) it would be obvious to a competent and careful driver that driving in that way would be dangerous.*
*(2) A person is also to be regarded as driving dangerously for the purposes of sections 1 and 2 above if it would be obvious to a competent and careful driver that driving the vehicle in its current state would be dangerous.*
*(3) In subsections (1) and (2) above 'dangerous' refers to danger either of injury to any person or of serious damage to property; and in determining for the purposes of those subsections what would be expected of, or obvious to, a competent and careful driver in a particular case, regard shall be had not only to the circumstances of which he could be expected to be aware but also to any circumstances shown to have been within the knowledge of the accused.*
*(4) In determining for the purposes of subsection (2) above the state of a vehicle, regard may be had to anything attached to or carried on or in it and to the manner in which it is attached or carried.*

**Keynote**

This is clearly an *objective* test which focuses, at s. 2A(1)(a) on the manner of driving rather than the defendant's state of mind and, at (b) on what would have been obvious to a hypothetical 'competent and careful driver'. An example is where a diabetic driver drives on a road in the knowledge that he/she is likely to suffer a hypoglycaemic episode (*R* v *Marison* [1997] RTR 457).

An example of the application of s. 2A(2) can be seen in a recent Scottish case where the defendant drove a small go-kart on a busy road. The nature of the kart and the likelihood of its not being seen by other motorists were held to be features which could be taken into account in assessing whether or not the defendant's driving was in fact 'dangerous' (*Carstairs* v *Hamilton* 1997 SCCR 311).

The standard of driving must be shown to have fallen far below that expected of a competent and careful driver; minor driver errors would not amount to such behaviour (but contrast offences under s. 3 below).

In determining what would have been obvious to a competent and careful driver, ss. 2A(3) and (4) introduce a *subjective* element by taking account of circumstances known to the defendant. This unusual mixture of tests means that, although a defendant's behaviour will be judged against the ordinary standards of competent and careful drivers, the defendant's conduct will also be assessed in the light of facts personally known to him/her (such as knowledge of the risk of a load falling off the vehicle (*R* v *Crossman* [1986] RTR 49)). If the vehicle involved was in a dangerous condition it is important that you prove either:

- that the dangerous condition would itself have been obvious to a competent or careful driver; or

- that the defendant actually *knew* of its dangerous condition

(see *R* v *Strong* [1995] Crim LR 428).

The defendant's belief, however honestly held, as to the conditions surrounding his/her driving at the time are not relevant to the issue of whether he/she drove competently and carefully (see *R* v *Collins* [1997] RTR 439). In *Collins* a police driver went through a red traffic light at almost 100 mph colliding with another vehicle and killing two people. His belief that the traffic at the lights was being operated by other officers was not a relevant factor for the jury in considering whether or not his driving had been dangerous. (For police drivers generally, **see para. 2.10**.)

## 2.3 Dangerous Driving

**Offence — Dangerous Driving — Road Traffic Act 1988, s. 2**
*Triable either way. Two years' imprisonment and/or a fine on indictment; six months' imprisonment and/or statutory maximum summarily. Obligatory disqualification. Compulsory re-test.*
**(*No specific power of arrest*)**

The Road Traffic Act 1988, s. 2 states:

*A person who drives a mechanically propelled vehicle dangerously on a road or other public place is guilty of an offence.*

**Keynote**

The elements of this offence are the same as those for s. 1.

Evidence showing how the particular vehicle was being driven before the incident itself may be given in support of the charge of dangerous driving. Where the dangerous driving leads to an accident, the court may allow a police officer who is an expert in the investigation of accidents to give evidence of opinion as to the cause of that accident (*R* v *Oakley* [1979] RTR 417).

In addition, there is a rarely used offence of causing bodily harm by wanton or furious driving or racing (Offences Against the Person Act 1861, s. 35). The offence applies to any vehicle or carriage and is not restricted to roads.

## 2.4 Careless and Inconsiderate Driving

**Offence — Careless and Inconsiderate Driving — Road Traffic Act 1988, s. 3**
*Triable summarily. Fine. Discretionary disqualification.*
**(*No specific power of arrest*)**

The Road Traffic Act 1988, s. 3 states:

> *If a person drives a mechanically propelled vehicle on a road or other public place without due care and attention, or without reasonable consideration for other persons using the road or place, he is guilty of an offence.*

**Keynote**

Like the offences under ss. 1 and 2, this offence also applies to a mechanically propelled vehicle and to public places as well as roads.

'Due care and attention' is the standard of driving that would be expected of a reasonable, prudent and competent driver in all the attendant circumstances.

There is one *objective* standard of driving which is expected of all drivers — even learner drivers (*McCrone* v *Riding* [1938] 1 All ER 157). Once you have proved that a defendant departed from that standard of driving, and that his/her actions were 'voluntary', then the offence is complete. There is no need to prove any *knowledge* or *awareness* by the defendant that their driving fell below that standard (*R* v *Lawrence* [1981] RTR 217).

The standard of driving that would be expected of a prudent and competent driver will be a question of fact for the court to decide and, in so deciding, the magistrate(s) may take into account local factors such as the expected level of traffic, the time of day, peculiar hazards etc. (*Walker* v *Tolhurst* [1978] RTR 513).

Evidence of earlier incidents involving careless or inconsiderate driving around the same time as the offence charged may be admissible to support that charge under some circumstances (*Hallet* v *Warren* (1929) 93 JP 225) as it may if the offence is charged as one continuing offence (*Horrix* v *Malam* [1984] RTR 112).

If a witness reports the driver of an unidentified vehicle as having committed a driving offence, it is critical that the witness provides direct evidence of what they actually saw. It would not be enough to produce evidence from the police to show that they had received details of the vehicle which they subsequently traced back to the driver. Both vehicle *and* driver must be linked by admissible and relevant evidence (*Ahmed* v *DPP* [1998] RTR 90).

If a driver falls asleep at the wheel he/she will be guilty of careless driving (*Henderson* v *Jones* (1955) 119 JP 304) but evidence of this fact from the driver alone will not be enough to support a charge under s. 3 (*Edwards* v *Clarke* (1951) 115 JPN 426).

In order to prove that a driver drove inconsiderately you must show that some other person using the road was actually inconvenienced (*Dilks* v *Bowman Shaw* [1981] RTR 4).

Other persons using the road/public place can include pedestrians who are deliberately sprayed with water from a puddle or passengers in a vehicle (see *Pawley* v *Wharldall* [1965] 2 All ER 757).

If a motorist takes action in response to an emergency situation, his/her actions are to be judged against what was a 'reasonable' course of action in those circumstances in assessing whether or not the driving amounted to an offence (*Jones* v *Chief Constable of Avon & Somerset* [1986] RTR 259).

Simply breaching the regulations at a pedestrian crossing (**see chapter 8**) is not of itself proof that the person's driving fell below the required standard (*Gibbons* v *Kahl* [1956] 1 QB 59).

## 2.5 Aiding and Abetting

It is possible for someone to aid and abet another to commit an offence under ss. 1–3. The supervisor of a learner driver may commit such an offence if he/she fails to supervise the other person properly (*Rubie* v *Faulkner* [1940] 1 All ER 285). (For the supervision of learner drivers generally, **see chapter 11**.) A driving test examiner however is in the vehicle for a different purpose and will not generally be liable for the driver's behaviour (*BSM Ltd* v *Simms* [1971] 1 All ER 317).

## 2.6 Dangerous, Careless and Inconsiderate Cycling

There are similar offences which regulate the standard of cycling *on roads*. These are found under ss. 28 and 29 of the Road Traffic Act 1988 and are summary offences punishable with a fine. The offence of causing bodily injury by 'furious driving' also applies to pedal cycles (**see para. 2.3**). For other offences involving pedal cycles, **see chapter 15**.

'Cycles' will include tricycles and any cycle having four or more wheels (s. 192 of the 1988 Act).

## 2.7 Causing Death by Careless Driving when under the Influence of Drink or Drugs

**Offence — Causing Death by Careless Driving when under the Influence of Drink or Drugs — Road Traffic Act 1988, s. 3A**
*Triable on indictment. Ten years' imprisonment. Obligatory disqualification – minimum two years.*
***(Serious arrestable offence)***

The Road Traffic Act 1988, s. 3A states:

*(1) If a person causes the death of another person by driving a mechanically propelled vehicle on a road or other public place without due care and attention, or without reasonable consideration for other persons using the road or place, and—*

*(a) he is, at the time when he is driving, unfit to drive through drink or drugs, or*

*(b) he has consumed so much alcohol that the proportion of it in his breath, blood or urine at that time exceeds the prescribed limit, or*

*(c) he is, within 18 hours after that time, required to provide a specimen in pursuance of section 7 of this Act, but without reasonable excuse fails to provide it,*

*he is guilty of an offence.*

*(2) For the purposes of this section a person shall be taken to be unfit to drive at any time when his ability to drive properly is impaired.*

*(3) Subsection (1)(b) and (c) above shall not apply in relation to a person driving a mechanically propelled vehicle other than a motor vehicle.*

**Keynote**

The elements in relation to the 'causing' of death and 'another person' are the same as those under s. 1 (**see para. 2.2.1**).

The elements relating to 'due care and attention' and 'reasonable consideration' are the same as those under s. 3 (**see para. 2.4**).

The elements relating to 'unfitness to drive' and the consumption of alcohol should be read in conjunction with those discussed in **chapter 5**.

Although the offence under s. 3A applies to a road or other public place, note that s. 3A(1)(b) and (c) can only be committed by a driver of a *motor vehicle* (**see para. 1.2.1**).

The requirement under s. 3A(1)(c) is for the provision of a specimen for *analysis* under s. 7 of the Road Traffic Act 1988 and not a screening breath test under s. 6.

It would appear that the request must be made within 18 hours *after the driving which caused the death* and not after the death itself.

## 2.8 The Highway Code

One way of illustrating the standard of driving expected of a prudent and competent driver is through the Highway Code. Section 38 of the Road Traffic Act 1988 states:

> *(7) A failure on the part of a person to observe a provision of the Highway Code shall not of itself render that person liable to criminal proceedings of any kind but any such failure may in any proceedings (whether civil or criminal, and including proceedings for an offence under the Traffic Acts, the Public Passenger Vehicles Act 1981 or sections 18 to 23 of the Transport Act 1985) be relied upon by any party to the proceedings as tending to establish or negative any liability which is in question in those proceedings.*

Among its many provisions, the Highway Code makes reference to the use of mobile phones and in-car communications equipment (rule 43) and this provision has supported a charge under s. 3 in a Scottish case (*Roe* v *Friel* 1993 SLT 791).

At the time of writing, a bill to make the use of a hand-held mobile phone an offence while driving a motor vehicle on the road was before the House of Lords.

The braking distances shown in the Highway Code however are not admissible in proving speeding cases as they amount to hearsay (*R* v *Chadwick* [1975] Crim LR 105; for hearsay generally, **see Evidence and Procedure, chapter 11**).

## 2.9 Identity of Drivers

Section 172 of the Road Traffic Act 1988 states:

> *(1) This section applies—*
> *(a) to any offence under the preceding provisions of this Act except—*
> *(i) an offence under Part V, or*
> *(ii) an offence under section 13, 16, 51(2), 61(4), 67(9), 68(4), 96 or 120,*
> *and to an offence under section 178 of this Act,*
> *(b) to any offence under sections 25, 26 or 27 of the Road Traffic Offenders Act 1988,*
> *(c) to any offence against any other enactment relating to the use of vehicles on roads, except an offence under paragraph 8 of Schedule 1 to the Road Traffic (Driver Licensing and Information Systems) Act 1989, and*
> *(d) to manslaughter, or in Scotland culpable homicide, by the driver of a motor vehicle.*
> *(2) Where the driver of a vehicle is alleged to be guilty of an offence to which this section applies—*
> *(a) the person keeping the vehicle shall give such information as to the identity of the driver as he may be required to give by or on behalf of a chief officer of police, and*
> *(b) any other person shall if required as stated above give any information which it is in his power to give and may lead to identification of the driver.*
> *(3) Subject to the following provisions, a person who fails to comply with a requirement under subsection (2) above shall be guilty of an offence.*

**Keynote**

Section 172 applies to offences other than those listed at s. 172(1)(a)–(d). The excepted offences listed at s. 172(1)(a) and (b) are offences relating to:

- driving instructors
- motoring events on public highways
- protective headgear
- testing of goods vehicles
- regulations for 'type approval'
- obstruction of a vehicle examiner
- requirements to proceed to a place of vehicle inspection
- uncorrected eyesight
- regulations for licensing of large goods vehicle/passenger carrying vehicle drivers
- unlawful vehicle taking in Scotland, and
- post-conviction offences under the Road Traffic Offenders Act 1988.

Therefore s. 172 will apply to regulations made under the applicable sections (e.g. the Road Vehicles (Construction and Use) Regulations 1986; **see chapter 9**)

The requirement under s. 172 applies to the person *keeping* the vehicle and will apply to a person who is the keeper of the vehicle at the time the requirement is made even if he/she was not the keeper at the time of the alleged offence (*Hateley* v *Greenough* [1962] Crim LR 329).

There is no particular form of words to be used when making the requirement. It must be shown that the person making the requirement did so by, or on behalf of, the chief officer of police. A computerised form stating that the author is so acting has been held by the Divisional Court to be sufficient for this purpose (*Arnold* v *DPP, The Independent*, 23 June 1997).

The information must be provided within a reasonable time which may, in the prevailing circumstances, mean immediately (see *Lowe* v *Lester* [1987] RTR 30).

Where the requirement is made in writing and served by post, it shall have effect as a requirement to provide the information within 28 days beginning with the day on which it is served (s. 172(7)(a) (see the defence below)).

If a person falsely claims to have been the driver, an offence of perverting the course of justice may be appropriate (**see Crime, chapter 15**).

Where the defendant is a company or corporate body, any director, secretary, manager or other officer of the company may also be prosecuted for the offence if it can be shown that the offence was committed with his/her 'consent or connivance' (s. 172(5)).

Compare the requirements of this section with those under the Vehicle Excise and Registration Act 1994 (**see chapter 12**).

### 2.9.1 Defence

Section 172(4) provides that a person shall not be convicted of an offence under s. 172(3) if that person can show that he/she did not know *and* could not have ascertained with reasonable diligence who the driver of the vehicle was.

Section 172(7)(b) provides that, where the requirement is made in writing by post, the person shall not be guilty of an offence if that person can show that either he/she gave the information as soon as reasonably practicable after the end of the 28 day period *or* that it has not been reasonably practicable for him/her to give it.

In both of these cases the burden of proof lies on the defendant.

## 2.10 Police Drivers

Police drivers will be judged against the same standard of care as other drivers (*Wood* v *Richards* [1977] RTR 201) and there is no special exemption for them or any other emergency crews (*R* v *O'Toole* (1971) 55 Cr App R 206).

The Traffic Signs Regulations and General Directions 1994, reg. 33 (**see chapter 10**) make allowances for emergency services drivers to pass through red traffic lights under certain circumstances. These regulations set out the conditions under which a driver may proceed through a red light and failure to meet those conditions will render the driver liable to a charge under s. 2 or 3 of the 1988 Act. Consequently the driver of a police surveillance vehicle following suspects to the scene of an intended armed robbery could not rely on the fact that he was required by the seriousness of the circumstances to go through a red light when he did so in a way which was not covered by the regulations (*DPP* v *Harris* [1995] RTR 100). See also *R* v *Collins* at **para. 2.2.2**.

For the provisions relating to emergency service vehicles at pedestrian crossings, see **para. 8.9.2**.

If a person drives in a way which creates a need for police officers to pursue him/her and an officer is subsequently injured in that pursuit, that person may owe a duty of care to the police officer and may therefore be sued for damages by the injured officer (*Langley* v *Dray* [1997] PIQR P508).

## 2.11 Defences

The very narrow defence(s) of *duress* and *necessity* (**see Crime, chapter 4**) will apply to cases of dangerous, careless and inconsiderate driving (they also apply to the offences of driving while disqualified (*R* v *Martin* [1989] RTR 63 and confirmed recently in *R* v *Backshall*, *The Times*, 10 April 1998) and driving with excess alcohol (*DPP* v *Bell* [1992] Crim LR 176). The defences will only apply where the driver was forced to commit the offence in order to avoid death or serious injury (*R* v *Conway* [1989] RTR 35).

The defence of 'self-defence' (**see Crime, chapter 4**) also appears to be available, where appropriate, to offences involving driving standards. This was made clear by the Court of Appeal in *R* v *Symonds* [1998] Crim LR 280 where the defendant was approached by a drunken pedestrian who tried to drag him from his car. It was held that, to allow the defence of 'self-defence' in relation to an *assault* caused by driving a vehicle (in this case, by driving off while the pedestrian had his arm through the driver's window), but not to allow it in relation to an offence such as dangerous driving arising from the same incident, was an anomaly. Therefore the defence of 'self-defence' should, where the circumstances require it, be open to someone who is charged with an offence involving the standard of their driving.

The defence afforded by the Criminal Law Act 1967, s. 3(1) (**see Crime, chapter 4**) — which allows the use of reasonable force in arresting offenders and preventing crime — may apply to cases of dangerous, careless or inconsiderate driving (*R* v *Renouf* [1986] 2 All ER 449). See also the 'defence' of automatism in **chapter 1**.

### 2.11.1 Mechanical Defect

If an unforeseen mechanical defect suddenly deprives the driver of control of the vehicle, he/she may have a defence similar to 'automatism' (**see chapter 1**). The reasoning for this seems to be that there is little distinction between a totally unexpected aberration in the bodily functions of a driver and a similar eventuality affecting the workings of their vehicle. In each case the driver has been deprived suddenly and unexpectedly of proper control of the vehicle and ought to be afforded the same 'defence' (*R* v *Spurge* [1961] 2 QB 205). As with automatism, if the possibility of such a defect ought to have been foreseeable by reasonable prudence, the defence will not be available.

# CHAPTER THREE

# NOTICES OF INTENDED PROSECUTION

## 3.1 Introduction

Under s. 1 of the Road Traffic Offenders Act 1988, before certain offences can be prosecuted:

- the defendant must have been warned of the possibility of that prosecution at the time of the offence (s. 1(1)(a)); or
- the defendant must have been served with a summons (or charged) within 14 days of the offence (s. 1(1)(b)); or
- a notice setting out the possibility of that prosecution must have been sent to the driver or registered keeper of the vehicle within 14 days of the offence (s. 1(1)(c)).

The notice or warning must be given by the 'prosecutor' which will ordinarily be the police. If the person giving it is not empowered to make a decision whether or not to prosecute (such as a vehicle examiner employed by the vehicle inspectorate), the warning or notice will not be deemed to have been served (*Swan* v *Vehicle Inspectorate* [1997] RTR 187).

The notice referred to is a Notice of Intended Prosecution (NIP). If a verbal warning is given at the time it must be shown that the defendant understood it (*Gibson* v *Dalton* [1980] RTR 410). Proof that they understood it will lie on the prosecution and, for that reason, it is common practice to send an NIP whether a verbal warning was given or not.

Where an offence is committed partly within the jurisdiction of one court and partly within that of another, either court may try the case. Consider the following scenario. A person whose home address is in county A commits a traffic offence in county B. Later, at their home address, that person is required to provide details of the driver at the time of the original traffic offence. The person fails to provide the details as required. The fact that the original offence was in county B does not stop the court in county A from hearing the case as the person's subsequent offence — failure to provide the details required — occurred within the jurisdiction of county A (*Kennet DC* v *Faroq*, *The Times*, 16 October 1998).

## 3.2 Relevant Offences

The offences which require an NIP are listed in sch. 1 of the Road Traffic Offenders Act 1988 and include:

- Dangerous, careless or inconsiderate driving (**see chapter 2**).
- Dangerous, careless or inconsiderate cycling (**see chapter 2**).
- Failing to comply with traffic signs and directions (**see chapter 10**).
- Leaving a vehicle in a dangerous position (**see chapter 8**).
- Speeding offences under ss. 16 and 17 of the Road Traffic Regulation Act 1984 (**see chapter 7**).

The list of offences in sch. 1 is exhaustive; other offences, even if similar in nature to those in the list, will not be covered by the requirements of s. 1(1) (*Sulston* v *Hammond* [1970] 1 WLR 1164).

## 3.3 Exceptions

Section 2(1) of the Road Traffic Offenders Act 1988 states that the requirement to serve an NIP does not apply in relation to an offence if:

- at the time or
- immediately afterwards and
- owing to the presence of the vehicle concerned
- on a road
- an accident occurred.

Each of these features must be present to remove the need for an NIP to be served or a warning given.

'Accident' is defined at **para. 1.2.7** and is broader than the expression used under s. 170 of the Road Traffic Act 1988 (**see chapter 1**).

Whether the accident occurred 'at the time' is a matter of fact and degree (*R* v *Okike* [1978] RTR 489).

If the driver is unaware that the accident has taken place because it is so minor, there *will* be a need to serve an NIP (*Bentley* v *Dickinson* [1983] RTR 356). The thinking behind this ruling is that the warning or NIP will allow the driver to gather evidence to answer any charge arising from the accident.

Where the accident is so severe that the driver has no recollection of it, there is no need to serve an NIP and the ruling in *Bentley* (above) will not apply (*DPP* v *Pidhajeckyj* [1991] RTR 136).

There must be some causal connection between the presence of the vehicle concerned and the accident (*Quelch* v *Phipps* [1955] 2 All ER 302).

The vehicle must have been on a 'road' (**see para. 1.2.7**).

Section 2 goes on to say:

*(2) The requirement of section 1(1) of this Act does not apply in relation to an offence in respect of which—*
*(a) a fixed penalty notice (within the meaning of Part III of this Act) has been given or fixed under any provision of that Part, or*
*(b) a notice has been given under section 54(4) of this Act.*
*(3) Failure to comply with the requirement of section 1(1) of this Act is not a bar to the conviction of the accused in a case where the court is satisfied—*
*(a) that neither the name and address of the accused nor the name and address of the registered keeper, if any, could with reasonable diligence have been ascertained in time for a summons or, as the case may be, a complaint to be served or for a notice to be served or sent in compliance with the requirement, or*
*(b) that the accused by his own conduct contributed to the failure.*

**Keynote**

For fixed penalty procedures generally, **see chapter 14**.

Failure to observe the requirements of s. 1(1) will not bar an alternative conviction which is allowed under s. 24, that is, where the original offence was not one requiring an NIP but where the alternative office *would* ordinarily require such a notice (s. 2(4)).

If the defendant contributes to the failure to serve the NIP, then that failure will not be a bar to conviction.

## 3.4 Presumption

Section 1 of the Road Traffic Offenders Act 1988 states that:

*(3) The requirement of subsection (1) above shall in every case be deemed to have been complied with unless and until the contrary is proved.*

**Keynote**

This places the burden of proving non-conformity with the requirement on the defence.

## 3.5 Proof

Section 1 of the Road Traffic Offenders Act 1988 states:

*(1A) A notice required by this section to be served on any person may be served on that person—*
*(a) by delivering it to him;*
*(b) by addressing it to him and leaving it at his last known address; or*
*(c) by sending it by registered post, recorded delivery service or first class post addressed to him at his last known address.*

*(2) A notice shall be deemed for the purposes of subsection (1)(c) above to have been served on a person if it was sent by registered post or recorded delivery service addressed to him at his last known address, notwithstanding that the notice was returned as undelivered or was for any other reason not received by him.*

*(3) The requirement of subsection (1) above shall in every case be deemed to have been complied with unless and until the contrary is proved.*

**Keynote**

As discussed above, the warning may be oral (under s. 1(1)(a)) but there are problems of proof where such warnings are given. If the defendant was preoccupied at the time or can show that he/she did not fully understand what was being said, the provisions of s. 1(1) will not have been complied with.

Serving an NIP personally on the spouse or partner of the defendant would appear to be enough (*Hosier* v *Goodall* [1962] 1 All ER 30).

If the defendant is not at his/her home address, for instance because he/she is in hospital or on holiday, service to his/her last known address will suffice even if the police are aware of that fact (*Phipps* v *McCormick* [1972] Crim LR 540).

If neither the defendant nor the registered keeper have any fixed abode, reasonable efforts must be made to serve the notice personally. If such efforts fail, s. 2(3) would apply and the need for service would be removed.

As the purpose of the warning or notice is to alert the defendant to the likelihood of prosecution, it is not necessary to specify exactly which offence is being considered; it is enough that the defendant is made aware of the *nature* of the offence (*Pope* v *Clarke* [1953] 2 All ER 704).

# CHAPTER FOUR

# ACCIDENTS

## 4.1 Introduction

Although there are many types of event involving vehicles which can be described as an 'accident' — including those brought about deliberately (**see chapter 1**) — there are specific circumstances where that 'accident' imposes duties on certain people involved. This chapter is concerned with these 'reportable' accidents.

## 4.2 Reportable Accidents

Section 170 of the Road Traffic Act 1988 states that:

> *(1) This section applies in a case where, owing to the presence of a mechanically propelled vehicle on a road, an accident occurs by which—*
>
> *(a) personal injury is caused to a person other than the driver of that mechanically propelled vehicle, or*
>
> *(b) damage is caused—*
>
> *(i) to a vehicle other than that mechanically propelled vehicle or a trailer drawn by that mechanically propelled vehicle, or*
>
> *(ii) to an animal other than an animal in or on that mechanically propelled vehicle or a trailer drawn by that mechanically propelled vehicle, or*
>
> *(iii) to any other property constructed on, fixed to, growing in or otherwise forming part of the land on which the road in question is situated or land adjacent to such land.*
>
> *(2) The driver of the mechanically propelled vehicle must stop and, if required to do so by any person having reasonable grounds for so requiring, give his name and address and also the name and address of the owner and the identification marks of the vehicle.*
>
> *(3) If for any reason the driver of the mechanically propelled vehicle does not give his name and address under subsection (2) above, he must report the accident.*
>
> *(4) . . .*
>
> *(5) If, in a case where this section applies by virtue of subsection (1)(a) above, the driver of a motor vehicle does not at the time of the accident produce such a certificate of insurance or security, or other evidence, as is mentioned in section 165(2)(a) of this Act—*
>
> *(a) to a constable, or*
>
> *(b) to some person who, having reasonable grounds for so doing, has required him to produce it, the driver must report the accident and produce such a certificate or other evidence.*
>
> *This subsection does not apply to the driver of an invalid carriage.*

*(6) To comply with a duty under this section to report an accident or to produce such a certificate of insurance or security, or other evidence, as is mentioned in section 165(2)(a) of this Act, the driver—*

*(a) must do so at a police station or to a constable, and*

*(b) must do so as soon as is reasonably practicable and, in any case, within twenty-four hours of the occurrence of the accident.*

*(7) . . .*

*(8) In this section 'animal' means horse, cattle, ass, mule, sheep, pig, goat or dog.*

**Keynote**

Accidents as defined under s. 170(1)(a) and (b) above are generally referred to as 'reportable' accidents. These should be distinguished from the wider definition of 'accident' used elsewhere in the Act (**see para. 1.2.7**).

Note that the duty upon the driver under s. 170(2) is to stop *and* give his/her name and address (and name and address of the owner) (*DPP* v *Bennett* [1993] RTR 175).

However, it has been held that, as the reason for this requirement to 'exchange details' is to allow future communications between interested parties, the address of the driver's solicitor would be enough to discharge the duty at s. 170(2) (*R* v *McCarthy*, *The Times*, 8 January 1999).

No mention is made of who may have been to blame for the accident. A driver will attract the duties imposed by s. 170 even if he/she is not at fault. In order to attract those duties, however, the driver must know of the accident (see *Harding* v *Price* [1948] 1 All ER 283).

In proving the offence you would not have to show that the driver was so aware; once the damage or injury is proved it is for the driver to show (on the balance of probabilities) that he/she was unaware of its occurrence (*Selby* v *Chief Constable of Avon and Somerset* [1988] RTR 216).

Damage caused under the circumstances set out at s. 170(1)(b) applies to any vehicle, not just one which is mechanically propelled (such as bicycles and trailers).

If the only damage caused is to the vehicle concerned or an animal in it then the accident will not fall within the criteria of being 'reportable'. Similarly if the only person injured is the driver of the vehicle concerned, the accident will not be reportable; it will, however, be reportable if a passenger in that vehicle is injured.

Where a bus driver braked hard, causing injury to one of his passengers, the Divisional Court held that he had a duty to stop at the place and the time that the passenger was caused to be injured. It was not open to the driver to claim that the bus itself was the scene of the accident. The fact that the driver failed to stop immediately meant that he was guilty of an offence under s. 170(4) (**see para. 4.3**) (*Hallinan* v *DPP* [1998] Crim LR 754).

The list of animals under s. 170(8) does not include one of the most common 'victims' of road traffic accidents — cats.

The accident must have been brought about owing to the vehicle's presence on a 'road' (**see chapter 1**); therefore s. 170 does not apply to accidents which occur on private premises.

In order to determine whether the motor vehicle was being driven without insurance (**see chapter 6**), s. 171 of the Road Traffic Act 1988 places a requirement on the *owner* of the vehicle to give such information as required the police. Failure to comply with such a requirement is a summary offence.

### 4.2.1 Stop

Stop under s. 170(2) means to stop and remain at the scene for such a time as would allow anyone having a right or reason for doing so to ask for information from the driver (*Lee* v *Knapp* [1967] 2 QB 442); it does not require the driver to make enquiries of his/her own to try and find such a person (see *Mutton* v *Bates* [1984] RTR 256).

This duty also appears to require the driver to stay with his/her vehicle for a reasonable time (*Ward* v *Rawson* [1978] RTR 498).

### 4.2.2 Injury

Injury under s. 170 has been held to include shock and, given the recent developments in the area of assaults (e.g. *R* v *Ireland* [1997] 3 WLR 534; *R* v *Chan-Fook* [1994] 1 WLR 689 (**see Crime, chapter 8**)), it would appear that psychological harm may well amount to an 'injury' for these purposes.

### 4.2.3 Duty to Report

If the driver does not give his/her name and address, he/she must report the accident to a police officer or at a police station. This must be done as soon as reasonably practicable (which will be a question of fact for the court to decide in each circumstance) and in any case within 24 hours of the occurrence of the incident. This latter requirement does not give the driver up to 24 hours to report the accident; that report must be made as soon as is reasonably practicable. The report to the police within 24 hours appears to apply even if it is not practicable — or even possible? — to do so within that time limit (see *Bulman* v *Lakin* [1981] RTR 1).

That duty is probably not discharged if the driver waits until the police call at his/her house and then tells them (see *Dawson* v *Winter* (1932) 49 TLR 128 *obiter*); neither is it discharged if the driver tells a friend who happens to be a police officer (*Mutton* v *Bates* [1984] RTR 256).

Any report must be made in person; telephoning (and presumably sending a fax or e-mail) a police station is not enough (*Wisdom* v *Macdonald* [1983] RTR 186).

## 4.3 The Offences

**Offence — Failing to Stop or Report an Accident —**
**Road Traffic Act 1988, s. 170(4)**
*Triable summarily. Six months' imprisonment and/or fine. Discretionary disqualification.*
***(No specific power of arrest)***

The Road Traffic Act 1988, s. 170 states:

> *(4) A person who fails to comply with subsections (2) or (3) above is guilty of an offence.*

### Offence — Failing to Produce Proof of Insurance after Injury Accident — Road Traffic Act 1988, s. 170(7)

*Triable summarily. Fine.*

***(No specific power of arrest)***

The Road Traffic Act 1988, s. 170 states:

*(7) A person who fails to comply with a duty under subsection (5) above is guilty of an offence, but he shall not be convicted by reason only of a failure to produce a certificate or other evidence if, within seven days after the occurrence of the accident, the certificate or other evidence is produced at a police station that was specified by him at the time when the accident was reported.*

**Keynote**

If a driver fails to stop *and* fails to report an accident he/she commits *two* offences (*Roper* v *Sullivan* [1978] RTR 181).

### Offence — Failing to Give, or Giving False Details after Allegation of Dangerous or Careless Driving or Cycling — Road Traffic Act 1988, s. 168

*Triable summarily. Fine.*

***(No specific power of arrest)***

The Road Traffic Act 1988, s. 168 states:

*Any of the following persons—*

*(a) the driver of a mechanically propelled vehicle who is alleged to have committed an offence under section 2 or 3 of this Act, or*

*(b) the rider of a cycle who is alleged to have committed an offence under section 28 or 29 of this Act,*

*who refuses, on being so required by any person having reasonable ground for so requiring, to give his name or address, or gives a false name or address, is guilty of an offence.*

**Keynote**

This requirement arises where the driver (or rider) is alleged to have committed an offence of dangerous or careless driving or cycling (**see chapter 2**).

There is no requirement for there to have been an accident of any sort.

# CHAPTER FIVE

# DRINK DRIVING

## 5.1 Introduction

The law regulating drinking and driving is contained in the Road Traffic Act 1988 and the Road Traffic Offenders Act 1988. It has been substantially developed by common law and entire books could be devoted to the cases which the subject has generated since its introduction over 30 years ago.

One of the good things about the subject, both from a practical point of view, and that of the student, is that virtually every conceivable circumstance, excuse or mitigating situation has been put before the courts. The result is that, when approaching a set of real or hypothetical circumstances under the drink/drive laws, the chances are that it has already been tried — both literally and judicially!

## 5.2 Unfit Through Drink or Drugs

**Offence — Driving or Attempting to Drive a Mechanically Propelled Vehicle when Unfit Through Drink or Drugs — Road Traffic Act 1988, s. 4(1)**
*Triable summarily. Six months' imprisonment and/or a fine. Obligatory disqualification.*
***(Statutory power of arrest)***

For the corresponding legislation applying to railways and tram systems, see **General Police Duties, chapter 13**.

The Road Traffic Act 1988, s. 4 states:

> *(1) A person who, when driving or attempting to drive a mechanically propelled vehicle on a road or other public place, is unfit to drive through drink or drugs is guilty of an offence.*

**Offence — Being in Charge of a Mechanically Propelled Vehicle when Unfit Through Drink or Drugs — Road Traffic Act 1988, s. 4(2)**
*Triable summarily. Three months' imprisonment and/or a fine. Discretionary disqualification.*
***(Statutory power of arrest)***

The Road Traffic Act 1988, s. 4 states:

> *(2) Without prejudice to subsection (1) above, a person who, when in charge of a mechanically propelled vehicle which is on a road or other public place, is unfit to drive through drink or drugs is guilty of an offence.*

**Keynote**

Section 4 creates three separate offences. For the definitions of 'driving', 'attempting to drive' and 'in charge', **see chapter 1**.

Under s. 4:

> *(3) . . . a person shall be deemed not to have been in charge of a mechanically propelled vehicle if he proves that at the material time the circumstances were such that there was no likelihood of his driving it so long as he remained unfit to drive through drink or drugs.*

**Keynote**

The onus is on the defendant to prove this fact. However, in determining whether the defendant was likely to drive the vehicle while unfit a court will disregard any injury to the defendant or damage to the vehicle (s. 4(4)).

For the definitions of 'mechanically propelled vehicle', 'road' and 'public place', **see chapter 1**.

Evidence of impairment must be produced by the prosecution. That evidence may be given by any 'lay' witness and does not require expert testimony (*R* v *Lanfear* [1968] 2 QB 77). Such a witness cannot, however, give evidence as to the defendant's ability to drive.

It is not necessary to show what quantity of alcohol or drug the defendant had in his/her system for this offence.

'Drugs' will include any intoxicant other than alcohol (s. 11); toluene found in some glues will amount to such a drug (*Bradford* v *Wilson* (1983) 78 Cr App R 77). (Contrast this situation with other offences of 'drunkenness'; see **General Police Duties, chapter 4**.)

### 5.2.1 Police Powers

A constable may arrest a person without warrant if he/she has reasonable cause to suspect that the person is, or has been committing an offence under s. 4 (s. 4(6)). For the purpose of arresting a person under the power above, a constable may enter (if need be by force) any place where that person is or where he/she, with reasonable cause, suspects them to be (s. 4(7)).

The suspicion need not be formed while the defendant is driving and can become apparent after he/she has been stopped or spoken to for some other reason (*R* v *Roff* [1976] RTR 7).

Note that, in both the power to arrest and the power to enter, the suspicion required is the lesser one of reasonable cause to *suspect*; contrast reasonable cause to *believe* (**para. 5.4.1**). In *Swales* v *Cox* [1981] QB 849 the Divisional Court held that officers would need to show that force was actually necessary before its use could be justified and therefore it would be prudent in every case to seek admittance first.

## 5.3 Over Prescribed Limit

**Offence — Driving or Attempting to Drive a Motor Vehicle while Over the Prescribed Limit — Road Traffic Act 1988, s. 5(1)(a)**
*Triable summarily. Six months' imprisonment and/or a fine. Obligatory disqualification.*
***(Statutory power of arrest)***

The Road Traffic Act 1988, s. 5 states:

> *(1) If a person—*
> *(a) drives or attempts to drive a motor vehicle on a road or other public place . . .*
> *after consuming so much alcohol that the proportion of it in his breath, blood or urine exceeds the prescribed limit he is guilty of an offence.*

**Offence — Being in Charge of a Motor Vehicle while Over the Prescribed Limit — Road Traffic Act 1988, s. 5(1)(b)**
*Triable summarily. Three months' imprisonment and/or a fine. Discretionary disqualification.*
***(Statutory power of arrest)***

The Road Traffic Act 1988, s. 5 states:

> *(1) If a person—*
> *(a) . . .*
> *(b) is in charge of a motor vehicle on a road or other public place,*
> *after consuming so much alcohol that the proportion of it in his breath, blood or urine exceeds the prescribed limit he is guilty of an offence.*

### Keynote

These offences apply to *motor vehicles* as defined in **para. 1.2.1**; contrast the previous offences in relation to unfitness to drive.

'Consuming' is not restricted to drinking and will encompass other methods of getting alcohol into the bloodstream (*DPP* v *Johnson* [1995] RTR 9).

The prescribed limit (at the time of writing) is:

- 35 microgrammes of alcohol in 100 millilitres of breath
- 80 milligrammes of alcohol in 100 millilitres of blood
- 107 milligrammes of alcohol in 100 millilitres of urine.

Section 11(2) which sets out these limits also allows for the levels to be changed and the present government is considering reducing them.

### 5.3.1 Defence

Section 5 goes on to say that:

> *(2) It is a defence for a person charged with an offence under subsection (1)(b) above to prove that at the time he is alleged to have committed the offence the circumstances were such that there was*

*no likelihood of his driving the vehicle whilst the proportion of alcohol in his breath, blood or urine remained likely to exceed the prescribed limit.*

*(3) The court may, in determining whether there was such a likelihood as is mentioned in subsection (2) above, disregard any injury to him and any damage to the vehicle.*

**Keynote**

For the defence of duress of circumstances or necessity, **see Crime, chapter 4**.

## 5.4 Preliminary Breath Tests

Section 6 of the Road Traffic Act 1988 provides for the administering of preliminary breath tests, sometimes referred to as 'screening' or 'roadside' breath tests (as opposed to evidential breath tests (**see para. 5.5**). The procedures for obtaining such breath tests are summarised in **appendix 8, diagrams 1 and 2**.

Section 6 provides that:

*(1) Where a constable in uniform has reasonable cause to suspect—*

*(a) that a person driving or attempting to drive or in charge of a motor vehicle on a road or other public place has alcohol in his body or has committed a traffic offence whilst the vehicle was in motion, or*

*(b) that a person has been driving or attempting to drive or been in charge of a motor vehicle on a road or other public place with alcohol in his body and that that person still has alcohol in his body, or*

*(c) that a person has been driving or attempting to drive or been in charge of a motor vehicle on a road or other public place and has committed a traffic offence whilst the vehicle was in motion, he may, subject to section 9 of this Act, require him to provide a specimen of breath for a breath test.*

**Keynote**

The breath test referred to is 'for the purpose of obtaining, by means of a device of a type approved by the Secretary of State, *an indication* whether the proportion of alcohol in a person's breath or blood is likely to exceed the prescribed limit' (s. 11(2) — emphasis added). This is an important distinction as the preliminary breath test is undertaken only to give an indication to the officer administering it of the likelihood of the offence, not for proving the relevant offence.

Failure to comply with the manufacturer's instructions on the use of approved devices (e.g. when assembling the tube on the Lion Alcolmeter or allowing the driver to smoke immediately before taking the test) will mean that the person has *not provided* a preliminary breath test and may be asked to provide another; refusing to do so will be an offence (see below) (*DPP* v *Carey* [1969] 3 All ER 1662).

The Divisional Court decided recently that an innocent failure by a police officer to follow the manufacturer's instructions should not be deemed to render either the test or any subsequent arrest unlawful (*DPP* v *Kay*, *The Times*, 13 April 1998).

The procedure specifies that a constable requiring the test must be in uniform (contrast the powers available under s. 4 above). The section does not specifically mention who may *administer* the test once the requirement has been made. At the time of writing there is no reliable authority on the point. When deciding on the issue of whether some other officer, in uniform or otherwise, can actually *administer* a breath test that has been lawfully required under s. 6(1), the following arguments may be brought:

- Parliament clearly intended to provide certain safeguards in relation to the taking of breath specimens in certain situations, under this and the previous legislation. The inclusion at s. 6(1) of the requirement for an officer to be in uniform when making the request must be seen as a deliberate restriction on the scope of that power, particularly when seen alongside the next subsection relating to accidents (**see para. 5.4.2**). The practical effect of such a safeguard would be considerably diluted if it was to be interpreted as allowing the actual *administration* of the breath test to be carried out by any other officer. If this were the case then, taken to its logical extreme, a plain clothes officer wishing to breathalyse someone sitting in a car in a public place might simply get one of their uniformed colleagues to make the request to the driver over their personal radio or by mobile phone! This cannot have been Parliament's intention.

- The courts *may* conclude that Parliament's assumption was that the officer making the request and the officer administering the test would be one and the same person, i.e., in the same way that they interpreted the former provisions of s. 5 of the Public Order Act 1986 (where the warning had to be given by the same officer who subsequently went on to arrest the defendant), necessitating the passing of the Public Order (Amendment) Act 1996 (**see General Police Duties, chapter** 4).

In the absence of an authority on this point, it is suggested that the officer administering the test under s. 6(1) should at least be in uniform when doing so (although the provisions of s. 15(2) of the Road Traffic Offenders Act 1988 means that any evidence obtained after an inadvertently flawed process may still be admissible (**see para. 5.5.2**).

Whether the constable (which includes an officer of any rank, including special constables) was in uniform at the time is a matter of fact for a court to determine in each case. What counts as uniform is unclear but, if the constable can be easily identified from his/her manner of dress as a police officer, the requirement has probably been met (*Wallwork* v *Giles* [1970] RTR 117; officer without helmet on held to be 'in uniform').

No specific form of words is needed; the officer must clearly convey a 'requirement' to take the preliminary test *(R* v *O'Boyle* [1973] RTR 445).

A traffic offence is generally any offence under the Road Traffic Act 1988 (except those relating to driving instructors), the Road Traffic Regulation Act 1984 and the Road Traffic Offenders Act 1988 (except the provisions of Part III which deal with fixed penalty procedures) (s. 6(8)). Such offences, which include offences under any regulations made under those Acts, must have been committed where the vehicle was moving.

The courts have accepted that the police are empowered to *stop* vehicles at random (under the Road Traffic Act 1988, s. 163), whether to establish the identity of the driver, to enquire whether the driver has been drinking or to train newly appointed officers in traffic procedures (see *Chief Constable of Gwent* v *Dash* [1986] RTR 41). That does not empower officers to conduct *random breath tests* but, having randomly stopped a vehicle, they may carry out preliminary breath tests provided they follow the procedure set out above.

## 5.4.1 Reasonable Cause to Suspect

As mentioned above (**para. 5.2.1**), there is a distinction between reasonable cause to 'suspect' and reasonable cause to 'believe' (see s. 6(2) at **para. 5.4.2** below).

Whether the constable had reasonable cause to suspect or believe will be a question of fact, to be determined in the light of all the available facts. The distinction between the two however, has been held to be a significant one, intended by Parliament (*Baker* v *Oxford* [1980] RTR 315). In that case it was held that the deliberate use of the word 'believe' in the Act imposed a requirement for a greater degree of certainty in the mind of the officers concerned.

Reasonable cause to suspect may arise from the behaviour of a driver but single errors of judgement or carelessness will not necessarily justify a suspicion of alcohol (*Williams* v *Jones* [1972] RTR 4).

In addition to first-hand observation of a driver's behaviour, reasonable cause to suspect may arise from the observations of another officer (*Erskine* v *Hollin* [1971] RTR 199); it may even arise from information provided by a member of the public (see *DPP* v *Wilson* [1991] RTR 284). An officer receiving a radio message that a driver had been seen driving erratically may give the officer receiving the message reasonable cause to suspect that the driver had committed an offence in relation to alcohol consumption (*R* v *Evans (Terrence)* [1974] RTR 232).

Reasonable cause to *believe* requires something more than suspicion (*R* v *Forsyth* [1997] Crim LR 589. Additionally, it is not enough to show that there are such grounds for the belief; the officer must actually hold that belief as well (*R* v *Banks* [1916] 2 KB 621).

The suspicion required of a constable under s. 6(1)(b) relates both to the fact that the person drove etc. with alcohol in their body *and* that they still have alcohol in their body at the time of the request.

Whether a test was carried out 'at or near' the place where the requirement was made is a question of fact for the court to determine in each case and, given previous decisions, it is unlikely that the magistrates' decision will be overruled by a higher court (**see Evidence and Procedure, chapter 2**). Note that there is no general power of entry in order to administer preliminary breath tests (**see para. 5.4.4** below).

For further discussion of the general statutory meaning of 'reasonable cause to suspect', **see General Police Duties, chapter 2**.

## 5.4.2 Procedure Following an Accident

Section 6(2) provides that:

> *(2) If an accident occurs owing to the presence of a motor vehicle on a road or other public place, a constable may, subject to section 9 of this Act, require any person who he has reasonable cause to believe was driving or attempting to drive or in charge of the vehicle at the time of the accident to provide a specimen of breath for a breath test.*

**Keynote**

The power under s. 6(2) is expressly subject to the provisions of s. 9 which deals with hospital patients (**see para. 5.5.4**). The specimen after an accident may be taken at or near the place where the requirement is made or, if the officer making the requirement thinks fit, at a police station specified by that officer.

The officer must show that an accident had taken place, not simply that he/she believed that to be the case (*Chief Constable of West Midlands* v *Billingham* [1979] RTR 446). For the definition of 'accident' in this context, **see para. 1.2.7**. The meaning is not restricted to that given to a 'reportable' accident under s. 170 (**see para. 4.2**).

The requirement here is for the officer to have 'reasonable cause to believe' that the person was driving or in charge of a relevant vehicle at the time of an accident (s. 6(2) and see *Johnson* v *Whitehouse* [1984] RTR 38). The issue of whether the officer had reasonable cause to *believe* that the person was so driving or in charge of the vehicle at the time of the accident will be a question of fact.

There is no need for the police officer making the requirement to suspect or believe that the driver has been drinking, nor that he/she has committed any offence; reasonable belief in his/her involvement in the accident is enough.

### Offence — Failing to Provide Breath Specimen for Preliminary Test — Road Traffic Act 1988, s. 6(4)

*Triable summarily. Fine. Discretionary disqualification.*

***(Statutory power of arrest)***

The Road Traffic Act 1988, s. 6 states:

> *(4) A person who, without reasonable excuse, fails to provide a specimen of breath when required to do so in pursuance of this section is guilty of an offence.*

**Keynote**

An example of 'reasonable excuse' would be where the defendant is physically unable to provide a specimen or where to do so would entail a substantial risk to his/her health (see *R* v *Lennard* [1973] 2 All ER 831).

The breath sample must be provided in such a way as to 'enable the objective of the test or analysis to be satisfactorily achieved' (s. 11(3) of the Road Traffic Act 1988). Therefore, if the person does not follow the instructions given or provides a sample in a way which does not fulfil the requirements of s. 11(3), he/she has 'failed' to provide.

Failing includes a refusal (s. 11(2)). Having been required to provide a specimen of breath, a person may also be required to wait until a device is brought to the scene; failing to wait for a reasonable time, or doing anything which demonstrates an intention not to provide the specimen can amount to a 'failure' (see *R* v *Wagner* [1970] Crim LR 535).

Simply producing enough breath to enable the device to give a positive reading does not necessarily mean the defendant has 'provided a specimen'; he/she must produce sufficient breath in the manner required to enable the device to give a reliable reading — positive or negative (*DPP* v *Heywood* [1998] RTR 1).

## 5.4.3 Trespassing

Many legal arguments have raged over the legitimacy of a breath test carried out, or requested where the officers concerned are in fact trespassing on the property of another. The results of these deliberations are:

- If police officers are trespassing *on the defendant's property* they are not entitled to require a breath test (*Fox* v *Chief Constable of Gwent* [1986] AC 281).

- If the officers are trespassing at the time they make the requirement, any subsequent arrest made by them is unlawful (*Clowser* v *Chaplin* [1981] RTR 317).

- Although the entry and the arrest may be unlawful, this will only affect the offence under s. 6(4) and not any other offences detected at the police station (see below).

- Any requirement for a sample of breath properly made, and any subsequent, arrest remains lawful *until* the officers become trespassers. A police officer, like any other member of the public, has an implied licence to go onto certain parts of someone's property (e.g. the front doorstep) unless and until that licence is withdrawn. If a police officer goes onto such a part of the defendant's property, he/she is not trespassing until told to leave and any requirement for a breath test, or any arrest made before this happens will be lawful. (See *Pamplin* v *Fraser* [1981] RTR 494 where the defendant drove onto his own land and locked himself in his car. It was held that the officers' licence to enter the land had not been withdrawn at that stage.) Telling officers to 'fuck off' is not necessarily enough to withdraw this implied licence (*Snook* v *Mannion* [1982] RTR 321).

- A person cannot seek refuge on someone else's land as a trespasser themselves; a requirement for a breath test and any subsequent arrest may be lawful if the person is a trespasser (see *Morris* v *Beardmore* [1980] RTR 321).

- If a person has been lawfully arrested on their own land, officers may remain on the land and enter premises to recapture them, even if asked to leave (*Hart* v *Chief Constable of Kent* [1983] Crim LR 117).

- Although the provisions of s.15(2) of the Road Traffic Offenders Act 1988 may render evidence from a specimen taken after an unlawful arrest admissible (**see para. 5.5.2**), any finding that the officer(s) concerned acted in a way that they know to be unlawful or unwarranted may lead to that evidence being excluded under s. 78 of the Police and Criminal Evidence Act 1984 (see *DPP* v *Godwin* [1991] RTR 303).

## 5.4.4 Powers of Entry

Clearly the above situations can be avoided where there is a power of entry. In addition to that provided under s. 4 (**see para. 5.2.1**), there is a specific power of entry provided by s. 6(6) which states that:

> *(6) A constable may, for the purpose of requiring a person to provide a specimen of breath under subsection (2) above in a case where he has reasonable cause to suspect that the accident involved injury to another person or of arresting him in such a case under subsection (5) above, enter (if need be by force) any place where that person is or where the constable, with reasonable cause, suspects him to be.*

**Keynote**

The entry may be made to:

- carry out the test
- arrest the person following such a test
- arrest a person after they have failed to provide a specimen for such a test.

In order for this power to apply you must show that:

- **there was an accident** (mere suspicion or belief by the officer, however strong, is not enough);
- **the officer had reasonable cause to *believe* that the person had been driving, attempting to drive or in charge of the vehicle concerned** (suspicion is not enough);
- **the officer had reasonable cause to *suspect* that the accident involved injury *to another person*** (for this part suspicion is enough provided there is reasonable cause for it);
- ***the officer had reasonable cause to suspect* the person to be in the place entered** (again suspicion is enough).

### 5.4.5 Power of Arrest

Under s. 6(5)(a) a police officer may (not *must*) arrest a person if, as a result of a preliminary breath test, the officer has reasonable cause to suspect that he/she is over the prescribed limit.

Under s. 6(5)(b) however, an officer may only arrest that person if he/she has failed to provide a breath specimen *and* the officer has reasonable cause to suspect that he/she has alcohol in his/her body. If a driver refuses to provide a breath specimen, an officer will need to show reasonable cause for suspecting the driver to have alcohol in his/her body — otherwise s. 6(5)(b) does not give a power of arrest.

## 5.5 Evidential Specimens

Sections 7–9 of the Road Traffic Act 1988 govern the procedure for obtaining specimens for analysis, or evidential specimens. Unlike the preliminary breath tests above, specimens taken under this part of the Act are retained for evidential purposes in subsequent hearings. Such specimens will either be by breath samples taken on an approved machine (e.g. the Lion Intoximeter or the Camic Breath Analyser) or by blood/urine samples.

The print outs from 'approved' machines will generally be admissible in evidence under s. 69 of the Police and Criminal Evidence Act 1984. Minor errors in the printing functions of such machines will not necessarily invalidate the evidence produced by the machine, provided it can be shown that the analytical function of the machine was calibrated and working properly (*Reid* v *DPP*, *The Times*, 6 March 1998).

Many of the difficulties which have been encountered during the police station process have now been addressed by police forces adopting a national pro-forma and strict adherence to those forms will significantly reduce the likelihood of convictions being quashed (see below).

### 5.5.1 Provision of Specimens for Analysis

Section 7 of the Road Traffic Act 1988 provides that:

*(1) In the course of an investigation into whether a person has committed an offence under section 3A, 4 or 5 of this Act a constable may, subject to the following provisions of this section and section 9 of this Act, require him—*

*(a) to provide two specimens of breath for analysis by means of a device of a type approved by the Secretary of State, or*

*(b) to provide a specimen of blood or urine for a laboratory test.*

*(2) A requirement under this section to provide specimens of breath can only be made at a police station.*

*(3) A requirement under this section to provide a specimen of blood or urine can only be made at a police station or at a hospital; and it cannot be made at a police station unless—*

*(a) the constable making the requirement has reasonable cause to believe that for medical reasons a specimen of breath cannot be provided or should not be required, or*

*(b) at the time the requirement is made a device or a reliable device of the type mentioned in subsection (1)(a) above is not available at the police station or it is then for any other reason not practicable to use such a device there, or*

*(bb) a device of the type mentioned in subsection (1)(a) above has been used at the police station but the constable who required the specimens of breath has reasonable cause to believe that the device has not produced a reliable indication of the proportion of alcohol in the breath of the person concerned, or*

*(c) the suspected offence is one under section 3A or 4 of this Act and the constable making the requirement has been advised by a medical practitioner that the condition of the person required to provide the specimen might be due to some drug;*

*but may then be made notwithstanding that the person required to provide the specimen has already provided or been required to provide two specimens of breath.*

*(4) . . .*

*(5) A specimen of urine shall be provided within one hour of the requirement for its provision being made and after the provision of a previous specimen of urine.*

*(6) . . .*

*(7) A constable must, on requiring any person to provide a specimen in pursuance of this section, warn him that a failure to provide it may render him liable to prosecution.*

**Keynote**

Section 7(3)(bb) was inserted into the 1988 Act by the Criminal Procedure and Investigations Act 1996 to cater for the arrival of the next generation of 'approved devices'.

At the time of writing the new devices that have been approved under s. 7(1) are:

- the CAMIC (Car and Medical Instrument Co.) **Datamaster**
- the Lion **Intoxylizer 6000UK**
- the **EC/IR Intoximeter**.

The key difference between these new evidential devices and their well-known predecessors lies in their ability to give an automatic indication of the reliability of their own read out in relation to the presence of alcohol. They are able to detect the presence of mouth alcohol and other interfering substances, giving an indication to that effect to the operator. They will also produce error messages in certain situations, such as where the difference between the first and second sample of breath exceeds 15%. The introduction of these new machines — expected to be installed in all police stations throughout England and Wales by December 1999 — may well increase the number of occasions where police officers have to exercise their discretion in requiring specimens of blood or urine.

## The Requirement

A requirement under s. 7 for a breath specimen can only be made at a police station.

That requirement can be made of more than one person in respect of the same vehicle (e.g. if it is believed that one of three defendants was driving the vehicle) (*Pearson* v *Metropolitan Police Commissioner* [1988] RTR 276).

A requirement for blood or urine can only be made at a police station if the conditions under s. 7(3)(a) to (c) are met.

**Medical Reasons**

For the officer making the requirement to have 'reasonable cause to *believe*' that medical reasons exist, there is no need to seek medical advice first (see *Dempsey* v *Catton* [1986] RTR 194). It is the objective *cause* of that belief which will be considered by the courts, not whether the officer actually did believe that a medical reason existed (*Davis* v *DPP* [1988] RTR 156).

If a person is too drunk to provide a breath specimen, that may be regarded as a 'medical' reason for requiring a sample of blood/urine (*Young* v *DPP* [1992] RTR 328).

**Device 'Available'?**

If the relevant machine at a police station will not calibrate or is in some other way unreliable, this would appear to make it 'unavailable'. In such a case, however, the driver may be taken to another police station where such a machine is 'available'; this may be done *even if the driver has already provided two samples on the inaccurate machine* (*Denny* v *DPP* [1990] RTR 417).

Whether a machine is 'available' if it produces an accurate reading of the analysis of the driver's breath but cannot, for some reason, produce a hard copy printout of that reading is open to some doubt. In one case (*Morgan* v *Lee* [1985] RTR 409) where the officer did not know of the machine's defect, his subsequent request for a blood sample was held to have been unlawful. However, in a later case the Divisional Court held that, if the officer knew at the time that the machine had any form of malfunction, he/she could require a specimen of blood/urine under s. 7(3)(b) (*Thompson* v *Thynne* [1986] Crim LR 629) and this *subjective* approach has been followed and approved many times since.

Where the requirement for blood/urine is made under s. 7(3)(b), that sample must be used and the prosecution cannot revert to evidence produced by the breath sample (*Badkin* v *Chief Constable of South Yorkshire, The Times,* 29 August 1987).

If the option to provide a blood sample is chosen then, again, the driver may be taken to another police station where a doctor is available (*Chief Constable of Kent* v *Berry* [1986] Crim LR 748).

Section 7(3)(b) also allows the officer (see below) the option of a blood/urine specimen when, 'for any other reason' it is not practicable to use a breath-testing device at the police station. This would clearly include the situation where no trained operator is available to work the machine (*Chief Constable of Avon and Somerset* v *Kelliher* [1986] Crim LR 635).

**Drugs**

In contrast to the condition at s. 7(3)(a), the advice of a medical practitioner *must* be sought before the power to request blood/urine can be made under s. 7(3)(c); even then, it can only be made in cases of being unfit (**see para. 5.2**) or causing death by careless driving when under the influence of drink or drugs (**see para. 2.7**).

When such medical advice is sought, the doctor must give the officer a clear verbal statement to the effect that the driver's condition was due to some drug (*Cole* v *DPP* [1988] RTR 224).

### Warning

The warning required by s. 7(7) is critical to a successful prosecution for failing to provide a specimen when required under s. 7(3). It is not needed when a driver elects to give an alternative sample under s. 8 below (see *Hayes* v *DPP* [1993] Crim LR 966 and also *DPP* v *Jackson*; *Stanley* v *DPP* [1998] 3 WLR 514 below).

### Choice by Officer

Section 7(4) provides that:

> *(4) If the provision of a specimen other than a specimen of breath may be required in pursuance of this section the question whether it is to be a specimen of blood or a specimen of urine shall be decided by the constable making the requirement, but if a medical practitioner is of the opinion that for medical reasons a specimen of blood cannot or should not be taken the specimen shall be a specimen of urine.*

### Keynote

In exercising the power under s. 7(3) and s. 8 below, the decision as to whether the specimen will be blood or urine will be made by the officer. The line of decided cases which allowed a 'drivers' preference' was ended by the House of Lords' ruling in *DPP* v *Warren* [1993] AC 319 where their Lordships stated unequivocally that the decision, in both situations, is to be made by the officer.

This area of law has now become quite complex and what follows is a brief summary of the key points arising from the case decisions. In cases of doubt, the advice of the CPS should be sought.

Following the decision in *DPP* v *Warren*, many forces adapted their pro-formas once again in order to close what Lord Bridge called *a variety of wholly unmeritorious avenues of escape from conviction*. For a while it was believed that Lord Bridge's *dicta* in *Warren* would avoid any further appeals based on the procedure followed by police officers when obtaining evidential specimens in line with their respective force forms. However, there have been several more recent cases where the defendants have argued that the *Warren* formula, as laid down by Lord Bridge, has not been followed. Most of those cases have concerned what information must be given, and when it must be given to a defendant when explaining the choices available under s. 7(4) above and s. 8(2) below. In the first case, *Fraser* v *DPP* [1997] RTR 373, Lord Bingham CJ examined many of the other authorities since *Warren*. In his judgment he endorsed the pro-forma used by the Northumbria police and said that there was a danger of putting *a new and heretical gloss* on the statute itself. His lordship held that there were many things which drivers ought to be told, but they need not be told them all at once. His lordship went on to say that there was no requirement for an officer to explain to a defendant *at the time of making a decision under s. 7(4)* that any blood sample taken would only be so taken by a doctor.

In the second case, *DPP* v *Jackson*; *Stanley* v *DPP* [1998] 3 WLR 514, the House of Lords stressed the distinction between the roles of the police officer and the doctor. The police officer decides *which* evidential sample(s) should be obtained and the medical practitioner decides *on the validity of the reasons put forward by the defendant* as to why a specimen of blood should not be taken. Their lordships held that, with three exceptions, the rules laid down in *Warren* were not mandatory elements of the procedure for taking evidential specimens but were guidelines indicating matters which should be brought to a defendant's attention before he/she exercised any choice that might be available.

The three elements that **are** mandatory are:

- In a s. 7(3) case (see above), the warning required under s. 7(7) above;
- a statement as to why, in a case under s. 7(3), a breath specimen could not be used; and
- a statement, in a case under s. 8(2) below, that the specimen of breath containing the lower proportion of alcohol did not exceed 50 microgrammes in 100 millilitres of breath. In such a case, the police offer should ask whether there are any medical reasons why a particular specimen could not or should not be taken.

As with other decisions involving when and where to give information to a defendant (e.g. cautioning; **see General Police Duties, chapter 2**), there are probably fewer dangers in giving more than is required, sooner than required than vice versa. Many of the cases before and since *Warren* have turned on the fact that drivers claim that they were not given the chance to reveal medical reasons as to why they could not give blood, or that they were not told that it would be a doctor who took the blood rather than a police officer. Although it is now clear from the House of Lords' decisions above that such opportunity and information need not be given out as a general requirement, there seems to be little harm in following an approach that errs on the side of caution and there are not many cases in this area where drunk drivers go free solely as a result of the police officer giving them too many opportunities or too much information! The arrival of new pro-formas may also close a few more avenues of appeal, although history has shown the extent of ingenuity of some defendants and their advisors in this area.

The officer should explain what the options are and that the decision as to which will be chosen is his or hers; the driver should also be given the opportunity to state any reasons why blood should not be taken so that the officer may take the appropriate advice (*Edge* v *DPP* [1993] RTR 146).

### Choice by Defendant

Section 8 of the Road Traffic Act 1988 states that:

> *(1) Subject to subsection (2) below, of any two specimens of breath provided by any person in pursuance of section 7 of this Act that with the lower proportion of alcohol in the breath shall be used and the other shall be disregarded.*
>
> *(2) If the specimen with the lower proportion of alcohol contains no more than 50 microgrammes of alcohol in 100 millilitres of breath, the person who provided it may claim that it should be replaced by such specimen as may be required under section 7(4) of this Act and, if he then provides such a specimen, neither specimen of breath shall be used.*

**Keynote**

Under s. 8(2) the driver does have a choice; that being to ask for the specimen of breath to be replaced by an option under s. 7(4) above. As discussed, once that request has been made, the choice as to whether it will be blood or urine will be the officer's.

If a driver elects to give blood and, through no fault of his/her own, the sample then proves unsuitable for evidential use, the original reading from the machine cannot be used in its place (*Archbold* v *Jones* [1985] Crim LR 740).

Although the choice is to be made by the requesting officer, the possibility of medical reasons for not giving blood must still be considered. An alleged fear of needles by the driver (which has provided the courts with a number of opportunities to explore this area) is a relevant consideration when making a decision as to whether a blood sample should be taken (*DPP* v *Jackson*; *Stanley* v *DPP* above and also *Johnson* v *West Yorkshire Metropolitan Police* [1986] RTR 167).

The medical advice may be given to the officer over the telephone if appropriate (*Andrews* v *DPP* [1992] RTR 1).

### Offence — Failing to Provide Evidential Specimen — Road Traffic Act 1988, s. 7(6)

*Triable summarily. Six months' imprisonment and/or a fine. Obligatory disqualification.*
***(No specific power of arrest)***

The Road Traffic Act 1988, s. 7 states:

> *(6) A person who, without reasonable excuse, fails to provide a specimen when required to do so in pursuance of this section is guilty of an offence.*

**Keynote**

Section 11(3) of the Road Traffic Act 1988 states that a breath specimen must be provided in such a way as to enable the analysis to be carried out. If a driver produces it in any other way, they will have 'failed to provide'.

As with preliminary breath tests (**see para. 5.4**), 'fail' will include a refusal. If a driver elects to substitute a breath specimen (which gave a reading below 50 microgrammes) with one of blood/urine under s. 8 (above), and subsequently fails or refuses to do so, he/she does not commit an offence under s. 7(6); you revert to the original breath specimen.

Provision of only one specimen of breath is a 'failure to provide' (*Cracknell* v *Willis* [1987] 3 All ER 801).

#### Reasonable Excuse

What amounts to a 'reasonable excuse' is a matter of law; whether the defendant actually *had* such an excuse is a question of fact for the court to determine having regard to the particular circumstances in each case. There have been many cases where 'excuses' have been put forward. The following is a brief summary:

*Not reasonable*

- Refusal until legal advice has been sought

- Refusal until solicitor present
- Refusal on advice by solicitor
- Refusal until driver had read the Codes of Practice under PACE
- Mistaken belief by the defendant
- Belief that the officer did not have the authority to make the requirement
- Religious beliefs
- Self-induced intoxication
- Mental anguish caused by custody officer's behaviour.

*Reasonable*

- Mental incapacity
- Physical incapacity
- Inability to understand requirement caused by factors other than drink or drugs (e.g. language barrier).

Where any physical or mental incapacity (to provide the specimen or to understand the warning which accompanies it) is put forward, there will need to be clear, independent support for the claim being genuine (e.g. from a medical practitioner).

The courts have warned of the need for caution when accepting a defendant's claim of such incapacity, particularly given the generally stressful nature of the police station procedure, together with the possible effects following an accident or motoring incident leading up to the request.

Where a defendant's mental capacity to understand the warning is impaired by his/her drunkenness, this is not a 'reasonable' excuse (*DPP* v *Beech* [1992] Crim LR 64).

**Blood**

Section 11(4) of the Road Traffic Act 1988 provides that a specimen of blood must be taken by a medical practitioner with the defendant's consent; s. 15 of the Road Traffic Offenders Act 1988 (**see below**) states that any sample of blood will be disregarded unless it is so taken.

Once that consent is given, it is for the doctor to say from which part of the body it will be taken. Any insistence on a different course of action will be a refusal (*Rushton* v *Higgins* [1972] Crim LR 440).

**Urine**

Urine samples do not need to be taken by a medical practitioner.

The samples will be admissible as long as they are provided within the time set out under s. 7(5) and there are two distinct samples (as opposed to two samples taken during the same act of urinating) (*Prosser* v *Dickeson* [1982] RTR 96).

### 5.5.2 Use of Specimens

Section 15 of the Road Traffic Offenders Act 1988 states that:

> *(1) This section and section 16 of this Act apply in respect of proceedings for an offence under section 3A, 4 or 5 of the Road Traffic Act 1988 (driving offences connected with drink or drugs); and*

*expressions used in this section and section 16 of this Act have the same meaning as in sections 3A to 10 of that Act.*

*(2) Evidence of the proportion of alcohol or any drug in a specimen of breath, blood or urine provided by the accused shall, in all cases (including cases where the specimen was not provided in connection with the alleged offence), be taken into account and, subject to subsection (3) below, it shall be assumed that the proportion of alcohol in the accused's breath, blood or urine at the time of the alleged offence was not less than in the specimen.*

*(3) That assumption shall not be made if the accused proves—*

*(a) that he consumed alcohol before he provided the specimen and—*

*(i) in relation to an offence under section 3A, after the time of the alleged offence, and*

*(ii) otherwise, after he had ceased to drive, attempt to drive or be in charge of a vehicle on a road or other public place, and*

*(b) that had he not done so the proportion of alcohol in his breath, blood or urine would not have exceeded the prescribed limit and, if it is alleged that he was unfit to drive through drink, would not have been such as to impair his ability to drive properly.*

*(4) A specimen of blood shall be disregarded unless it was taken from the accused with his consent by a medical practitioner.*

*(5) Where, at the time a specimen of blood or urine was provided by the accused, he asked to be provided with such a specimen, evidence of the proportion of alcohol or any drug found in the specimen is not admissible on behalf of the prosecution unless—*

*(a) the specimen in which the alcohol or drug was found is one of two parts into which the specimen provided by the accused was divided at the time it was provided, and*

*(b) the other part was supplied to the accused.*

**Keynote**

Section 15(2) requires the court to:

- take into account evidence of the proportion of alcohol *or any drug* in a specimen of breath, blood or urine *in all cases*; and
- assume that the proportion of alcohol (though apparently not drugs) in the defendant's breath, blood or urine at the time of the alleged offence was *not less* than that found in the specimen, subject to the circumstances in subsection (3).

### Taking Evidence into Account

The first requirement, to take the evidence into account in all cases, was accepted by the House of Lords in *Fox* v *Chief Constable of Gwent* [1986] AC 281 as meaning that evidence obtained following an unlawful arrest was still admissible. However, their lordships did not hold this to be an exception to the general law on the admissibility of improperly or unfairly obtained evidence (as to which **see Evidence and Procedure, chapter 13**). Under the general discretion given to courts by s. 78 of the Police and Criminal Evidence Act 1984, to exclude unfair evidence, evidence of specimens could be so excluded in spite of the provisions of subsection (2) above.

### Making the Assumption

Section 15(3) allows the defendant to produce evidence which prevents that presumption from being made. This enables a defendant to prove that the alcohol had been consumed between the time of the alleged offence and the provision of the specimen and, that if the defendant had not consumed it, then he/she would not have been over the limit/unfit. That is, the defendant can prove that the alcohol level at the time of the alleged offence was lower than shown in the analysis. The burden of proof upon the defence in making such a case would, as ever, be 'on the balance of probabilities' (**see Evidence and Procedure, chapter 11**).

The assumption does not prevent the prosecution from adducing evidence to show that the proportion of alcohol in the defendant's body was in fact *higher* than that in the specimen. To do so, however, requires a process of 'back calculation', a process accepted by the House of Lords in *Gumbley* v *Cunningham* [1989] RTR 49. In that case their lordships said that such a process should be used with caution and evidence of back calculation should not be relied upon unless it is easily understood and clearly persuasive. In a later case Lord Lane CJ said that such calculations should be treated with great care and that they would be less helpful in deciding cases involving driving while over the prescribed limit than they would in offences involving the *standard* of driving (**see chapter 2**) (*R* v *Downes* [1991] RTR 395).

The effect of subsection (2) is to limit any use of back calculation to the *prosecution*. Other than in the context of subsection (3), a defendant may not adduce back calculation evidence to show that the level of alcohol in his/her body was in fact *below* the amount in the specimen (*Millard* v *DPP* (1990) 91 Cr App R 108).

### Specimen of Blood

Under s. 15(4) the prosecution must prove that the defendant consented to the taking of blood and that burden will only be discharged if this is proved beyond a reasonable doubt (see *Friel* v *Dickinson* [1992] RTR 366). This may generally be proved by documentary evidence signed by a medical practitioner, subject to certain provisos (s. 16(2)).

### Provision of Specimen *to* Defendant

Under s. 15(5), the prosecution must show that the defendant, if he/she asked for one, was provided with a specimen divided and supplied as set out in the subsection. Although the specimen must be divided 'at the time' it is taken and as part of the same continuing event, there is no need for it to be done in the defendant's presence (*DPP* v *Elstob* [1992] RTR 45). Again, although the *division* of the specimen must be made at the time it is taken, there is no requirement that the defendant be *provided* with his/her part 'at the time' — only that it be provided within a reasonable time thereafter — see *R* v *Sharp* [1968] 2 QB 564. The part-specimen must be in such a quantity and of such a quality that it is capable of being analysed (*Smith* v *Cole* [1971] 1 All ER 200). Whether or not this has been done is a question of fact for the court to determine on its own merits.

Where a police officer supplied the defendant with a part-specimen but did not follow the local procedure of sealing it inside an envelope and subsequently convinced the defendant that the part-specimen could not then be submitted for analysis, the conviction based on the specimen was quashed (*Perry* v *McGovern* [1986] RTR 240). Although a 'principle' of law grew up around this case to the effect that actions by the police must not mislead or deter a defendant from submitting the part-specimen for analysis, the provisions of s. 78 of the Police and Criminal Evidence Act 1984 would appear to cover any such eventualities (**see Evidence and Procedure, chapter 13**).

Section 16 of the Road Traffic Offenders Act 1988 sets out the provisions for documentary evidence to be used when proving the proportion of alcohol *or drugs* in specimens of breath, blood or urine. This has proved to be another fertile ground for litigation and there are many case decisions surrounding the interpretation of the provisions of s. 16. In summary the section allows for proof of the proportion of alcohol or drugs in a specimen to be made by a statement produced by the approved device that measured the specimen together with a certificate as to its truth signed by a police officer (s. 16(1)(a)). It also provides for evidence to be given in the form of a certificate signed by an authorised analyst as to the proportion of alcohol or drug found in a specimen of blood or urine (s. 16(1)(b)).

Section 16(3) and (4) set out the requirements for service of a copy of any such statement and certificate on the defendant before it can become admissible. Any such copy or other document must be served on the defendant not later than seven days before the hearing (s. 16(3)). Certificates will not be admissible if the defendant serves notice not later than three days before the hearing (or longer if the court allows) on the prosecutor requiring the attendance of the person by whom the certificate purports to be signed (s. 16(4)). It has been held that there is no requirement for the *copy* to be signed by the police officer (*Chief Constable of Surrey* v *Wickens* [1985] RTR 277).

The effect of failing to serve the copies on the defendant is that the evidence contained within them is inadmissible. This does not prevent the relevant witnesses — police officers, analysts or medical practitioners — from providing oral evidence in person.

It would appear that oral evidence as to a defendant's breath-alcohol level may be given by the police officer who operated the machine, provided that evidence also proves that the approved device was properly calibrated (*Owen* v *Chesters* [1985] RTR 191).

## 5.5.3 Detention of Person Affected

Section 10 of the Road Traffic Act 1988 provides that:

*(1) Subject to subsections (2) and (3) below, a person required to provide a specimen of breath, blood or urine may afterwards be detained at a police station until it appears to the constable that, were that person then driving or attempting to drive a mechanically propelled vehicle on a road, he would not be committing an offence under section 4 or 5 of this Act.*

*(2) A person shall not be detained in pursuance of this section if it appears to a constable that there is no likelihood of his driving or attempting to drive a mechanically propelled vehicle whilst his ability to drive properly is impaired or whilst the proportion of alcohol in his breath, blood or urine exceeds the prescribed limit.*

*(3) A constable must consult a medical practitioner on any question arising under this section whether a person's ability to drive properly is or might be impaired through drugs and must act on the medical practitioner's advice.*

**Keynote**

The requirement to consult a doctor under s. 10(3) is mandatory.

There is no guidance as to how the officer might form his/her view as to the fitness of a person to drive when released. A further screening breath test may be used if appropriate but it is not required as it was under the former legislation.

If there is no likelihood of the person driving any mechanically propelled vehicle while impaired or over the limit, the person must be released.

## 5.5.4 Hospital Procedure

Section 9 provides that:

*(1) While a person is at a hospital as a patient he shall not be required to provide a specimen of breath for a breath test or to provide a specimen for a laboratory test unless the medical practitioner in immediate charge of his case has been notified of the proposal to make the requirement; and—*

*(a) if the requirement is then made, it shall be for the provision of a specimen at the hospital, but*

*(b) if the medical practitioner objects on the ground specified in subsection (2) below, the requirement shall not be made.*

*(2) The ground on which the medical practitioner may object is that the requirement or the provision of a specimen or, in the case of a specimen of blood or urine, the warning required under section 7(7) of this Act, would be prejudicial to the proper care and treatment of the patient.*

## Keynote

A 'hospital' will include an institution providing medical treatment for in-patients or out-patients (s. 11(2) of the Road Traffic Act 1988). It will also include anywhere within the precincts of that hospital.

Whether the person is there as a 'patient' or in another capacity will be a question of fact. In assessing this fact the courts will be helped by reference to hospital records which show names of patients, together with their times of admission and discharge (see *Askew* v *DPP* [1988] RTR 303), although these records will not be conclusive.

If a person has been treated and then discharged from the hospital, he/she ceases to be a 'patient' for these purposes even if he/she has to return at a future date for further, related treatment (e.g. to have stitches removed).

A useful case illustrating this area is *Webber* v *DPP* [1998] RTR 111. In *Webber* the driver of a vehicle involved in an accident was taken to a hospital where she was requested to provide a specimen of breath under s. 6. She refused. While she was still a patient at the hospital, the driver was required to provide a blood specimen for analysis under ss. 7(1)(b) and 9(1). She agreed but, before she was able to provide the specimen, she was discharged. She was then arrested under s. 6(5)(b) as a result of her earlier refusal. The driver was taken to a police station where she provided a specimen of blood on the strength of which she was subsequently convicted of driving while over the prescribed limit. She appealed, by way of case stated, on the ground that s. 9(1)(a) required the blood specimen to be taken *at the hospital*, which in this case it was not. The Divisional Court held that, once the obligation to provide a specimen for analysis has been made, it is not to be discharged simply by an 'irrelevant change of *locus*'. The court went on to say, by making the requirement, the police officer set in train a procedure which carries a sanction (s. 7(6)), a procedure that was not to be altered by the mere fact that the defendant, for whatever reason, had left the hospital before complying with the requirement.

The restriction applies to both preliminary breath tests and evidential tests.

If the patient provides a positive reading or fails to provide a specimen of breath, he/she cannot then be arrested while still a 'patient' (s. 6(5)).

The procedure for requiring a specimen for analysis is generally the same as that employed when requiring blood/urine at a police station, with the exception that the officer requiring the sample ought to inform the patient that a breath specimen cannot be taken at a hospital (*Ogburn* v *DPP* [1994] RTR 241).

# CHAPTER SIX

# INSURANCE

## 6.1 Introduction

People using or driving vehicles on roads necessarily present an element of risk to others. In addition to the many provisions which minimise that risk so far as is practicable there is a requirement that most road users are insured against third party risk.

## 6.2 Requirement for Insurance

Section 143(1) of the Road Traffic Act 1988 states that:

*(1) Subject to the provisions of this Part of this Act—*

*(a) a person must not use a motor vehicle on a road unless there is in force in relation to the use of the vehicle by that person such a policy of insurance or such a security in respect of third party risks as complies with the requirements of this Part of this Act, and*

*(b) a person must not cause or permit any other person to use a motor vehicle on a road unless there is in force in relation to the use of the vehicle by that other person such a policy of insurance or such a security in respect of third party risks as complies with the requirements of this Part of this Act.*

**Offence — Contravening Requirement for Insurance — Road Traffic Act 1988, s. 143(2)**
*Triable summarily. Fine. Discretionary disqualification.*
***(No specific power of arrest)***

The Road Traffic Act 1988, s. 143 states:

*(2) If a person acts in contravention of subsection (1) above he is guilty of an offence.*

**Keynote**

Unless the insurer of a vehicle delivers a certificate of insurance to the person taking out the policy, the requirements of s. 143(1) will not have been met (s. 147(1)). Therefore, anyone using, or causing or permitting to be used, a motor vehicle on a road before the delivery of such a certificate, commits this offence.

A driver may be required under s. 165 (**see para. 6.2.6**) or s. 170 (**see para. 4.2**) of the Road Traffic Act 1988 to produce a certificate of insurance (or other acceptable form of security). In such cases, in order to determine whether a motor vehicle was being driven in contravention of s. 143 above, s. 171 of the Road Traffic Act 1988 places a requirement on the *owner* of the vehicle to give such information as required the police. Failure to comply with such a requirement is a summary offence.

Many insurance companies appear now to issue instant insurance cover over the telephone by creating an 'agency' to which the insurance certificate is delivered on behalf of the insured.

For the difference between 'using', 'causing' and 'permitting' and the proof required for each, **see chapter 1**. Note that if the driver is employed by the vehicle's owner you must prove that the driver was acting in the course of his/her employment before you can convict the owner of using, causing or permitting the use of the vehicle without insurance. The driver's own inadmissible statement to that effect will not suffice (*Jones* v *DPP*, *The Times*, 23 April 1998).

The risks which must be covered by any insurance policy for the purposes of s. 143 are set out in s. 145(3). These are generally:

- Liability in relation to bodily injury caused to others when the vehicle on a road in Great Britain.
- Civil liability in relation to the use of a vehicle from another EU member State in Great Britain.
- Civil liability in relation to the use of a vehicle from Great Britain in another EU member State.

### 6.2.1 Absolute Liability

Generally the offence under s. 143 is one of absolute liability (**see Crime, chapter 1**), that is, you need not prove any intent or guilty knowledge by the defendant in order to convict (*Tapsell* v *Maslen* [1967] Crim LR 53).

If, however, a person allows another to use their vehicle on the express condition that the other person insures it first, the lender cannot be convicted of 'permitting' (*Newbury* v *Davis* [1974] RTR 367).

### 6.2.2 Defence

The Road Traffic Act 1988, s. 143 states:

> *(3) A person charged with using a motor vehicle in contravention of this section shall not be convicted if he proves—*
> *(a) that the vehicle did not belong to him and was not in his possession under a contract of hiring or of loan,*
> *(b) that he was using the vehicle in the course of his employment, and*
> *(c) that he neither knew nor had reason to believe that there was not in force in relation to the vehicle such a policy of insurance or security as is mentioned in subsection (1) above.*

**Keynote**

Note that s. 143(3) provides a special defence for employees using their employer's vehicle in the course of their employment.

The burden of proof in such a case is on the defendant and will be judged on the balance of probabilities (*R* v *Carr-Briant* [1943] 2 All ER 156).

### 6.2.3 Check 'This'

As with other areas of law involving documentation (e.g. firearms (**see General Police Duties, chapter 5**)), when considering vehicle insurance it is useful to ask:

Does

- **This** policy
  cover
- **This** person
  to drive/use
- **This** vehicle
  for
- **This** purpose
  on
- **This** day?

Each of these elements is considered in turn.

**This Policy**

The form in which certificates must appear, together with the requirement for insurers to keep and supply copies of records are contained in the Motor Vehicles (Third Party Risks) Regulations 1972 (SI 1972 No. 1217) as amended.

Cover notes are included, by s. 161(1) of the Road Traffic Act 1988, in the meaning of 'policy of insurance'.

The internationally recognised 'green card scheme' allows for the insurance of British vehicles abroad and overseas vehicles in Great Britain (see the Motor Vehicles (International Motor Insurance Card) Regulations 1971 (SI 1971 No. 792)).

There is a requirement (under s. 145(3)(b) of the 1988 Act) however, for insurance policies to provide cover which extends to other European Union countries, removing the need for the 'green card' scheme within the EU by vehicles from member States.

**This Person**

If a policy is restricted to a named person, only that person will generally be covered by it.

If, as often happens, the policy covers any person who holds a current driving licence, that description may include the holder of a provisional licence (see *Rendlesham* v *Dunne* [1964] 1 Lloyd's Rep 192) or even the holder of a licence issued in another country.

If a policy refers to 'agents' or 'employees', you will need to establish whether or not the relevant person fits into those categories. Garage proprietors returning vehicles to the owner after repairing them are not in the owner's employment (*Lyons* v *May* [1948] 2 All ER 1062). However, an employee driving an employer's vehicle in an unauthorised manner will not negate the effect of a policy of insurance (*Marsh* v *Moores* [1949] 2 All ER 27).

Generally, an insurance policy obtained by false representations will be valid for the purposes of s. 143 and will remain so until the contract has been 'avoided' (ended) by the insurer (*Durrant* v *MacLaren* [1956] Crim LR 632).

### This Vehicle

Generally the question of whether or not a policy applies to the particular vehicle will not present a problem. Trailers can create difficulties, both in relation to the vehicles covered by the policy, and the use to which they are being put. Trailers are themselves 'vehicles' (**see para. 1.2.5**) at times and may be included in the definition of motor vehicle when charging an offence under s. 143 (see *Rogerson* v *Stephens* [1950] 2 All ER 144).

When motor vehicles are being towed by other vehicles, they remain 'motor vehicles' and, as such, require insurance when used on roads (*Milstead* v *Sexton* [1964] Crim LR 474).

### This Purpose

Insurance policies will often exclude certain uses (e.g. racing and time trials); many stipulate 'social and domestic purposes'. Lending vehicles to friends in return for payment reimbursing petrol costs will amount to such use, as will using the vehicle to help a friend move house (see *Lee* v *Poole* [1954] Crim LR 942).

Such an expression does not include business trips (see *Wood* v *General Accident etc. Assurance Co.* (1948) 65 TLR 53).

Insurance cover in respect of 'the insured's business' does not extend to other businesses of friends or colleagues (see *Passmore* v *Vulcan etc. Insurance Co.* (1935) 154 LT 258)). If employees deviate from the ordinary course of their duties or employment, on what is often termed a 'frolic of their own', they may not be covered by the terms of the employer's policy. Simply taking a two-mile detour in order to give someone a lift has been held not to invalidate the employer's insurance policy (*Ballance* v *Brown* [1955] Crim LR 384) but each case will have to be decided on its own facts.

### This Day

Clearly any insurance policy must be shown to have been in force at the relevant time. Many business users have arrangements whereby they pass the risk to their insurers at short notice and it will always be necessary to establish whether a particular policy is actually operative at the time (see e.g. *Samuelson* v *National Insurance etc. Ltd* [1986] 3 All ER 417).

In a Scottish case a defendant telephoned his insurer and arranged cover to start at a particular time once he had paid the appropriate premium. Three hours before he paid the premium he was stopped by the police. Although his insurers later issued a certificate covering the time at which he was stopped, the defendant was held not to have been covered by the policy *at that time* as he had not yet paid the required premium (*McCulloch* v *Heywood* 1995 SLT 1009).

Although many policies exclude use of the particular vehicle for payment or reward, s. 150 of the 1988 Act makes provision for 'car-sharing' agreements, provided that they meet the criteria set out.

### 6.2.4 Exclusions

Section 148(1) of the Road Traffic Act 1988 makes the effects of some restrictions in a policy void in relation to s. 143. This means that, if a policy purports to restrict the extent of its cover by reference to any of these features, breach of them by the insured person will not affect the validity of that policy for the purposes of s. 143.

Those features (under s. 148) are:

*(1) . . .*
*(a) the age or physical or mental condition of persons driving the vehicle,*
*(b) the condition of the vehicle,*
*(c) the number of persons that the vehicle carries,*
*(d) the weight or physical characteristics of the goods that the vehicle carries,*
*(e) the time at which or the areas within which the vehicle is used,*
*(f) the horsepower or cylinder capacity or value of the vehicle,*
*(g) the carrying on the vehicle of any particular apparatus, or*
*(h) the carrying on the vehicle of any particular means of identification other than any means of identification required to be carried by or under the Vehicle Excise and Registration Act 1994.*

### 6.2.5 Exemptions

Crown vehicles do not appear to require insurance *while being used as such*; if they are being used for some other purpose, they will need insurance on a road (see the Scottish case of *Salt* v *MacKnight* 1947 SC (J) 99).

Section 144 of the 1988 Act sets out other occasions where vehicles will be exempt. Such occasions include police authority vehicles and vehicles being used for police purposes; this will include an off duty police officer using his/her own vehicle for police purposes (*Jones* v *Chief Constable of Bedfordshire* [1987] RTR 332).

By virtue of s. 144(2)(ba), the exemption will extend to vehicles owned by the National Criminal Intelligence Service (NCIS) and the National Crime Squad at a time when they are being used by those organisations by the appropriate officers and employees (as to which **see General Police Duties, chapter 1**).

### 6.2.6 Producing Documents

Section 165 of the Road Traffic Act 1988 states that:

*(1) Any of the following persons—*
*(a) a person driving a motor vehicle (other than an invalid carriage) on a road, or*
*(b) a person whom a constable or vehicle examiner has reasonable cause to believe to have been the driver of a motor vehicle (other than an invalid carriage) at a time when an accident occurred owing to its presence on a road, or*
*(c) a person whom a constable or vehicle examiner has reasonable cause to believe to have committed an offence in relation to the use on a road of a motor vehicle (other than an invalid carriage), must, on being so required by a constable or vehicle examiner, give his name and address and the name and address of the owner of the vehicle and produce the following documents for examination.*
*(2) Those documents are—*
*(a) the relevant certificate of insurance or certificate of security (within the meaning of Part VI of this Act), or such other evidence that the vehicle is not or was not being driven in contravention of section 143 of this Act as may be prescribed by regulations made by the Secretary of State,*

*(b) in relation to a vehicle to which section 47 of this Act applies, a test certificate issued in respect of the vehicle as mentioned in subsection (1) of that section, and*

*(c) in relation to a goods vehicle the use of which on a road without a plating certificate or goods vehicle test certificate is an offence under section 53(1) or (2) of this Act, any such certificate issued in respect of that vehicle or any trailer drawn by it.*

*(3) Subject to subsection (4) below, a person who fails to comply with a requirement under subsection (1) above is guilty of an offence.*

*(4) A person shall not be convicted of an offence under subsection (3) above by reason only of failure to produce any certificate or other evidence . . . if in proceedings against him for the offence he shows that—*

*(a) within seven days after the date on which the production of the certificate or other evidence was required it was produced at a police station that was specified by him at the time when its production was required, or*

*(b) it was produced there as soon as was reasonably practicable, or*

*(c) it was not reasonably practicable for it to be produced there before the day on which the proceedings were commenced,*

*and for the purposes of this subsection the laying of the information . . . shall be treated as the commencement of the proceedings.*

*(5) A person—*

*(a) who supervises the holder of a provisional licence granted under Part III of this Act while the holder is driving on a road a motor vehicle (other than an invalid carriage), or*

*(b) whom a constable or vehicle examiner has reasonable cause to believe was supervising the holder of such a licence while driving, at a time when an accident occurred owing to the presence of the vehicle on a road or at a time when an offence is suspected of having been committed by the holder of the provisional licence in relation to the use of the vehicle on a road,*

*must, on being so required by a constable or vehicle examiner, give his name and address and the name and address of the owner of the vehicle.*

**Keynote**

Production of the certificate need not be in person but the certificate must be shown to the officer for long enough to allow proper inspection of it (applying the 'This' rules above); waving it in front of an officer or snatching it back shortly afterwards will not be enough to comply with the s. 165 (see *Tremelling* v *Martin* [1971] RTR 196).

In cases where a requirement has been made under s. 165, s. 171 of the Road Traffic Act 1988 places a requirement on the *owner* of the vehicle to give such information as required by the police in order to determine whether the motor vehicle was being driven without insurance. Failure to comply with such a requirement is a summary offence.

For additional requirements following an accident, **see chapter 4**.

For the obligations under s. 165 on the supervision of learner drivers, **see chapter 11**.

Traffic wardens may also demand a person's name and address under s. 165. They may *not*, however, demand driving documents under these particular circumstances (see Functions of Traffic Wardens Order 1970 (SI 1970 No. 1958) and also **para. 10.4.2**).

## 6.3 Motor Insurers' Bureau

All insurers in Great Britain are required to be members of the Motor Insurers' Bureau (MIB) (s. 145 of the Road Traffic Act 1988).

The purpose of the MIB is to provide compensation where someone is unable to pursue a valid claim against another following a road traffic accident because the other party is:

- not insured
- not known/traceable
- insured by a company now in liquidation.

The MIB has drawn up an agreement with the Secretary of State which sets out its terms of operation. Generally it will not pay compensation to those who are victims of deliberate criminal acts involving motor vehicles (including those who allow themselves to be carried in vehicles taken without the owner's consent), neither will it compensate those who 'use' vehicles without insurance ('use' here will be taken in the wide sense discussed in **chapter 1** and will include some passengers (see e.g. *Stinton* v *Stinton and Another* [1995] RTR 167 and *O'Mahoney* v *Joliffe, The Times*, 24 February 1999)). The Court of Appeal decided recently that a person injured by an uninsured or untraced driver cannot enforce a claim to compensation against the MIB by citing the 'direct effect' of EC Council Directive 8415 which provides certain rights for citizens of EU member States (*Mighell* v *Reading*; *Evans* v *Motor Insurers' Bureau*; *White* v *White*, *The Times*, 12 October 1998).

# CHAPTER SEVEN

# SAFETY MEASURES

## 7.1 Introduction

This chapter deals with the main areas of legislation aimed at increasing — and enforcing — safety in the use of vehicles.

## 7.2 Seat Belts

The law governing the fitting of seat belts to vehicles comes under the Road Vehicles (Construction and Use) Regulations 1986 (SI 1986 No. 1078) (**see chapter 9**); that which regulates the *wearing* of seat belts is provided by the Motor Vehicles (Wearing of Seat Belts) Regulations 1993) (SI 1993 No. 176) for people over 14 years old, and by the Road Traffic Act 1988, s. 15 for children under that age.

The regulations are made under s. 14 of the Road Traffic Act 1988.

**Offence — Contravention of Regulation Relating to Seat Belts — Road Traffic Act 1988, s. 14(3)**
*Triable summarily. Fine.*
**(*No specific power of arrest*)**

It is an offence to:

- *drive* a **motor vehicle** or
- *ride* in a *front seat* of a **motor vehicle** or
- *ride* in the *rear seat* of a **motor car** or **passenger car**

in each case without wearing an adult seat belt.

Section 14(3) creates these offences by virtue of reg. 5 of the 1993 Regulations.

The above offences can only be committed by people aged 14 and over.

In these and the offences which follow, it is important to note the different definitions used (e.g. *drive, ride, motor vehicle, passenger car, rear seat* etc.).

The definitions can be found in the Road Traffic Act 1988, ss. 15(9) and 185; the Motor Vehicles (Wearing of Seat Belts) Regulations 1993, reg. 3; the Motor Vehicles (Wearing of Seat Belts by Children in Front Seats) Regulations 1993 (SI 1993 No. 31), regs 2 and 3 and the Road Vehicles (Construction and Use) Regulations 1986 (see **chapter 9**).

Section 14(3) goes on to say that, notwithstanding any enactment or rule of law, no person *other than the person actually committing the contravention* is guilty of an offence by reason of the contravention. This means that, irrespective of the general law relating to the aiding and abetting of offences (**see Crime, chapter 2**), the driver of a vehicle will not be responsible for a passenger not wearing a seat belt. This is similar to the wording used at s. 16 of the 1988 Act (**see para. 7.3**) in relation to motor cycle crash helmets.

This should be contrasted with the position under s. 15 of the 1988 Act in respect of children under 14 years of age who are not wearing seat belts (see below). In those cases the driver *is* responsible and, in theory at least, it would be possible for the child to be guilty of aiding and abetting the driver by not wearing a seat belt. It is also useful to contrast these provisions with those relating to the wearing of motor cycle helmets (**see para. 7.3**).

### 7.2.1 Exemptions

There are several general exemptions to the requirements of the regulations, many of them following common sense. Drivers of delivery vans, prisoner escorts, taxis and people reversing are all subject *to some degree* of exemption under reg. 6 of the Motor Vehicles (Wearing of Seat Belts) Regulations 1993, as are vehicles being used for police or fire brigade purposes. An exemption may give a specific description, not only of the activity (e.g. taxis on hire business), but also of the *vehicle* to which it will apply (for instance, making deliveries in the family car would not attract the exemption because the vehicle used by delivery drivers must *be made or adapted* for making deliveries in order to be exempt).

In addition to these general exemptions, there are other occasions where the requirements will not apply. If there is no adult seat belt provided for the driver, or available for passengers aged 14 and over, the requirements will not apply (reg. 6).

Schedule 2 to the Regulations expands on a number of occasions where seat belts will be deemed not to be 'available'. These occasions include:

- where the seat is properly occupied by someone wearing the seat belt
- where the seat is being used for a carry cot containing a child under one year old which cannot go anywhere else in the vehicle
- where the seat is occupied by someone with a medical exemption.

If a person is unable to wear a seat belt owing to a disability, the seat belt will not be regarded for this purpose as being 'available'.

If a person holds a medical certificate signed by a doctor stating that the wearing of a seat belt by that person is inadvisable on medical grounds, that person will be exempt. Any such certificate must state the period over which it applies and carry the symbol prescribed in the regulations. If it is to be used in evidence in answer to a charge under

s. 14(3) of the 1988 Act, such a certificate must be produced to a constable on request or to a police station within seven days (s. 14(4)).

### 7.2.2 Children Under 14

The law in relation to the wearing of seat belts by children is contained in the Road Traffic Act 1988. The fact that it appears in primary legislation (**see Evidence and Procedure, chapter 1**) perhaps gives an indication of the added importance which Parliament has ascribed to this area of safety.

Further evidence of this importance can be seen in the fact that, unlike the foregoing offences, it is the *driver* who carries most responsibility in relation to the wearing of seat belts by children.

Section 15(1) of the Road Traffic Act 1988 states that, where a child under the age of 14 is in the front of a motor vehicle, a person must not without reasonable excuse drive the motor vehicle on a road unless the child is wearing a seat belt in conformity with the regulations.

Section 15 states that:

> *(3) Except as provided by regulations, where a child under the age of fourteen years is in the rear of a motor vehicle and any seat belt is fitted in the rear of that vehicle, a person must not without reasonable excuse drive the vehicle on a road unless the child is wearing a seat belt in conformity with regulations.*
> *(3A) Except as provided by regulations, where—*
> *(a) a child who is under the age of 12 years and less than 150 centimetres in height is in the rear of a passenger car.*
> *(b) no seat belt is fitted in the rear of the passenger car, and*
> *(c) a seat in the front of the passenger car is provided with a seat belt but is not occupied by any person,*
> *a person must not without reasonable excuse drive the passenger car on a road.*

**Offence — Driving Motor Vehicle in Contravention of Requirement for Seat Belts for Under 14's — Road Traffic Act 1988, s. 15(2) and 15(4)**
*Triable summarily. Fine.*
**(*No specific power of arrest*)**

The Road Traffic Act 1988, s. 15 states:

> *(2) It is an offence for a person to drive a motor vehicle in contravention of subsection (1) above.*
> . . .
> *(4) It is an offence for a person to drive a motor vehicle in contravention of subsections (3) and (3A) above.*

**Keynote**

If all the seats in a vehicle are properly occupied, there is no general requirement to make a child wear a seat belt or to move an adult out of a seat in order to give the child access to a seat belt. There is also no general requirement to move a child from the back seat of a vehicle where there are no seat belts, into the front (or vice versa). However, s. 15(3A) creates additional protection for children who are both under 12 and less than 150cms tall travelling in vehicles which have no rear seat belts fitted but where a front seat with a seat belt is unoccupied. References are to children *in the rear* of the vehicle, not to the *seating*. Therefore, unlike the situation where adults are concerned, it would appear that children under 14 who are standing up in the rear of vehicles are subject to the requirements, irrespective of the seating provided.

The suitability of seat belts, types of seat belts and the manner in which they must be worn by children are set out in the Regulations, as are the further provisions which distinguish between smaller and larger children using them.

Vehicles which do not fall within the definition of a 'motor car' under s. 185 of the 1988 Act (**see chapter 1**) are exempt from the requirements of s. 15(3) and (3A) above (reg. 9).

Many of the exemptions above, including the exemption in relation to medical certificates above, also apply to children (s. 15(6)).

There are separate requirements which govern the wearing of seat belts in the *front* seats of motor vehicles and they are, unsurprisingly, contained in the Motor Vehicles (Wearing of Seat Belts by Children in Front Seats) Regulations 1993 (SI 1993 No. 31) which set out further conditions. In essence the Regulations require any child under 14 to wear a seat belt or other restraint when *in the front of a vehicle* — the requirement is not restricted to *seating*, and would again appear to apply even if the child were standing up.

If a person drives a motor vehicle in contravention of those Regulations, he/she commits the offence under s. 15(2) above.

Note that these offences have a defence of 'reasonable excuse' which is not available in relation to seat belt offences involving adults. Whether an excuse is reasonable will be a matter for the court to determine in each case.

The Motor Vehicles (Safety Equipment for Children) Act 1991 introduced a new summary offence into s. 15A of the Road Traffic Act 1988. Under s. 15A a person commits an offence by selling or letting on hire carry cot restraining devices and other related safety equipment which is not of the type prescribed or which contravenes the Regulations.

## 7.3 Motor Cycle Helmets

Under s. 16 of the Road Traffic Act 1988, the Secretary of State may make Regulations relating to the wearing of protective headgear by people riding motor cycles. The relevant regulations are the Motor Cycles (Protective Helmets) Regulations 1998 (SI 1998 No. 1807).

The Regulations require every person driving or riding on a motor *bicycle* on a road to wear protective headgear (reg. 4).

**Offence — Driving or Riding on Motor Cycle in Contravention of Regulations — Road Traffic Act 1988, s. 16(4)**

*Triable summarily. Fine.*

**(*No specific power of arrest*)**

The Road Traffic Act 1988, s. 16 states:

> *(4) A person who drives or rides on a motor cycle in contravention of regulations under this section is guilty of an offence . . .*

**Keynote**

The Regulations do not apply to all motor cycles; they only apply to motor bicycles. A motor *bi*cycle is a two-wheeled motor cycle, whether having a side-car attached thereto or not. In counting the wheels, any wheels the centre of which in contact with the road surface are less than 460mm apart are to be treated as one wheel.

Certain motor mowers are exempted by reg. 4(2) of the 1998 Regulations.

The helmet worn must either conform to one of the British Standards specified (in reg. 5) and be marked as such or they must give a similar (or greater) degree of protection as one which meets those Standards *and* be of a type manufactured for motor cyclists (reg. 4(3)(a). If the helmet is unfastened or improperly fastened (e.g. with part of the chinstrap undone) the offence will be complete (reg. 4(3)(b) and (c)).

It is a summary offence under s. 17(2) to sell or let on hire a helmet for these purposes which does not meet the prescribed requirements. That offence will be committed even if the helmet is sold for off-road use (*Losexis Ltd* v *Clarke* [1984] RTR 174).

The wording of the Regulations suggests that no helmet is required by someone who is pushing a motor bicycle along but, if they straddled it and pedalled it along with their feet, they would require one (see *Crank* v *Brooks* [1980] RTR 441 and **chapter 1**).

Section 16(2) creates an exemption for 'a follower of the Sikh religion while he is wearing a turban'.

The Motor Cycles (Eye Protectors) Regulations 1999 (SI 1999 No. 535) as amended create an offence (under s. 18(3)) of using non-prescribed eye protectors when driving or riding on a motor cycle. These Regulations do not require the use of eye protectors; they impose standards on those appliances which motor cyclists choose to use. The definition of eye protector includes any appliance placed on the head intended for the protection of the eyes (which might include sunglasses). It is also an offence (s. 18(4)) to sell or let on hire eye protectors which do not meet the prescribed requirements.

### 7.3.1 Passengers

'Riding on' in the above offence means that pillion passengers must wear helmets but s. 16(1) of the 1988 Act exempts people in side-cars.

As with the seat belt provisions above, there is an exception to the general rule on aiding and abetting. Section 16(4) provides that only the person committing the offence of not wearing a helmet shall be liable *unless the person is under 16*. This means that, where a 16 year old rider of a motor bicycle carries a 15 year old pillion passenger who is not wearing a helmet, the 16 year old will be responsible for the commission of the offence by the passenger as well as the passenger themselves. If the passenger were 16 years old, they alone would be responsible for their offence.

**Offences — Passengers on Motor Cycles — Road Traffic Act 1988, s. 23**
*Triable summarily. Fine. Discretionary disqualification.*
**(*No specific power of arrest*)**

The Road Traffic Act 1988, s. 23 states:

*(1) Not more than one person in addition to the driver may be carried on a motor bicycle.*

*(2) No person in addition to the driver may be carried on a motor bicycle otherwise than sitting astride the motor cycle and on a proper seat securely fixed to the motor cycle behind the driver's seat.*

*(3) If a person is carried on a motor cycle in contravention of this section, the driver of the motor cycle is guilty of an offence.*

**Keynote**

Under this section it is the *driver* who commits the offence (s. 23(3)), and the passenger can be convicted of aiding and abetting.

There is no specific requirement for the passenger to face the *front* — though this is presumably because it did not occur to the legislators. Any person travelling as a passenger astride a motor cycle but facing the rear may commit an offence under the Road Vehicles (Construction and Use) Regulations 1986 (**see chapter 9**); he/she may also commit an offence of aiding and abetting the driver to drive dangerously (**see chapter 2**).

Note that under the 1986 Regulations suitable supports for a passenger must be provided on a motor bicycle if it is to carry a passenger (reg. 102). There is no requirement that the supports be used by a passenger.

Note also the restrictions on learner drivers carrying passengers (**see chapter 11**).

## 7.4 Speed Limits

Speed limits may apply to particular roads (e.g. 'restricted' roads), particular vehicles (e.g. heavy commercial vehicles) or temporary conditions imposed in a given area. There are also further conditions regulating speed limits on motorways. As a general rule, the limit on most motorways and dual carriageways for most cars will be 70 mph. However, there are many exceptions and local regulations and orders should be consulted in cases of doubt.

Note that since the Road Traffic Act 1991, increasing reliance has been placed on the use of automatic devices for detecting speeding offences and that the procedure of 'conditional offers' of fixed penalties are available for such offences (**see chapter 14**).

### 7.4.1 Speed Limits on Restricted Roads

Section 82 of the Road Traffic Regulation Act 1984 defines a 'restricted road' as:

*(1) Subject to the provisions of this section and of section 84(3) of this Act, a road is a restricted road for the purposes of section 81 of this Act if—*

*(a) in England and Wales, there is provided on it a system of street lighting furnished by means of lamps placed not more than 200 yards apart;*

*(b) (applies to Scotland only).*

*(2) The traffic authority for a road may direct—*

*(a) that the road which is a restricted road for the purposes of section 81 of this Act shall cease to be a restricted road for those purposes, or*

*(b) that the road which is not a restricted road for those purposes shall become a restricted road for those purposes.*

By virtue of s. 85(5), where a road has such a system of street lamps the lack of any traffic signs specifically saying that the road is not a 'restricted' road will be evidence that it *is* a 'restricted' road.

If there are no such street lamps then there must be traffic signs stating what the speed limit is (s. 85(4)).

### 7.4.2 Traffic Signs

Traffic signs must generally conform to the Traffic Signs Regulations and General Directions 1994 (SI 1994 No. 1519) (as to which **see chapter 10**) and the specifications of signs relating to speed limits in particular are contained in sch. 2 to those Regulations.

Section 81(1) of the 1984 Act states that it shall be unlawful for a person to drive a motor vehicle on a restricted road at a speed exceeding 30 mph (**see para. 7.4.6**).

Section 84 allows for speed limits to be imposed on roads other than restricted roads and motorways.

### 7.4.3 Temporary Speed Limits

Section 88 of the 1984 Act provides for both maximum and minimum temporary speed limits to be imposed on certain roads (**see para. 7.4.6**).

Traffic authorities may impose temporary speed *restrictions* in connection with road works or similar operations near to the road which present a danger to the public or serious damage to the highway (see ss. 14–16 of the Road Traffic Regulation Act 1984). These restrictions cannot exceed 18 months without approval from the Secretary of State.

As *restrictions* rather than speed limits, offences under this heading do not require notices of intended prosecution (**see chapter 3**) (*Platten* v *Gowing* [1983] Crim LR 184), neither do they require corroboration (**see para. 7.4.6**).

### 7.4.4 Speed Limits for Particular Classes of Vehicle

Section 86 of the Road Traffic Regulation Act 1984 states:

> *(1) It shall not be lawful for a person to drive a motor vehicle of any class on a road at a speed greater than the speed specified in Schedule 6 to this Act as the maximum speed in relation to a vehicle of that class.*
> *(2) Subject to subsections (4) and (5) below, the Secretary of State may by regulations vary, subject to such conditions as may be specified in the regulations, the provisions of that Schedule.*
> *(3) Regulations under this section may make different provision as respects the same class of vehicles in different circumstances.*
> *(4) . . .*
> *(5) The Secretary of State shall not have power under this section to vary the speed limit imposed by section 81 of this Act.*

Schedule 6 of the 1984 Act is set out at **appendix 2**.

### 7.4.5 Exemption for Police, Fire and Ambulance Purposes

Section 87 of the Road Traffic Regulation Act 1984 states:

> *No statutory provisions imposing a speed limit on motor vehicles shall apply to any vehicle on an occasion when it is being used for fire brigade, ambulance or police purposes, if the observance of that provision would be likely to hinder the use of the vehicle for the purpose for which it is being used on that occasion.*

**Keynote**

It is the *purpose* to which the vehicle is being put which matters here. Consequently, a privately-owned vehicle used for police purposes may attract the exemption under s. 87 if it is driven in excess of the speed limit. However, a police vehicle being used for private purposes (i.e. doing some unauthorised 'shopping') would not attract the exemption.

Section 87 only applies to *speed*; it does not absolve drivers of emergency vehicles from any breaches of driving *standards*, **see chapter 2**.

### 7.4.6 Proof of Speed

Section 89(2) of the 1984 Act requires that a person prosecuted for driving a motor vehicle at a speed exceeding the limit shall not be convicted solely on the evidence of one witness to the effect that, in his/her opinion, the defendant was exceeding the speed limit. Section 88(7) includes a similar provision for failing to attain a minimum speed limit.

The requirements for corroboration do not apply to general speeding offences on motorways (but they do for special classes of vehicle exceeding motorway speed limits).

Corroboration may be provided by the equipment in a police vehicle or by *Vascar* or similar speed measuring equipment (*Nicholas* v *Penny* [1950] 2 All ER 89). While it may be preferable, it is not *necessary* in such cases to prove the accuracy of the equipment being used (see e.g. *Darby* v *DPP* [1995] RTR 294).

Two police officers may provide sufficient evidence in a case of speeding but the court will decide how much weight (**see Evidence and Procedure, chapter 11**) to give to such evidence. It is important to show that both officers saw the vehicle at exactly the same time (*Brighty* v *Pearson* [1938] 4 All ER 127).

The signal emitted by a hand-held radar speed gun has been deemed *not* to amount to a 'communication' for the purposes of the Wireless Telegraphy Act 1949 and a person intercepting such signals cannot be prosecuted under that legislation (*R* v *Crown Court of Knightsbridge, ex parte Foot, The Times* 18 February 1998 (**see General Police Duties, chapter 3**). See, however, the offences of obstruction and incitement (**Crime, chapters 3 and 8**).

### 7.4.7 Punishment of Speeding Offences

Speeding offences are punishable under the following Acts:

- Contravening speed limits generally (s. 89(1) of the Road Traffic Regulation Act 1984 and sch. 2 to the Road Traffic Offenders Act 1988).
- Contravening motorway speed limits (other than special classes of vehicle) (s. 17(4) of the Road Traffic Regulation Act 1984 and sch. 2 to the Road Traffic Offenders Act 1988).
- Contravening *minimum* speed limits made under s. 88(1)(b) of the Road Traffic Regulation Act 1984 (s. 88(7) of the Road Traffic Regulation Act 1984 and sch. 2 to the Road Traffic Offenders Act 1988).

- Contravening temporary speed *restrictions* made under s. 14 of the Road Traffic Regulation Act 1984 (s. 16(1) of the Road Traffic Regulation Act 1984 and sch. 2 to the Road Traffic Offenders Act 1988).

Section 89(1) of the Road Traffic Regulation Act 1984 states:

> *(1) A person who drives a motor vehicle on a road at a speed exceeding a limit imposed by or under any enactment to which this section applies shall be guilty of an offence.*

**Keynote**

The enactments to which this section applies are the Road Traffic Regulation Act 1984 itself *except s. 17(2)* (ordinary classes of vehicles on motorways).

## 7.5 Motorways

The classes of vehicle which can use motorways at any time are those falling under Class I and Class II in sch. 4 to the Highways Act 1980. These include:

*Class I*

- Motor cars and motor cycles with an engine/cylinder capacity not less than 50cc which comply with the Road Vehicles (Construction and Use) Regulations 1986 (**see chapter 9**).
- Heavy and light locomotives and heavy motor cars.
- Trailers drawn by the above.

*Class II*

- Motor vehicles and trailers authorised to carry abnormal indivisible loads.
- Armed forces vehicles.
- 'Special type' vehicles.

All other vehicles may only use a motorway under the conditions set out in reg. 15 of the Motorways Traffic (England and Wales) Regulations 1982 (SI 1982 No. 1163), as amended.

Regulation 15(1)(b) of the 1982 Regulations prohibits the use of motorways by pedestrians who, if they refuse to leave a motorway, may be arrested for obstructing the highway (**see chapter 8**) (*Reed* v *Wastie* [1972] Crim LR 221).

The Motorways Traffic (Amendment) Regulations 1992 (SI 1992 No. 1364) set out a number of key definitions including 'hard shoulder', 'carriageway' and 'verge'. They contain further prohibitions on activities such as stopping (reg. 7), reversing (reg. 8) and using the central reservation (reg. 10).

Learner drivers (**see chapter 11**) are excluded from using motorways (by reg. 11), but these will not include drivers who hold ordinary licences but who are learning to drive large goods vehicles and passenger carrying vehicles.

Regulation 12 lists those vehicles which are prohibited from using the outside lane of a motorway (principally goods vehicles exceeding 7.5 tonnes, passenger vehicles over 12m long and vehicles drawing trailers).

For a list of motorway offences and penalties, **see appendix 3**.

### 7.5.1 Speeding on Motorways

Schedule 6 to the Road Traffic Regulation Act 1984 sets speed limits for particular classes of vehicles using motorways. Otherwise the offence of exceeding the speed limit on a motorway is punishable under s. 17(4) of the Road Traffic Regulation Act 1984 and sch. 2 to the Road Traffic Offenders Act 1988.

# CHAPTER EIGHT

# OTHER MEASURES AFFECTING SAFETY

## 8.1 Introduction

In addition to the legislation regulating driver fitness and competence, there are many other provisions aimed at improving — and enforcing — safety. This chapter addresses some of the more common measures affecting safety, including the parking of vehicles.

## 8.2 Obstruction

**Offence — Obstruction of the Highway — Highways Act 1980, s. 137**
*Triable summarily. Fine.*
***(Power of arrest under Police and Criminal Evidence Act 1984, s. 25(3)(d)(v) general conditions)***

The Highways Act 1980, s. 137 states:

> *(1) If a person, without lawful authority or excuse, in any way wilfully obstructs the free passage along a highway he is guilty of an offence . . .*

**Offence — Obstruction on a Road — Road Vehicles (Construction and Use) Regulations 1986, reg. 103**
*Triable summarily. Fine.*
***(No specific power of arrest)***

The Road Vehicles (Construction and Use) Regulations 1986, reg. 103 states:

> *No person in charge of a motor vehicle or trailer shall cause or permit the vehicle to stand on a road so as to cause any unnecessary obstruction of the road.*

**Offence — Obstruction of Street — Town Police Clauses Act 1847, s. 28**
*Triable summarily. Fourteen days' imprisonment and/or fine.*
***(No specific power of arrest)***

The Town Police Clauses Act 1847, s. 28 states:

*Every person who in any street, to the obstruction, annoyance, or danger of the residents or passengers, . . . wilfully interrupts any public crossing, or wilfully causes any obstruction in any public footpath or other public thoroughfare . . .*

**Keynote**

What amounts to an obstruction is a question of fact for the magistrate(s) to decide in each case (*Wade* v *Grange* [1977] RTR 417; see also *DPP* v *Jones (Margaret)* [1999] 2 WLR 625). In arriving at that decision they will have regard to, amongst other things: 'the length of time the obstruction continued, the place where it occurred, the purpose for which it was done and whether it caused an actual as opposed to a potential obstruction' (Lord Parker CJ in *Nagy* v *Weston* [1965] 1 All ER 78).

Each of the above offences has different elements which are important in selecting the appropriate charge. The Highways Act 1980 offence can be committed by anyone using anything whereas the offence under reg. 103 refers to a person in charge of a motor vehicle or trailer. Similarly, the *place* being obstructed differs from a 'highway', 'road' or 'street' according to the enactment, while the *way* in which that place is obstructed may be either 'wilful' or 'unnecessary'.

Both of the offences, however, appear to require an unreasonable use of the road. contrast the situation where the power to require vehicles to be moved or the power to move them applies (see **para. 8.6.2**).

Some examples of what might amount to obstruction have included:

- Parking a van in a lay-by to sell food and drink to passers by (*Waltham Forest LBC* v *Mills* [1980] RTR 201).
- Creating a queue of vehicles at a security gate at the entry to a factory (*Lewis* v *Dickson* [1976] RTR 431).
- Putting displays out on the footpath in front of a shop (*Hertfordshire County Council* v *Bolden, The Times,* 9 December 1986).
- Street entertainers in a shopping street (*Waite* v *Taylor* (1985) 149 JP 551).

A refusal to move a vehicle that is obstructing the highway when requested by a police officer can amount to an 'obstruction' of the officer under what is now s. 89(2) of the Police Act 1996 (**see Crime, chapter 8**) (*Gelberg* v *Miller* [1961] 1 WLR 153).

A continuing or repeated obstruction may amount to the offence of a public nuisance (as to which, **see General Police Duties, chapter 3**).

## 8.3 Causing Danger

**Offence — Causing Danger to Other Road Users — Road Traffic Act 1988, s. 22A**

*Triable either way. Seven years' imprisonment and/or a fine on indictment; six months' imprisonment and/or a fine summarily.*

***(Arrestable offence)***

The Road Traffic Act 1988, s. 22A states:

*(1) A person is guilty of an offence if he intentionally and without lawful authority or reasonable cause—*
*(a) causes anything to be on or over a road, or*
*(b) interferes with a motor vehicle, trailer or cycle, or*
*(c) interferes (directly or indirectly) with traffic equipment,*
*in such circumstances that it would be obvious to a reasonable person that to do so would be dangerous.*
*(2) In subsection (1) above 'dangerous' refers to danger either of injury to any person while on or near a road, or of serious damage to property on or near a road; and in determining for the purposes of that subsection what would be obvious to a reasonable person in a particular case, regard shall be had not only to the circumstances of which he could be expected to be aware but also to any circumstances shown to have been within the knowledge of the accused.*
*(3) In subsection (1) above 'traffic equipment' means—*
*(a) anything lawfully placed on or near a road by a highway authority;*
*(b) a traffic sign lawfully placed on or near a road by a person other than a highway authority;*
*(c) any fence, barrier or light lawfully placed on or near a road—*
*(i) in pursuance of section 174 of the Highways Act 1980, or section 65 of the New Roads and Street Works Act 1991 (which provide for guarding, lighting and signing in streets where works are undertaken), or*
*(ii) by a constable or a person acting under the instructions (whether general or specific) of a chief officer of police.*
*(4) For the purposes of subsection (3) above anything placed on or near a road shall unless the contrary is proved be deemed to have been lawfully placed there.*

**Keynote**

This offence requires a defendant to act both intentionally and without lawful authority Although crimes requiring 'intention' are generally more difficult to prove than those capable of commission by some lesser state of mind (such as recklessness) (**see Crime, chapter 1**), the intention in s. 22A only applies to the causing or interfering described. There is no need to show that the defendant *intended* to create danger — only that it would have been obvious to a reasonable person that to do so would be dangerous.

Like the requirements for dangerous driving under ss. 1 and 2 of the 1988 Act, the test here is primarily *objective* (the 'reasonable person' test) but it also has a *subjective* element in that regard will be had to any circumstances shown to be known to the defendant.

A 'road' for the purpose of this offence does not include a footpath (or bridleway) (s. 22A(5)).

## 8.4 Parking

### 8.4.1 Parking on Verges

**Offence — Parking of Heavy Commercial Vehicles on Verges — Road Traffic Act 1988, s. 19**
*Triable summarily. Fine.*
**(*No specific power of arrest*)**

The Road Traffic Act 1988, s. 19 states:

*(1) Subject to subsection (2) below, a person who parks a heavy commercial vehicle (as defined in section 20 of this Act) wholly or partly—*

*(a) on the verge of a road, or*
*(b) on any land situated between two carriageways and which is not a footway, or*
*(c) on a footway,*
*is guilty of an offence.*

## Defence

The Road Traffic Act 1988, s. 19 states:

*(2) A person shall not be convicted of an offence under this section in respect of a vehicle if he proves to the satisfaction of the court—*
*(a) that it was parked in accordance with permission given by a constable in uniform, or*
*(b) that it was parked in contravention of this section for the purpose of saving life or extinguishing fire or meeting any other like emergency, or*
*(c) that it was parked in contravention of this section but the conditions specified in subsection (3) below were satisfied.*
*(3) The conditions mentioned in subsection (2)(c) above are—*
*(a) that the vehicle was parked on the verge of a road or on a footway for the purpose of loading or unloading, and*
*(b) that the loading or unloading of the vehicle could not have been satisfactorily performed if it had not been parked on the footway or verge, and*
*(c) that the vehicle was not left unattended at any time while it was so parked.*
*(4) In this section 'carriageway' and 'footway', in relation to England and Wales, have the same meanings as in the Highways Act 1980.*

**Keynote**

'Heavy commercial vehicle' means any goods vehicle which has an operating weight exceeding 7.5 tonnes (Road Traffic Act 1988, s. 20(1)).

The operating weight of a goods vehicle for the purposes of this section is:

- in the case of a motor vehicle not drawing a trailer or in the case of a trailer, its maximum laden weight,
- in the case of an articulated vehicle, its maximum laden weight (if it has one) and otherwise the aggregate maximum laden weight of all the individual vehicles forming part of that articulated vehicle, and
- in the case of a motor vehicle (other than an articulated vehicle) drawing one or more trailers, the aggregate maximum laden weight of the motor vehicle and the trailer or trailers attached to it.

## 8.4.2 Leaving Vehicles in Dangerous Positions

**Offence — Leaving Vehicles in Dangerous Positions — Road Traffic Act 1988, s. 22**
*Triable summarily. Fine. Discretionary disqualification.*
**(*No specific power of arrest*)**

The Road Traffic Act 1988, s. 22 states:

*If a person in charge of a vehicle causes or permits the vehicle or a trailer drawn by it to remain at rest on a road in such a position or in such condition or in such circumstances as to involve a danger of injury to other persons using the road, he is guilty of an offence.*

**Keynote**

This offence involves presenting a danger of injury to other road users by the *position*, *condition* or *circumstances* of the vehicle/trailer.

The danger presented by the condition or circumstances of the vehicle is not confined to occasions when it is stationary but will also apply to a vehicle/trailer which presents a danger by moving (such as where a driver fails to set the handbrake (*Maguire* v *Crouch* (1940) 104 JP 445)).

The risk must be to 'other persons using the road'.

### 8.4.3 Parking Regulations

Much of the responsibility for regulating the parking of vehicles on roads falls on local authorities. The Road Traffic Regulation Act 1984, ss. 45–56 makes provision for the parking of motor vehicles on highways and for the operation of parking meters. The designation of parking places by local authorities is provided for under s. 46 while s. 47 creates an offence of failing to comply with the conditions of such a designated parking place.

The type of parking meters approved by the Secretary of State come under the British Standard No. BS 6571 and, by virtue of s. 47(5) of the 1984 Act, parking meters shall be presumed to be of the approved type and design.

The Road Traffic Regulation Act 1984, ss. 1–8 allows for the creation of 'no waiting' orders. When creating these orders, local authorities must follow the procedure laid out in the Local Authorities' Traffic Orders (Procedure) (England and Wales) Regulations 1989 (SI 1989 No. 1120).

**Offence — Contravention of Traffic Regulation Order —**
**Road Traffic Regulation Act 1984, s. 5(1) (outside London);**
**s. 8(1) (inside London)**
*Triable summarily. Fine.*
**(*No specific power of arrest*)**

The Road Traffic Regulation Act 1984, ss. 5 and 8 state:

*5.—(1) A person who contravenes a traffic regulation order, or who uses a vehicle, or causes or permits a vehicle to be used in contravention of a traffic regulation order, shall be guilty of an offence.*

*8.—(1) Any person who acts in contravention of, or fails to comply with, an order under section 6 of this Act shall be guilty of an offence.*
*(1A) Subsection (1) above does not apply in relation to any order under section 6 of this Act so far as it designates any parking places.*

**Keynote**

In order to be effective, signs showing 'no waiting' areas must be properly marked and displayed as required by the Road Traffic Regulation Act 1984, s. 64 and the Traffic Signs Regulations and General Directions 1994 (SI 1994 No. 1519). If they are not then no offence of contravention can be prosecuted (see *Hassan* v *DPP* [1992] RTR 209).

### 8.4.4 Orange Badge Scheme: Disabled Drivers

Local authorities are empowered to issue 'orange badges' under the Chronically Sick and Disabled Persons Act 1970 (as amended) for motor vehicles driven by, or used for the carriage of disabled persons.

Exemptions for disabled people driving or being carried in vehicles using an orange badge are covered by the Local Authorities' Traffic Orders (Exemptions for Disabled Persons) (England and Wales) Regulations 1986 (SI 1986 No. 178) as amended. These Regulations (which do not apply in certain areas within London) require exemptions in certain local no waiting and parking orders. Their effect is generally to increase or remove altogether the waiting time allowed for orange badge holders, and to allow such people to park without charge in certain areas. The orange badge scheme applies only to orders made under the Road Traffic Regulation Act 1984 and does not provide some form of general exemption from other legislation controlling traffic.

The badges themselves are issued under the Disabled Persons (Badges for Motor Vehicles) Regulations 1982 (SI 1982 No. 1740), as amended.

**Offence — Wrongful Use of Disabled Person's Badge —**
**Road Traffic Regulation Act 1984, s. 117**
*Triable summarily. Fine.*
***(No specific power of arrest)***

The Road Traffic Regulation Act 1984, s. 117 states:

> *(1) A person who at any time acts in contravention of, or fails to comply with, any provision of an order under this Act relating to the parking of motor vehicles is also guilty of an offence under this section if at that time—*
> *(a) there was displayed on the motor vehicle in question a badge of a form prescribed under section 21 of the Chronically Sick and Disabled Persons Act 1970, and*
> *(b) he was using the vehicle in circumstances where a disabled person's concession would be available to a disabled person's vehicle,*
> *but he shall not be guilty of an offence under this section if the badge was issued under that section and displayed in accordance with regulations made under it.*
> *(3) In this section—*
> *'disabled person's concession' means—*
> *(a) an exemption from an order under this Act given by reference to disabled persons' vehicles; or*
> *(b) a provision made in any order under this Act for the use of a parking place by disabled persons' vehicles.*

**Keynote**

A local authority may require the return of an orange badge and may refuse to issue such a badge if the person concerned has misused an orange badge at least three times in a way which has led to a conviction or would give grounds for a conviction of the above offence.

A driver who commits a parking offence and misuses an orange badge at the same time commits both the relevant parking offence *and* an offence under s. 117 above.

### 8.4.5 Removal and Immobilisation of Parked Vehicles

Sections 104–106 of the Road Traffic Regulation Act 1984 provide for the clamping of vehicles on roads using an 'approved' device (listed at s. 104(12A)). The only roads currently affected by this power are in central London although the Secretary of State may identify further areas in which it will apply.

Wheel clamping on private land is a different matter. If an occupier of land decides to enforce a civil remedy of detaining the property of trespassers until compensation is paid (i.e. by clamping their vehicle), that is a civil matter. Where an occupier of private land displayed a clear notice that vehicles parking without authority would be clamped, the Divisional Court held that anyone who subsequently parked there without authority consented to their car being clamped. The vehicle owner could not be excused for causing criminal damage (**see Crime, chapter 14**) to the clamp by trying to remove it (*Lloyd* v *DPP* [1991] Crim LR 904).

Note that under the Vehicle Excise Duty (Immobilisation, Removal and Disposal of Vehicles) Regulations 1997 (SI 1997 No. 2439) vehicles may be clamped if they are not taxed (**see chapter 12**).

Interestingly, in Scotland wheel clamping has been held to be 'extortion' (*Black* v *Carmichael, The Times,* 25 June 1992) and there are strong arguments to suggest that the clamping of vehicles without statutory authority is unlawful (see the article by Kruse J. *Legal Action,* July 1998, p. 27).

Special provisions in relation to the disposal and immobilisation of vehicles in London are set out at s. 101 of the Road Traffic Regulation Act 1984. By a somewhat tortuous route (ss. 67, 68 and 69 of the Road Traffic Act 1991), some of these provisions were brought into effect in April 1998 by the Road Traffic Act 1991 (Commencement No. 15 and Transitional Provisions) Order 1998 (SI 1998 No. 967).

## 8.5 Tampering with and Getting on to Vehicles

**Offence — Tampering with Motor Vehicles — Road Traffic Act 1988, s. 25**
*Triable summarily. Fine.*
***(No specific power of arrest)***

The Road Traffic Act 1988, s. 25 states:

*If, while a motor vehicle is on a road or on a parking place provided by a local authority, a person—*
*(a) gets on to the vehicle, or*
*(b) tampers with the brake or other part of its mechanism,*
*without lawful authority or reasonable cause he is guilty of an offence.*

**Keynote**

This offence, which only applies to 'motor vehicles' and not trailers, can only be committed where the vehicle is on a road or local authority parking place.

What constitutes a part of its mechanism — other than the brake — is open to interpretation but it would appear that anything falling within the ordinary meaning of 'mechanism' would suffice.

If a defendant has got on to or tampered with the vehicle in order to steal it or part of its load then the offence under s. 9 of the Criminal Attempts Act 1981 (interfering) may be appropriate (**see Crime, chapter 3**).

If a defendant gets on to a *moving* vehicle — or trailer — he/she may commit the following offence.

**OTHER MEASURES AFFECTING SAFETY**

**Offence — Holding or Getting on to Vehicle in Motion — Road Traffic Act 1988, s. 26**
*Triable summarily. Fine.*
**(*No specific power of arrest*)**

The Road Traffic Act 1988, s. 26 states:

*(1) If, for the purpose of being carried, a person without lawful authority or reasonable cause takes or retains hold of, or gets on to a motor vehicle or trailer while in motion on a road he is guilty of an offence.*
*(2) If, for the purpose of being drawn, a person takes or retains hold of a motor vehicle or trailer while in motion on a road he is guilty of an offence.*

**Keynote**

For this offence the vehicle or trailer must both be in motion and on a road.

## 8.6 Abandoning Vehicles

**Offence — Abandoning Motor Vehicle — Refuse Disposal (Amenity) Act 1978, s. 2(1)**
*Triable summarily. Fine.*
**(*No specific power of arrest*)**

The Refuse Disposal (Amenity) Act 1978, s. 2 states:

*(1) Any person who, without lawful authority,—*
*(a) abandons on any land in the open air, or on any other land forming part of a highway, a motor vehicle or anything which formed part of a motor vehicle and was removed from it in the course of dismantling the vehicle on the land; or*
*(b) abandons on any such land any thing other than a motor vehicle, being a thing which he has brought to the land for the purpose of abandoning it there,*
*shall be guilty of an offence.*

**Keynote**

For police powers in relation to bringing vehicles on to land under the Criminal Justice and Public Order Act 1994, **see General Police Duties, chapter 9**).

### 8.6.1 Duty of Local Authority to Remove Abandoned Vehicles

Section 3 of the Refuse Disposal (Amenity) Act 1978 states:

*(1) Where it appears to a local authority that a motor vehicle in their area is abandoned without lawful authority on any land in the open air or on any other land forming part of a highway, it shall be the duty of the authority, subject to the following provisions of this section, to remove the vehicle.*

'Motor vehicle' is defined under s. 11 of the Act as:

*. . . a mechanically propelled vehicle intended or adapted for use on roads, whether or not it is in a fit state for such use, and includes any trailer intended or adapted for use as an attachment to such a vehicle, any chassis or body, with or without wheels, appearing to have formed part of such a vehicle or trailer, and anything attached to such a vehicle or trailer.*

**Keynote**

Before it can remove a vehicle under this section, a local authority must follow the requirements of the Act in relation to affixing of notices advising the owner of its intention.

## 8.6.2 Police Power to Remove Vehicles from Roads

Under certain circumstances police officers can require a vehicle to be removed from a road.

Regulation 3 of the Removal and Disposal of Vehicles Regulations 1986 (SI 1986 No. 183) provides that:

> *(1) A constable may require the owner, driver or other person in control or in charge of any vehicle to which this Regulation applies to move or cause to be moved the vehicle and any such requirement may include a requirement that the vehicle shall be moved from that road to a place which is not on that or any other road, or that the vehicle shall not be moved to any such road or to any such position on a road as may be specified.*

**Keynote**

These regulations are made under s. 99 of the Road Traffic Regulation Act 1984.

The vehicles to which this regulation applies are vehicles which:

- have broken down, or been permitted to remain at rest, on a road in such a position or in such condition or in such circumstances as to cause obstruction to persons using the road or as to be likely to cause danger to such persons, or
- have been permitted to remain at rest or have broken down and remained at rest on a road in contravention of a prohibition or restriction contained in, or having effect under, any of the enactments mentioned in sch. 1 to these Regulations.

Note that this Regulation is not restricted to 'motor' vehicles and it applies to any vehicle, whatever its condition, including chassis or bodies, with or without wheels appearing to have formed part of a vehicle (Road Traffic Regulation Act 1984, s. 99(5)).

'Obstruction' for these purposes is not to be construed in the same way as an obstruction under the Highways Act 1980 or reg. 103 of the Road Vehicles (Construction and Use) Regulations 1986 (**see para. 8.2**). There, an obstruction requires an unreasonable use of the road or highway. Under reg. 3 above the requirement to move the vehicle can be made, not only where the vehicle is *actually* obstructing other traffic, but also where it is *potentially* obstructing other road users that may be expected at some time in the future (*Carey* v *Chief Constable of Avon and Somerset* [1995] RTR 405). This power can be used if the offending vehicle is considered (by the officer) to be 'obstructing the passage of road users along the highway; hindering them or preventing them from getting past' (per Hutchinson LJ in *Carey* above).

Regulation 4A provides traffic wardens with a power to remove or arrange for the removal of vehicles to which reg. 3 applies under certain circumstances.

Schedule 1 lists most offences relating to unlawful parking (e.g. 'no waiting' areas, pedestrian crossing areas etc.).

Regulation 4 provides that:

*Where a vehicle—*

*(a) is a vehicle to which Regulation 3 of these Regulations applies, or*

*(b) having broken down on a road or on any land in the open air, appears to a constable to have been abandoned without lawful authority, or*

*(c) has been permitted to remain at rest on a road or on any land in the open air in such a position or in such condition or in such circumstances as to appear to a constable to have been abandoned without lawful authority,*

*then, subject to the provisions of sections 99 and 100 of the Road Traffic Regulation Act 1984, a constable may remove or arrange for the removal of the vehicle, and, in the case of a vehicle which is on a road he may remove it or arrange for its removal from that road to a place which is not on that or any other road, or may move it or arrange for its removal to another position on that or another road.*

**Keynote**

Section 99 of the Road Traffic Regulation Act 1984 provides for the removal of vehicles illegally parked or abandoned, while s. 100 deals with the interim disposal of such vehicles.

This power might be used where an officer wishes to move a vehicle and either cannot find the driver or the driver refuses to move it.

Regulation 4 also empowers a police officer to remove vehicles that have broken down on land in the open air.

Regulation 4 confers two powers on the police officer; a personal power to remove the vehicle and a power to arrange for the vehicle's removal by another (*Rivers* v *Cutting* [1983] RTR 105). If the officer arranges for a reputable contractor to remove the vehicle under this power and chooses that contractor with reasonable care, the officer is not liable for any damage caused by the contractor.

## 8.7 Off-road Driving

**Offence — Driving Motor Vehicle on Land other than a Road — Road Traffic Act 1988, s. 34(1)**
*Triable summarily. Fine.*
**(*No specific power of arrest*)**

The Road Traffic Act 1988, s. 34 states:

*(1) Subject to the provisions of this section, if without lawful authority a person drives a motor vehicle—*

*(a) on to or upon any common land, moorland or land of any other description, not being land forming part of a road, or*

*(b) on any road being a footpath or bridleway, he is guilty of an offence.*

### 8.7.1 Defence

Section 34 goes on to state:

*(2) It is not an offence under this section to drive a motor vehicle on any land within fifteen yards of a road, being a road on which a motor vehicle may lawfully be driven, for the purpose only of parking the vehicle on that land.*

**Keynote**

This exception only applies if the driver's purpose in driving on the land is to park on it. Although s. 34(2) could be interpreted as limiting such driving to 15 yards the point is unclear. If, however, the driver's purpose is to do something other than park on the land (e.g. to turn round) the offence will be made out. The section includes any land 'of any other description' which is not part of a road.

There is a further, general defence under s. 34 which states:

*(3) A person shall not be convicted of an offence under this section with respect to a vehicle if he proves to the satisfaction of the court that it was driven in contravention of this section for the purpose of saving life or extinguishing fire or meeting any other like emergency.*

**Keynote**

Note that it is still a summary offence under the Highways Act 1835, s. 72 wilfully to ride or drive on the footway and the offence is not limited to 'motor vehicles'. 'Wilfully' means doing so on purpose and any accidental or inadvertent driving onto the footway would not come under this offence (*Fearnley* v *Ormsby* (1879) 43 JP 384).

## 8.8 Skips

**Offence — Depositing Builders' Skip on the Highway — Highways Act 1980, s. 139**
*Triable summarily. Fine.*
**(*No specific power of arrest*)**

The Highways Act 1980, s. 139 states:

*(1) A builder's skip shall not be deposited on a highway without the permission of the highway authority for the highway.*
*(2) A permission under this section shall be a permission for a person to whom it is granted to deposit, or cause to be deposited, a skip on the highway specified in the permission, and a highway authority may grant such permission either unconditionally or subject to such conditions as may be specified in the permission including, in particular, conditions relating to—*
*(a) the siting of the skip;*
*(b) its dimensions;*
*(c) the manner in which it is to be coated with paint and other material for the purpose of making it immediately visible to oncoming traffic;*
*(d) the care and disposal of its contents;*
*(e) the manner in which it is to be lighted or guarded;*
*(f) its removal at the end of the period of permission.*
*(3) . . .*
*(4) Where a builder's skip has been deposited on a highway in accordance with a permission granted under this section, the owner of the skip shall secure—*
*(a) that the skip is properly lighted during the hours of darkness and, where regulations made by the Secretary of State under this section require it to be marked in accordance with the regulations (whether with reflecting or fluorescent material or otherwise), that it is so marked;*
*(b) that the skip is clearly and indelibly marked with the owner's name and with his telephone number or address;*
*(c) that the skip is removed as soon as practicable after it has been filled;*

*(d) that each of the conditions subject to which that permission was granted is complied with; and, if he fails to do so, he is, subject to subsection (6) below, guilty of an offence . . .*

**Keynote**

Any permission has to be given in writing and it is an offence to fail to comply with any condition imposed upon that permission. 'Blanket' permissions are not permitted (*York City Council* v *Poller* [1976] RTR 37) and the offence will be complete if the owner fails to remove the skip after the permission has expired (*Craddock* v *Green* [1983] RTR 479).

Under s. 139(11) skips for this purpose are containers:

*. . . designed to be carried on a road vehicle and to be placed on a highway or other land for the storage of builders' materials, or for the removal and disposal of builders' rubble, waste, household and other rubbish or earth . . .*

**Keynote**

They must also comply with the Builders' Skips (Markings) Regulations 1984 (SI 1984 No. 1933).

The owner of a skip that is the subject of a hiring or hire purchase agreement is defined under s. 139(11) as the person in possession of it, provided that the agreement is for a period of *not less than* one month.

### 8.8.1 Defence

Section 139 of the 1980 Act states:

*(6) In any proceedings for an offence under this section it is a defence, subject to subsection (7) below, for the person charged to prove that the commission of the offence was due to the act or default of another person and that he took all reasonable precautions and exercised all due diligence to avoid the commission of such an offence by himself or any person under his control.*

### 8.8.2 Police Powers

Under s. 140 of the 1980 Act a constable in uniform may require the removal of a skip from the highway. Failure to do so is an offence under s. 140(3) but the requirement must be made *in person*. If the requirement to remove the skip is made by the officer telephoning the owner, the offence will not be made out (*R* v *Worthing Justices, ex parte Waste Management Ltd* [1988] Crim LR 458).

## 8.9 Pedestrian Crossings

Section 25 of the Road Traffic Regulation Act 1984 allows the Secretary of State to make regulations with respect to pedestrian crossings.

The current regulations are the Zebra, Pelican and Puffin Pedestrian Crossings Regulations and General Directions 1997 (SI 1997 No. 2400) and these regulations are the ones referred to throughout the following section. It should be noted, however, that the earlier regulations (the Zebra Pedestrian Crossings Regulations 1971 (SI 1971 No. 1524) as amended, and the Pelican Pedestrian Crossings Regulations and General Directions 1987 (SI 1987 No. 16)) continue to apply to older crossings until the relevant changes have been made to those crossings (estimated to be December 2002).

**Offence — Contravening Regulations made under s. 25 of the Road Traffic Regulation Act 1984 — Road Traffic Regulation Act 1984, s. 25(5)**
*Triable summarily. Fine. Discretionary disqualification.*
***(No specific power of arrest)***

The Road Traffic Regulation Act 1984, s. 25 states:

*(5) A person who contravenes any regulations made under this section shall be guilty of an offence.*

**Keynote**

Offences committed against the following crossings regulations will generally be prosecuted under the Road Traffic Regulation Act 1984, s. 25. However, some behaviour will involve a breach of a regulation made under *s. 64* of the Road Traffic Regulation Act 1984 (e.g. ignoring a crossing light). In such cases the offence will be triable summarily, attracting a fine but no endorsement or liability to be disqualified (see sch. 2 of the Road Traffic Offenders Act 1988, **appendix 3**).

### 8.9.1 The Regulations

Somewhat tortuously, the puffin crossing gets its name from the new Pedestrian User-friendly Intelligent crossing! Puffin crossings will differ from their less intelligent counterparts by incorporating a pedestrian sensor that delays traffic as long as is necessary while people are on the crossing but not once the crossing is clear.

The Zebra, Pelican and Puffin Pedestrian Crossings Regulations and General Directions 1997 (SI 1997 No. 2400) set out the relevant requirements for each type of crossing, together with the obligations on drivers when at a crossing.

Regulation 3 provides the many definitions found within the 1997 Regulations. The various dimensions of each type of crossing and their respective markings are laid out in regs 5–7 and in schs 1–4.

Under regs 8 and 9, provision is made for traffic authorities to add further apparatus or equipment at crossings (e.g. equipment to help people with disabilities).

Although the prescribed dimensions and markings must be adopted by traffic authorities when erecting such crossings, minor irregularities which do not materially affect the appearance or proper operation of a crossing will not prevent it from being treated as ‘a crossing’ for the purposes of offences and traffic regulation (reg. 10).

### 8.9.2 Lights at Crossings

Lights placed at crossings are ‘traffic signs’ (**see chapter 10**) for the purposes of the Road Traffic Regulation Act 1984 (reg. 11).

Regulations 12 and 13 set out the significance of the lights and signals at pelican and puffin crossings respectively. These regulations state what meanings each signal shall have and what action may or may not be taken by drivers on seeing those signals.

Special provision is made within regs 12 and 13 in relation to vehicles being used for the purposes of:

- police;
- fire brigade;
- ambulance; or
- national blood service.

If a vehicle is being used for one of those purposes *and* if the observance of the steady amber or red signal (or the red-with-amber at a puffin crossing) would be likely to hinder the use of the vehicle for that purpose, the driver of the vehicle may proceed beyond the 'stop' line under certain conditions (regs 12(e) and 13(f)).

Those conditions are that the driver:

- accords precedence to any pedestrian who is on the carriageway within the limits of the crossing; *and*
- does not proceed in a manner *or* at a time likely to endanger any person/vehicle approaching or waiting at the crossing; or
- does not proceed in a manner *or* at a time likely to cause the driver of any such vehicle to change its speed or course in order to avoid an accident.

For a discussion of the standards of police driving in general, **see para. 2.10**.

### 8.9.3 Give-Way Lines at Zebra Crossings

Regulation 14 of the 1997 Regulations states:

*A give-way line included in the markings placed pursuant to regulation 5(1)(b) and Part II of Schedule 1 shall convey to vehicular traffic proceeding towards a Zebra crossing the position at or before which a vehicle should be stopped for the purpose of complying with regulation 25 (precedence of pedestrians over vehicles at Zebra crossings).*

### 8.9.4 Pedestrian Light Signals

Regulation 15 of the 1997 Regulations states:

*(1) The significance of the red and steady green pedestrian light signals whilst they are illuminated at a Pelican crossing and of the red and green figures on a pedestrian demand unit whilst they are illuminated at a Puffin crossing shall be as follows—*

*(a) the red pedestrian light signal and the red figure shall both convey to a pedestrian the warning that, in the interests of safety, he should not cross the carriageway; and*

*(b) the steady green pedestrian light signal and the steady green figure shall both indicate to a pedestrian that he may cross the carriageway and that drivers may not cause vehicles to enter the crossing.*

*(2) The flashing green pedestrian light signal at a Pelican crossing shall convey—*

*(a) to a pedestrian who is already on the crossing when the flashing green signal is first shown the information that he may continue to use the crossing and that, if he is on the carriageway or a central reservation within the limits of that crossing (but not if he is on a central reservation which lies between two crossings which form part of a system of staggered crossings) before any part of a vehicle has entered those limits, he has precedence over that vehicle within those limits; and*

*(b) to a pedestrian who is not already on the crossing when the flashing green light is first shown the warning that he should not, in the interests of safety, start to cross the carriageway.*

*(3) Any audible signal emitted by any device for emitting audible signals provided in conjunction with the steady green pedestrian light signal or the green figure, and any tactile signal given by any device for making tactile signals similarly provided, shall convey to a pedestrian the same indication as the steady green pedestrian light signal or as the green figure as the case may be.*

## 8.9.5 Movement of Traffic at Crossings

Section IV of the 1997 Regulations contains the relevant regulations which restrict the movement of vehicles at crossings. Regulations 18 to 26 state:

***18.*** *The driver of a vehicle shall not cause the vehicle or any part of it to stop within the limits of a crossing unless he is prevented from proceeding by circumstances beyond his control or it is necessary for him to stop to avoid injury or damage to persons or property.*

***19.*** *No pedestrian shall remain on the carriageway within the limits of a crossing longer than is necessary for that pedestrian to pass over the crossing with reasonable despatch.*

***20.****—(1) For the purposes of this regulation and regulations 21 and 22 the word 'vehicle' shall not include a pedal bicycle not having a sidecar attached to it, whether or not additional means of propulsion by mechanical power are attached to the bicycle.*

*(2) Except as provided in regulations 21 and 22 the driver of a vehicle shall not cause it or any part of it to stop in a controlled area.*

***21.*** *Regulation 20 does not prohibit the driver of a vehicle from stopping it in a controlled area—*

*(a) if the driver has stopped it for the purpose of complying with regulation 25 or 26;*

*(b) if the driver is prevented from proceeding by circumstances beyond his control or it is necessary for him to stop to avoid injury or damage to persons or property; or*

*(c) when the vehicle is being used for police, fire brigade or ambulance purposes.*

***22.****—(1) Regulation 20 does not prohibit the driver of a vehicle from stopping it in a controlled area—*

*(a) for so long as may be necessary to enable the vehicle to be used for the purposes of—*

*(i) any building operation, demolition or excavation;*

*(ii) the removal of any obstruction to traffic;*

*(iii) the maintenance, improvement or reconstruction of a road; or*

*(iv) the laying, erection, alteration, repair or cleaning in or near the crossing of any sewer or of any main, pipe or apparatus for the supply of gas, water or electricity, or of any telecommunications apparatus kept installed for the purposes of a telecommunications code system or of any other telecommunications apparatus lawfully kept installed in any position, but only if the vehicle cannot be used for one of those purposes without stopping in the controlled area; or*

*(b) if the vehicle is a public service vehicle being used—*

*(i) in the provision of a local service; or*

*(ii) to carry passengers for hire or reward at separate fares,*

*and the vehicle, having proceeded past the crossing to which the controlled area relates, is waiting in that area in order to take up or set down passengers; or*

*(c) if he stops the vehicle for the purpose of making a left or right turn.*

*(2) In paragraph (1) 'local service' has the meaning given in section 2 of the Transport Act 1985 but does not include an excursion or tour as defined by section 137(1) of that Act.*

***23.*** *When vehicular light signals at a Pelican or Puffin crossing are displaying the red light signal the driver of a vehicle shall not cause it to contravene the prohibition given by that signal by virtue of regulation 12 or 13.*

***24.**—(1) Whilst any motor vehicle (in this regulation called 'the approaching vehicle') or any part of it is within the limits of a controlled area and is proceeding towards the crossing, the driver of the vehicle shall not cause it or any part of it—*

*(a) to pass ahead of the foremost part of any other motor vehicle proceeding in the same direction; or*

*(b) to pass ahead of the foremost part of a vehicle which is stationary for the purpose of complying with regulation 23, 25 or 26.*

*(2) In paragraph (1)—*

*(a) the reference to a motor vehicle in sub-paragraph (a) is, in a case where more than one motor vehicle is proceeding in the same direction as the approaching vehicle in a controlled area, a reference to the motor vehicle nearest to the crossing; and*

*(b) the reference to a stationary vehicle is, in a case where more than one vehicle is stationary in a controlled area for the purpose of complying with regulation 23, 25 or 26, a reference to the stationary vehicle nearest the crossing.*

***25.**—(1) Every pedestrian, if he is on the carriageway within the limits of a Zebra crossing, which is not for the time being controlled by a constable in uniform or traffic warden, before any part of a vehicle has entered those limits, shall have precedence within those limits, over that vehicle and the driver of the vehicle shall accord such precedence to any such pedestrian.*

*(2) Where there is a refuge for pedestrians or central reservation on a Zebra crossing, the parts of the crossing situated on each side of the refuge for pedestrians or central reservation shall, for the purposes of this regulation, be treated as separate crossings.*

***26.** When the vehicular light signals at a Pelican crossing are showing the flashing amber signal, every pedestrian, if he is on the carriageway or a central reservation within the limits of the crossing (but not if he is on a central reservation which forms part of a system of staggered crossings) before any part of a vehicle has entered those limits, shall have precedence within those limits over that vehicle and the driver of the vehicle shall accord such precedence to any such pedestrian.*

**Keynote**

The expression 'pedestrian' replaced the former one of 'foot passengers' which had given rise to many debates about people pushing bicycles and skateboarders, roller-bladers, etc. It remains to be seen how the expression will be interpreted in relation to crossings.

Failing to observe the 1997 Regulations will amount to an offence under s. 25 of the 1984 Act above.

If a police officer or traffic warden is directing traffic at a crossing, it will for the time being cease to be 'uncontrolled' and their directions must be followed, even if they contravene the regulations. Failure to follow such directions may amount to an offence (**see chapter 10**).

Part I of sch. 1 to the 1997 Regulations requires Zebra crossings to be marked with yellow globes mounted at or near each end of the crossing. The globes must show a flashing or — where so authorised — a constant light (para. 1). If the globes have been disfigured, discoloured or have failed to light, the crossing will be still deemed to be properly marked for the purposes of enforcement (para. 4).

The globes may be fitted with boards to increase their visibility or prevent their light from reaching adjoining properties (para. 3).

The 'limits' of a Zebra crossing will be defined by the line of studs on each side of the black and white stripes. Anything or anyone who is outside those lines of studs is consequently outside the limits of the crossing (*Moulder* v *Neville* [1974] RTR 53).

Although the failure of a driver to stop at a crossing in contravention of the Regulations is *absolute* (that is, you need not show any particular state of mind, **see Crime, chapter 1**), if control of the vehicle is temporarily and unavoidably taken from the driver — say, by being shunted from behind by another vehicle — the driver will not commit an offence (*Burns* v *Bidder* [1966] 3 All ER 29).

Failure to observe crossing regulations is not of itself conclusive proof of driving without due care or consideration (*Gibbons* v *Kahl* [1956] 1 QB 59) (**see para. 2.4**).

## 8.9.6 School Crossings

The Road Traffic Regulation Act 1984 makes provision for the patrolling of school crossings (ss. 26–29). Section 28 states:

> *(1) When between the hours of eight in the morning and half-past five in the afternoon a vehicle is approaching a place in a road where children on their way to or from school, or from one part of a school to another, are crossing or seeking to cross the road, a school crossing patrol wearing a uniform approved by the Secretary of State shall have power, by exhibiting a prescribed sign, to require the person driving or propelling the vehicle to stop it.*
>
> *(2) When a person has been required under subsection (1) above to stop a vehicle—*
>
> *(a) he shall cause the vehicle to stop before reaching the place where the children are crossing or seeking to cross and so as not to stop or impede their crossing, and*
>
> *(b) the vehicle shall not be put in motion again so as to reach the place in question so long as the sign continues to be exhibited.*

**Offence — Failing to Comply — Road Traffic Regulation Act 1984, s. 28(3)**

*Triable summarily. Fine. Discretionary disqualification.*

***(No specific power of arrest)***

The Road Traffic Regulation Act 1984, s. 28 states:

> *(3) A person who fails to comply with paragraph (a) of subsection (2) above, or who causes a vehicle to be put in motion in contravention of paragraph (b) of that subsection, shall be guilty of an offence.*

**Keynote**

This section creates two separate offences:

- s. 28(2)(a) — failing to stop in a way which does not impede the people crossing; and
- s. 28(2)(b) — *having stopped*, putting the vehicle in motion again while the sign continues to be exhibited.

It is not necessary, in proving the first offence, that children on the crossing are impeded; if the adults who are with them are so impeded the offence is complete (*Franklin* v *Langdown* [1971] 3 All ER 662).

Section 28 does not appear to restrict crossings to children on foot and there is no reason why its provisions should not extend to children going to school on bicycles or roller blades.

Section 28 goes on to say:

*(4) In this section—*
*(a) 'prescribed sign' means a sign of a size, colour and type prescribed by regulations made by the Secretary of State or, if authorisation is given by the Secretary of State for the use of signs of a description not so prescribed, a sign of that description;*
*(b) 'school crossing patrol' means a person authorised to patrol in accordance with arrangements under section 26 of this Act;*
*and regulations under paragraph (a) above may provide for the attachment of reflectors to signs or for the illumination of signs.*
*(5) For the purposes of this section—*
*(a) where it is proved that a sign was exhibited by a school crossing patrol, it shall be presumed, unless the contrary is proved, to be of a size, colour and type prescribed, or of a description authorised, under subsection (4)(b) above, and, if it was exhibited in circumstances in which it was required by the regulations to be illuminated, to have been illuminated in the prescribed manner;*
*(b) where it is proved that a school crossing patrol was wearing a uniform, the uniform shall be presumed, unless the contrary is proved, to be a uniform approved by the Secretary of State; and*
*(c) where it is proved that a prescribed sign was exhibited by a school crossing patrol at a place in a road where children were crossing or seeking to cross the road, it shall be presumed, unless the contrary is proved, that those children were on their way to or from school or from one part of a school to another.*

**Keynote**

School crossings may also be marked with warning lights and both these and the crossing sign exhibited by crossing patrol staff are provided for under the Traffic Signs Regulations and General Directions 1994 (SI 1994 No. 1519).

Traffic wardens may act as school crossing patrols under the Functions of Traffic Wardens Order 1970 (SI 1970 No. 1958) and when they do there is no need for them to wear the prescribed uniform (although they must display the approved sign).

## 8.10 Playgrounds

Section 29 of the Road Traffic Regulation Act 1984 makes provision for local traffic authorities to create orders prohibiting or restricting vehicular access to certain roads so that the roads may be used as 'street playgrounds'.

**Offence — Contravention of Street Playground Order — Road Traffic Regulation Act 1984, s. 29(3)**
*Triable summarily. Fine. Discretionary disqualification.*
***(No specific power of arrest)***

The Road Traffic Regulation Act 1984, s. 29 states:

*(3) A person who uses a vehicle, or causes or permits a vehicle to be used, in contravention of an order in force under this section shall be guilty of an offence.*

**Keynote**

This offence does not apply to vehicles or drivers in the public service of the Crown.

For a discussion of the meaning of 'use, cause or permit', **see chapter 1**.

# CHAPTER NINE

# CONSTRUCTION AND USE

## 9.1 Introduction

The law governing the construction and use of road vehicles is mainly to be found — as the name suggests — in the Road Vehicles (Construction and Use) Regulations 1986 (SI 1986 No. 1078). The Regulations deal with everything from motor cycle sidestands (reg. 38) to the placing of mascots (reg. 53). These Regulations are frequently amended and continue to be amended as the law develops. Amendments over the last year have included new requirements in relation to braking systems and seat belt anchorage points. (For full details of the current Regulations, see *The Encyclopedia of Road Traffic Law & Practice* (Sweet & Maxwell).)

Although 'vehicles' for many purposes, pedal cycles have their own construction and use regulations (**see chapter 15**).

Lights on vehicles are dealt with at **para. 9.5** below.

Helpfully, the Road Vehicle (Construction and Use) Regulations 1986 have been drafted in two key parts. Part I deals with the construction, weight and equipment of vehicles (including trailers), while the second concentrates on the way in which those vehicles are used on roads. Invariably, all the features with which a vehicle must be fitted (brakes, wipers, warning instruments etc.) can be found under Part I of the Regulations, while the need to keep those features in good working order, other issues of vehicle maintenance and use on roads are addressed in Part II.

So far as the *use* of road vehicles is concerned, in addition to the offences and safety measures outlined elsewhere in this work, the Road Traffic Reduction (National Targets) Act 1998 makes provision for the Secretary of State to set reduction targets for road traffic. Section 2 of the Act imposes a duty on the Secretary of State to set such targets in order to reduce the adverse effects of road traffic and to publish those targets. In discharging those duties the Secretary of State must have regard to a number of specified issues including:

- congestion
- danger to other road users

- the social impact of traffic levels
- the needs of people with disabilities, and
- the needs of rural communities.

For the purposes of the 1998 Act, road traffic generally means mechanically propelled vehicles using roads, with the exception of vehicles constructed or adapted to carry more than eight passengers in addition to the driver. Although proposals to introduce significant legislative changes in the regulation of road traffic were put on hold during this last parliamentary session, the above Act came into force in July 1998 and there is no doubt as to the Government's intention to introduce further measures to regulate road usage in the UK.

## 9.2 Vehicle Defect Rectification Scheme

The Vehicle Defect Rectification Scheme (VDRS) was introduced to streamline the process for dealing with vehicles having minor defects and to ensure that those defects were in fact rectified rather than simply punished. The scheme is voluntary and a motorist does not have to participate. The VDRS, which represents the next non-prosecution stage after a verbal warning, involves the person responsible being issued with a form by a police officer setting out the relevant defect in his/her vehicle. Once the defect has been pointed out and the person has accepted the form, he/she must have the defect remedied and then submit the vehicle for examination at a Department of Transport approved testing station. The testing station will certify that the defect has been rectified and the form, so endorsed, must be returned to the central police ticket office by the responsible person within 14 days. Failure to return the form within that time will result in the matter being considered for prosecution in the normal manner. A copy of the form is returned to the originating officer after 21 days.

## 9.3 Type Approval

Part I of the Regulations, which govern the way in which vehicles are built and equipped, are gradually being replaced by the 'type approval' system.

The type approval system has come about as a result of the United Kingdom's membership of the European Union whose common transport policy has had a significant impact on this area of law (see the Motor Vehicles (EC Type Approval) Regulations 1992 (SI 1992 No. 3107) as amended).

The eventual aim of the policy is standardisation of the construction of all vehicles and their component parts.

When dealing with any potential breach of the legislation in this area, it is important to make sure whether a type approval system applies. In doing so you should refer to reg. 6 which contains guidance on the compliance with Community Directives and EC Regulations.

Whether or not a particular type approval scheme applies to a vehicle or a part used in one will largely be determined by the date of its first use or of its manufacture. It is important to distinguish which of these applies in any particular case.

The law which currently regulates this area is to be found in ss. 54–65 of the Road Traffic Act 1988 which makes it an offence to use, cause or permit to be used, a vehicle subject to the type approval requirements on a road without a certificate of conformity (s. 63(1)).

Additionally, under s. 80 of the 1988 Act the Secretary of State may designate the marking of motor vehicle parts to indicate conformity with a type approved by any country. Examples of such 'type approval marks' can be found under the Motor Vehicles (Designation of Approval Marks) Regulations 1979 (SI 1979 No. 1088), as amended, which relate to braking systems and seat belt anchorage systems. Applying a 'mark' in a way that is likely to deceive is an offence under the Trade Descriptions Act 1968, ss. 24 and 25.

## 9.4 The Road Vehicles (Construction and Use) Regulations 1986

Regulation 3 sets out the relevant definitions; where there is no specific definition, those used under the Road Traffic Act 1988 will usually apply (**see chapter 1**).

In bringing a prosecution for an offence under these Regulations it is important to establish whether the correct offence is 'using', 'causing' or 'permitting'. These expressions are explained in **chapter 1**.

It is also important to establish whether a particular regulation applies to vehicles *first used* on or after a certain date; *first registered* on or after a certain date; or *manufactured* on or after a certain date (see e.g. *Mackinnon* v *Peate* [1936] 2 All ER 240).

Certain vehicles are exempted from the Regulations (see reg. 4) and again it is important to check that a vehicle in a particular case does fall within those categories.

### 9.4.1 Brakes

Regulations 15–18 set out the requirements as to braking systems on vehicles, together with those for their maintenance. It is not absolutely *necessary* for the person testing the braking system of a vehicle to be a 'qualified examiner' (see *Stoneley* v *Richardson* [1973] RTR 229 where a constable testified to being able to push the defendant's car along with the handbrake applied).

The offence for breaching the requirement in relation to brakes is prosecuted under s. 41A of the Road Traffic Act 1988 (**see para. 9.4.10**).

See also s. 75 of the Road Traffic Act 1988 for the offence of selling unroadworthy vehicles.

### 9.4.2 Tyres

Section 41A of the 1988 Act also applies where the requirements in relation to tyres have been breached.

Regulation 24 sets out the requirements as to what tyres must be fitted to which vehicles, while reg. 25 restricts the speed limits and loads for such vehicles. Regulation 27 sets out a number of specific defects that will make tyres unlawful. It also contains exemptions for certain vehicles. The defects, in reg. 27 are where:

*(1) . . .*

*(a) the tyre is unsuitable having regard to the use to which the motor vehicle or trailer is being put or to the types of tyres fitted to its other wheels;*

*(b) the tyre is not so inflated as to make it fit for the use to which the motor vehicle or trailer is being put;*

*(c) the tyre has a cut in excess of 25 mm or 10% of the section width of the tyre, whichever is the greater, measured in any direction on the outside of the tyre and deep enough to reach the ply or cord;*

*(d) the tyre has any lump, bulge or tear caused by separation or partial failure of its structure;*

*(e) the tyre has any of the ply or cord exposed;*

*(f) the base of any groove which showed in the original tread pattern of the tyre is not clearly visible;*

*(g) either—*

*(i) the grooves of the tread pattern of the tyre do not have a depth of at least 1 mm throughout a continuous band measuring at least three-quarters of the breadth of the tread and round the entire outer circumference of the tyre; or*

*(ii) if the grooves of the original tread pattern of the tyre did not extend beyond three-quarters of the breadth of the tread, any groove which showed in the original tread pattern does not have a depth of at least 1 mm; or*

*(h) the tyre is not maintained in such condition as to be fit for the use to which the vehicle or trailer is being put or has a defect which might in any way cause damage to the surface of the road or damage to persons on or in the vehicle or to other persons using the road.*

Regulation 27 also places restrictions on 're-cut' tyres (reg. 27(5)) and provides for many exemptions from the above conditions.

**Keynote**

The entire outer circumference of a tyre does not usually include the outer walls or shoulder as they are not in contact with road (see *Coote* v *Parkin* [1977] RTR 61).

In the case of:

- passenger motor cars other than cars constructed or adapted to carry more than eight passengers (in addition to the driver)
- goods vehicles with a maximum gross weight not exceeding 3,500 kg
- light trailers first used on or after 3 January 1933

the depth of tread requirement is increased to 1.6 mm throughout a continuous band across the central 3/4 section of the tyre and around the entire circumference (see the Road Vehicles (Construction and Use) (Amendment) (No. 4) Regulations 1990 (SI 1990 No. 1981)).

To avoid the defect at reg. 27(1)(b) the tyre must be inflated so as to make it fit for the use to which the vehicle is being put at the material time; it does not have to be so inflated as to make it fit for some *future* use, however probable that use might be (*Connor* v *Graham* [1981] RTR 291).

Evidence as to the defective condition of a tyre may be given by anyone who saw it and it is no defence to argue that the tyre was not examined by an authorised vehicle examiner (*Phillips* v *Thomas* [1974] RTR 28).

Regulation 26 generally prohibits the mixing of different types of tyre (e.g. diagonal ply, bias-belted or radial ply) on both the same axle or different axles (although some combination is permissible). The use on roads of some 'knobbly' tyres or others which are designed for off-road use (on vehicles such as quad-bikes) may be prosecuted under reg. 27(1)(a) if it can be shown that the tyres were 'unsuitable having regard to the use to which the vehicle was put'.

'Tread pattern' includes plain surfaces as well as cut grooves but it does *not* cover tie-bars and tread wear indicators as used on many goods and heavy vehicles.

In relation to the selling of unsafe tyres, see the Motor Vehicles Tyres (Safety) Regulations 1994 (SI 1994 No. 3117) and the Consumer Protection Act 1987, s. 12(5).

### Exemptions

Regulation 27(4) sets out a number of exemptions to the provisions at (a)–(g) above, the main ones being:

- agricultural motor vehicles driven at not more than 20 mph
- agricultural trailers
- broken down vehicles or vehicles proceeding to a place to be broken up, being drawn in either case, by a motor vehicle at not more than 20 mph.

The onus appears to be on the defendant to show that his/her vehicle falls into an exempted category and that burden is not discharged simply by showing that the vehicle's excise licence describes it as being in one such category (*Wakeman* v *Catlow* [1977] RTR 174).

## 9.4.3 Mirrors

Regulation 33 sets out the requirements for mirrors on vehicles, including exemptions for certain types of vehicle. At reg. 33(1) there is a complex table showing the various types of mirror(s) required by different vehicles. Regulation 33(4) sets out the requirement for the stability and visibility of a vehicle's mirrors, together with the ability of the driver to adjust them.

## 9.4.4 Noise

Given the Government's commitment to exerting greater control over the effects that road traffic has on the community, these regulations in particular may become more prominent.

Regulations 54 and 57 regulate the fitting and use of silencers (including the rather sad attempts of some to increase the sound of their mopeds), while regs 37 and 99 apply to the types of audible warning instruments which are allowed on certain vehicles.

Regulation 97 provides that no motor vehicle shall be used on a road in such a manner as to cause any excessive noise which could have been avoided by the exercise of reasonable care by the driver.

A general prohibition on the use of an audible warning instrument while the vehicle is stationary on a road (except to warn of danger) is made by reg. 99, which also prohibits the use of such instruments between 11.30pm and 7am on a restricted road.

### 9.4.5 Quitting

Regulation 107 prohibits the leaving of a motor vehicle unattended on a road unless the engine has been stopped *and* the brake set; both must be done (*Butterworth* v *Shorthouse* [1956] Crim LR 341). Any person left 'attending' the vehicle must be someone who is licensed to drive it and in a position to intervene otherwise reg. 107 is breached. This sort of behaviour is very common (particularly outside cashpoints or video rental outlets) and, owing to the danger it presents, can often be dealt with under s. 22 of the Road Traffic Act 1988 (**see chapter 8**).

There are some exceptions to this prohibition when the vehicle is being used for certain purposes (e.g. for police, ambulance or fire services).

### 9.4.6 Stopping of Engine

Regulation 98 provides that the driver of a vehicle when it is stationary shall stop the action of any machinery attached to or forming part of the vehicle so far as may be necessary for the prevention of noise *or exhaust emissions*. The italicised addition was inserted by the Road Vehicles (Construction and Use) (Amendment) Regulations 1998 (SI 1998 No. 1) and has significant implications for vehicles such as taxis waiting at ranks. The exceptions to reg. 98 are:

- when the vehicle is stationary owing to the necessities of traffic;
- where it is necessary to examine machinery following its failure or derangement, or where it is required to be worked for a purpose other than driving the vehicle; or
- where a vehicle is propelled by gas produced in plant carried on the vehicle, the exception applies to that plant itself.

### 9.4.7 Dangerous Use or Condition

Regulation 100 contains a catch-all provision to prevent the use of vehicles in a way which presents a danger to others. There are many ways in which that danger can be brought about (e.g. insecure loading, using the vehicle in a way which causes a nuisance, having the vehicle in a poor general condition). This regulation, which would apply to vehicles carrying too many people or vehicles being used for an unsuitable purpose, overlaps to a large extent with the offence under s. 22A of the Road Traffic Act 1988 (**see chapter 8**).

Regulation 104 makes provision to ensure that drivers maintain proper control of their vehicles and maintain a full view of the traffic ahead together with restrictions on the distances which drivers can reverse.

### 9.4.8 Reversing

Regulation 106 prohibits the reversing of a motor vehicle on a road further than may be requisite for the safety or reasonable convenience of the occupants or of other traffic (unless the vehicle is a road roller engaged in the construction, maintenance or repair of the road).

### 9.4.9 Special Types of Vehicle

The much amended Motor Vehicles (Authorisation of Special Types) General Order 1979 (SI 1979 No. 1198) exempts a diverse collection of vehicles from the provisions of the 1986 Regulations.

Reading like an old Pepsi advert, the list of exemptions includes some track-laying, hedge-trimming, grass-cutting, life-saving, rotavating and excavating vehicles, together with some military and pedestrian-controlled vehicles. In the case of any vehicle which falls outside the conventional classes of cars, motor cycle, lorries and buses in terms of its size, construction or use, it is worth checking these exemptions.

The 1979 General Order also defines an *abnormal indivisible load.*

## 9.4.10 Offences

### Offence — Breach of Requirement: Brakes, Steering Gear or Tyres — Road Traffic Act 1988, s. 41A

*Triable summarily. Fine. Discretionary disqualification under specified conditions.*

***(No specific power of arrest)***

The Road Traffic Act 1988, s. 41A states:

*A person who—*

*(a) contravenes or fails to comply with a construction and use requirement as to brakes, steering-gear or tyres, or*

*(b) uses on a road a motor vehicle or trailer which does not comply with such a requirement, or causes or permits a motor vehicle or trailer to be so used,*

*is guilty of an offence.*

### Offence — Breach of Weight Requirements — Goods and Passenger Vehicles — Road Traffic Act 1988, s. 41B

*Triable summarily. Fine.*

***(No specific power of arrest)***

The Road Traffic Act 1988, s. 41B states:

*(1) A person who—*

*(a) contravenes or fails to comply with a construction and use requirement as to any description of weight applicable to—*

*(i) a goods vehicle, or*

*(ii) a motor vehicle or trailer adapted to carry more than eight passengers, or*

*(b) uses on a road a vehicle which does not comply with such a requirement, or causes or permits a vehicle to be so used,*

*is guilty of an offence.*

### Defence

The Road Traffic Act 1988, s. 41B states:

*(2) In any proceedings for an offence under this section in which there is alleged a contravention of or failure to comply with a construction and use requirement as to any description of weight applicable to a goods vehicle, it shall be a defence to prove either—*

*(a) that at the time when the vehicle was being used on the road—*

*(i) it was proceeding to a weighbridge which was the nearest available one to the place where the loading of the vehicle was completed for the purpose of being weighed, or*

*(ii) it was proceeding from a weighbridge after being weighed to the nearest point at which it was reasonably practicable to reduce the weight to the relevant limit, without causing an obstruction on any road, or*

*(b) in a case where the limit of that weight was not exceeded by more than 5 per cent—*

*(i) that that limit was not exceeded at the time when the loading of the vehicle was originally completed, and*

*(ii) that since that time no person has made any addition to the load.*

**Offence — Breach of Other Construction and Use Requirements — Road Traffic Act 1988, s. 42**
*Triable summarily. Fine.*
***(No specific power of arrest)***

The Road Traffic Act 1988, s. 42 states:

*A person who—*
*(a) contravenes or fails to comply with any construction or use requirement other than one within section 41A(a) or 41B(1)(a) of this Act, or*
*(b) uses on a road a motor vehicle or trailer which does not comply with such a requirement, or causes or permits a motor vehicle or trailer to be so used,*
*is guilty of an offence.*

## 9.5 Lights

The law which governs the fitting and use of lights on vehicles is to be found in the Road Vehicles Lighting Regulations 1989 (SI 1989 No. 1796). They are made under s. 41 of the Road Traffic Act 1988, for all vehicles except cycles (which are made under s. 81).

Parts of the 1989 Regulations are extremely detailed and reference should be made to the specific wording or diagram in each case. This chapter addresses only the broader aspects of the lighting regulations.

As with the Road Vehicles (Construction and Use) Regulations 1986 above, the lighting regulations can be divided into regulations which address fitting, maintenance and use.

The main lights are themselves divided into:

- headlamps (main beam and dipped)
- front and rear position lamps (side lights)
- front and rear fog lamps
- stop lamps
- reversing lamps
- optional lamps
- rear registration plate lamps.

Also included in the 1989 Regulations are reflectors and markers.

### 9.5.1 Offences

Offences contravening the lighting regulations are charged under s. 41 of the Road Traffic Act 1988 in the same ways as the other construction and use offences above.

Note the wording of a prohibition under the relevant regulation may be aimed at the fitting of a light and not necessarily its use.

### 9.5.2 Definitions

Regulation 3 sets out the definitions for the purposes of the 1989 Regulations. Again, where none is specified, the corresponding definition under the Road Traffic Act 1988 will usually apply.

The Regulations separate a 24-hour period into:

- the period between sunset and sunrise
- the period between sunrise and sunset.

Where the old distinction of 'daytime hours' and 'hours of darkness' apply, reg. 3 defines them as 'the time between half an hour before sunrise and half an hour after sunset' and 'the time between half an hour after sunset and half an hour before sunrise' respectively.

### 9.5.3 Exemptions

Regulations 4–9A list the exemptions which include:

> *4. . . .*
> *(3) Nothing in these Regulations shall require any lamp or reflector to be fitted between sunrise and sunset to—*
> *(a) a vehicle not fitted with any front or rear position lamp,*
> *(b) an incomplete vehicle proceeding to a works for completion,*
> *(c) a pedal cycle,*
> *(d) a pedestrian-controlled vehicle,*
> *(e) a horse-drawn vehicle,*
> *(f) a vehicle drawn or propelled by hand, or*
> *(g) a combat vehicle.*
>
> *5. [Temporarily imported vehicles and vehicles proceeding to a port for export]*
>
> *6. [Vehicles towing or being towed]*
>
> *7. [Military vehicles]*
>
> *8. [Invalid carriages]*
>
> *9. [Vehicles drawn or propelled by hand]*
>
> *9A. [Tram cars]*

Other exemptions will apply to some parked vehicles (see e.g. reg. 24).

### 9.5.4 Fitting of Lights

Regulations 11–22 cover the fitting of lights, reflectors and rear markings. The vehicles shown in sch. 1 must be fitted with the corresponding lights etc. and it is an offence to use, or to cause or permit to be used (**see chapter 1**) such a vehicle which does not comply with those regulations.

Regulation 11 deals with the colours of lights and reflectors which must or must not be fitted, while regs 13 and 16 address the fitting of flashing lights and warning beacons.

Regulations 21 and 22 deal with the fitting of additional lights to long vehicles and trailers.

### 9.5.5 Rear Registration Lamps

Although rear registration lamps are addressed under the 1989 Regulations, there is also an offence under the Vehicle Excise and Registration Act 1984 (**see chapter 12**).

### 9.5.6 Headlamps

Schedules 4 and 5 contain the specifications for headlamps.

Regulation 25 makes it an offence to use or cause or permit to be used, a vehicle with obligatory headlamps on a road unless they are kept lit during the hours of darkness and in seriously reduced visibility. (There is an exception to this requirement which applies to vehicles on 'restricted' roads per s. 81 of the Road Traffic Regulation Act 1984 where the street lights are on.)

### 9.5.7 Position Lamps

Schedules 2 and 10 set out the specification for front and rear position lamps respectively. Regulation 24 makes it an offence to use, or to cause or permit to be used, a vehicle on a road between sunset and sunrise or in motion in seriously reduced visibility, unless every position lamp, rear registration lamp and side-marker lamp required by it are lit.

### 9.5.8 Maintenance and Use

Regulations 23–27 govern the maintenance of lights and reflectors, together with their use. Regulation 23 makes it an offence to use, or to cause or permit to be used, a vehicle on a road unless the relevant lamps and reflectors (including some optional ones) are clean and in good working order.

The general exception to reg. 23 is if the vehicle is being used during daytime hours and the defect only happened during the journey or if arrangements have been made to rectify it with all reasonable expedition (reg. 23(3)).

Regulation 27 sets out a table showing the ways in which certain lights may/may not be used (**see appendix** 5). Regulation 27 states that no person shall use (or cause or permit to be used) on a road, any vehicle on which any lamp, hazard warning signal/device or beacon of a type specified in column 2 of the table in a manner specified in column 3.

### 9.5.9 Motor Cycles

A number of the construction and use regulations relate specifically to motor cycles.

Regulations 57 and 57A set out the construction requirements in relation to noise limits and exhaust systems on motor cycles.

Regulation 84 imposes restrictions on the drawing of trailers by motor cycles on a road, while regs 92 and 93 make provision for the attachment and use of side cars.

## 9.6 Testing

Section 47 of the Road Traffic Act 1988 requires all motor vehicles which were first registered more than three years before the time when they are being used on a road to pass a test. That requirement includes vehicles manufactured abroad (s. 47(2)(b)).

Some vehicles need to be tested after one year, notably:

- motor vehicles having more than eight seats (excluding the driver's seat) which are used to carry passengers
- taxis

- ambulances
- larger goods vehicles

need to be tested after one year.

The procedure for testing of vehicles is set out in the Motor Vehicles (Tests) Regulations 1981 (SI 1981 No. 1694), as amended. These and their many amending Regulations lay down both the instructions for carrying out a test and also specify those items which will be tested.

Tests can only be carried out by 'authorised examiners' and others listed in s. 45(3) and many garages are so authorised.

For the scope of Regulations that may be made in relation to the testing of vehicles, see the Road Traffic Act 1988, s. 46 as amended by the Road Traffic (Vehicle Testing) Act 1999. The 1999 Act also amends the summary offence of impersonating an authorised examiner with intent to deceive under s. 177 of the Road Traffic Act 1988. At the time of writing, the Road Traffic (Vehicle Testing) Act 1999 had received Royal Assent but no commencement date had been published.

The items tested will include:

- brakes
- tyres
- seat belts
- steering
- certain lights/reflectors
- stop lights
- exhausts
- wipers and washers
- direction indicators
- suspension
- bodywork
- horn.

Satisfactory completion of the test will result in the issuing of a certificate under s. 45(2)(b).

The Motor Vehicles (Tests) Amendment Regulations 1998 (SI 1998 No. 1672) introduced new transitory classes of vehicle to allow for extra installation checks to be made to minibuses, buses and coaches in respect of their seat belts.

### Offence — Using, Causing or Permitting Use of Vehicle without Test Certificate — Road Traffic Act 1988, s. 47(1)

*Triable summarily. Fine.*

***(No specific power of arrest)***

The Road Traffic Act 1988, s. 47 states:

> *(1) A person who uses on a road at any time, or causes or permits to be so used, a motor vehicle to which this section applies, and as respects which no test certificate has been issued within the appropriate period before that time, is guilty of an offence.*
>
> *In this section and section 48 of this Act, the 'appropriate period' means a period of twelve months or such shorter period as may be prescribed.*

**Keynote**

As ever, there are numerous exemptions to the requirements of s. 47, most of which relate to larger vehicles, track-laying vehicles and some pedestrian controlled vehicles (see reg. 6 of the 1981 Regulations).

Some military vehicles, some electrically-powered goods vehicles and vehicles temporarily in Great Britain are also exempt.

Vehicles *provided* (as opposed to 'used') for police purposes are exempt if they are maintained in an approved police workshop (reg. 6(xiv)). Other exemptions exist in relation to vehicles seized or detained by the police or customs and excise officers.

Special provision is made (under s. 48) for the issue of temporary exemption certificates in the case of certain public service vehicles.

An exemption exists where the person using the vehicle is taking it to or from a testing centre. This exemption is only applicable where the test has been previously arranged with the garage. A further exemption exists where a test certificate has been refused and the vehicle is:

- being delivered by prior arrangement, or brought from the place where the relevant work is to be/has been carried out; or
- being towed to a place where it is to be broken up.

Provision is made in reg. 6 for the use of a vehicle by an authorised examiner or inspector during the test.

The provisions of s. 165 of the Road Traffic Act 1988 apply to test certificates (**see para. 6.2.6**).

This means that an officer may issue a form HO/RT 1 in respect of such a certificate.

Note that the offences under s. 173 (forging documents) and s. 175 (issuing false documents) of the Road Traffic Act 1988 apply to test certificates (**see chapter 16**).

### 9.6.1 Goods Vehicles

The testing of goods vehicles is governed by ss. 49–53 of the Road Traffic Act 1988 and the Goods Vehicles (Plating and Testing) Regulations 1988 (SI 1988 No. 1478), as amended.

They are tested and 'plated' at government testing stations under the ambit of the Secretary of State and these tests must be carried out annually.

Schedule 2 to the Regulations lists the many vehicles which are exempt, a list which includes snow ploughs, hearses, fire fighting vehicles and road rollers.

**Offence — Using, Causing or Permitting Use of Goods Vehicle without Test Certificate — Road Traffic Act 1988, s. 53(2)**

*Triable summarily. Fine.*

***(No specific power of arrest)***

The Road Traffic Act 1988, s. 53 states:

*(2) If any person at any time on or after the relevant date—*
*(a) uses on a road a goods vehicle of a class required by regulations under section 49 of this Act to have been submitted for a goods vehicle test, or*
*(b) causes or permits to be used on a road a goods vehicle of such a class, and at that time there is no goods vehicle test certificate in force for the vehicle, he is guilty of an offence.*
*In this subsection 'relevant date', in relation to any goods vehicle, means the date by which it is required by the regulations to be submitted for its first goods vehicle test.*

Section 53(1) creates a similar offence in relation to Plating Certificates.

## 9.6.2 Roadside Tests

Section 67 of the Road Traffic Act 1988 allows 'authorised examiners' to carry out roadside tests on motor vehicles, in relation to the brakes, steering, tyres, lights and noise and fume emission. Authorised examiners include constables so authorised by their chief officer of police. Other examiners may be appointed (e.g. by the Secretary of State or a police authority) but they must produce their authority to act as such if required to do so (s. 67(5)). Obstructing such an examiner is a summary offence under s. 67(9) (for the offence of obstructing a police officer generally, **see Crime, chapter 8**).

Section 67(6) allows for drivers to ask for the examination to be deferred (in accordance with the time limits set out at sch. 2 to the 1988 Act). However, s. 67 goes on to provide that:

*(7) Where it appears to a constable that, by reason of an accident having occurred owing to the presence of the vehicle on a road, it is requisite that a test should be carried out forthwith, he may require it to be so carried out and, if he is not to carry it out himself, may require that the vehicle shall not be taken away until the test has been carried out.*
*(8) Where in the opinion of a constable the vehicle is apparently so defective that it ought not to be allowed to proceed without a test being carried out, he may require the test to be carried out forthwith.*
*(9) If a person obstructs an authorised examiner acting under this section, or fails to comply with a requirement of this section or Schedule 2 to this Act, he is guilty of an offence.*
*(10) In this section and in Schedule 2 to this Act—*
*(a) 'test' includes 'inspect' or 'inspection', as the case may require, and*
*(b) references to a vehicle include references to a trailer drawn by it.*

**Keynote**

Section 68 provides a power for vehicle examiners to inspect goods vehicles, PSVs and some larger passenger carrying vehicles. It also provides a power for a police officer in uniform to direct such a vehicle to a suitable place of inspection when found on a road, provided that that place of inspection is not more than five miles from the place where the requirement is made. Refusal or neglect to comply is a summary offence. The power is only available in relation to vehicles that are 'stationary' on a road. Presumably if the vehicle is moving, the officer need only stop it (using the general power under s. 163) before directing it to be driven to a place of inspection.

## 9.6.3 Testing and Inspection

Regulation 74 of the Road Vehicles (Construction and Use) Regulations 1986 provides a power to test and inspect the:

- brakes
- silencers
- steering gear
- tyres

of any vehicle on any premises where that vehicle is located.

The power applies to police officers in uniform and other authorised vehicle examiners (see reg. 74(a)–(f). Regulation 74 provides no power of entry and stipulates that the person empowered shall produce his/her authorisation if required to do so. It also provides that no such test or inspection shall be carried out unless:

- the owner of the vehicle consents;

- notice has been given to that owner (either personally or left at his/her address not less than 48 hours before the time of the proposed test/inspection, or sent to him/her by recorded delivery at least 72 hours before the proposed test/inspection); or

- the test or inspection is made within 48 hours of a reportable accident in which the vehicle was involved.

# CHAPTER TEN

# TRAFFIC SIGNS

## 10.1 Introduction

A 'traffic sign' is defined under the Road Traffic Regulation Act 1984, s. 64 which states:

> *In this Act 'traffic sign' means any object or device (whether fixed or portable) for conveying, to traffic on roads or any specified class of traffic, warnings, information, requirements, restrictions or prohibitions of any description—*
> *(a) specified by regulations made by the Ministers acting jointly; or*
> *(b) authorised by the Secretary of State,*
> *and any line or mark on a road for so conveying such warnings, information, requirements, restrictions or prohibitions.*

Such a traffic sign will include temporary signs and road markings (e.g. double white lines).

The restrictions on prosecution imposed by s. 1 of the Road Traffic Offenders Act 1988 (notices of intended prosecution) should be borne in mind when considering offences in this chapter.

Note that, since the Road Traffic Act 1991, increasing reliance has been placed on the use of automatic devices for detecting traffic light offences and that the procedure of 'conditional offers' of fixed penalties is available for such offences (**see chapter 14**).

## 10.2 Authorised Traffic Signs

The colour, size and other specifications for traffic signs are to be found in the Traffic Signs Regulations and General Directions 1994 (SI 1994 No. 1519). (For Wales see also the Traffic Signs (Welsh and English Language Provisions) Regulations 1985 (SI 1985 No. 713).)

If a traffic sign is to have any legal effect you must show that it was placed or displayed by someone who was authorised to do so under the circumstances.

Traffic signs, whether temporary or permanent, may not be placed on or near a road unless the person placing them is specifically authorised to do so (Road Traffic Regulation Act 1984, s. 64(4)).

Among those authorised are:

- **the local traffic authority** — in respect of roads in their area;
- **a constable or other person authorised by the chief officer of police** — under certain circumstances;
- **any other person** — in respect of a temporary obstruction.

### 10.2.1 Traffic Authority

Section 65 of the Road Traffic Regulation Act 1984 empowers a traffic authority to cause or permit traffic signs to be placed on or near any road in their area. These signs must be placed in accordance with certain directions issued by the Secretary of State and/or Minister, most of which fall under the Traffic Signs Regulations and General Directions 1994.

The civil liability of a traffic authority when placing, or deciding not to place, traffic signs under this section must be judged against the House of Lords' decision in *Stovin* v *Wise and Norfolk CC* [1996] RTR 354. There it was held that there are only limited grounds for apportioning civil liability to a traffic authority where it has taken a decision in relation to its statutory powers. In exercising its powers under s. 65, a traffic authority owes a duty of care to motorists when selecting a suitable position for a particular traffic sign (*Levine* v *Morris* [1970] 1 WLR 71).

### 10.2.2 Constable or Other Person Authorised by Chief Officer of Police

Sections 66 and 67 of the Road Traffic Regulation Act 1984 provide powers for police officers (and others acting under the instructions of a chief officer) to place traffic signs. Section 66 applies to the placing of signs and 'structures' in relation to local traffic regulations and includes:

- Races or speed trials authorised under s. 31(4) of the Road Traffic Act 1988.
- Measures taken to avoid obstruction on public occasions or near public buildings in London under s. 52 of the Metropolitan Police Act 1839.
- Similar measures authorised under other statutes (e.g. the Town Police Clauses Act 1847 or enactments relating to the City of London).

Section 67 of the 1984 Act states:

> *(1) A constable, or a person acting under the instructions (whether general or specific) of the chief officer of police, may place on a road, or on any structure on a road, traffic signs (of any size, colour and type prescribed or authorised under section 64 of this Act) indicating prohibitions, restrictions or requirements relating to vehicular traffic, as may be necessary or expedient to prevent or mitigate congestion or obstruction of traffic, or danger to or from traffic, in consequence of extraordinary circumstances; and the power to place signs conferred by this subsection shall include power to maintain a sign for a period of seven days or less from the time when it was placed, but no longer.*

**Keynote**

The offence of failing to comply with traffic directions (s. 36 of the Road Traffic Act 1988 (**see para. 10.3**) applies to signs placed under the authority granted by s. 67(1) (s. 67(2)).

## 10.2.3 Temporary Obstructions

The placing of traffic signs to warn of temporary obstructions is now governed by the Traffic Signs (Temporary Obstructions) Regulations 1997 (SI 1997 No. 3053) which came into force on 1 March 1998.

The 1997 Regulations introduce a new sign, the road vehicle sign, which is intended to warn of a temporary obstruction caused by stationary vehicles. They also make provision for someone in charge of, or accompanying emergency or breakdown vehicles, to place 'Keep Right' signs under certain circumstances.

### Authorisation to Place Temporary Signs

Regulation 15 provides that:

> *(1) Subject to paragraph (4) of this regulation, a person who is in charge of or accompanies an emergency or a breakdown vehicle which is temporarily obstructing a road is hereby authorised to place a keep right sign for the purpose of warning vehicular traffic of the obstruction created by the vehicle and to indicate the way past the vehicle.*
>
> *(2) Subject to paragraph (4) of this regulation, any person not otherwise authorised to do so is hereby authorised to place a road vehicle sign on a vehicle or a flat traffic delineator, traffic cone, traffic pyramid, traffic triangle or warning lamp on any road for the purpose of warning traffic of a temporary obstruction in the road, other than one caused by the carrying out of works.*

**Keynote**

Regulation 16 requires that signs be placed in an upright position and in such a way as to guide traffic past the obstruction. It also requires that they should be removed as soon as the relevant obstruction has itself been removed.

'Emergency vehicles' here will generally include vehicles used for fire, ambulance and police purposes, rescue vehicles and vehicles used in connection with blood transfusions and tissue transplant. The full definition can be found in the Road Vehicles Lighting Regulations 1989 (SI 1989 No. 1796).

'A breakdown vehicle' here is a vehicle used to attend an accident or a breakdown or to draw a broken down vehicle.

Finally, reg. 16 sets out a table showing the way in which the various signs may be used. A sign indicated in column 2 may be placed only if the conditions specified in column 3 are complied with.

Regulation 16 provides that:

> *(1) In this regulation—*
>
> *(a) 'placed' in relation to a traffic sign means placed in pursuance of an authorisation given by regulation 15;*
>
> *(b) references to 'the obstruction' are to the temporary obstruction in relation to which a traffic sign is placed; and*
>
> *(c) references to 'the road' are to the road on which the obstruction is situated.*
>
> *(2) A traffic sign which has been placed shall be removed as soon as the obstruction has been removed.*
>
> *(3) A flat traffic delineator, keep right sign, traffic cone, traffic pyramid or traffic triangle shall be placed in an upright position.*
>
> *(4) A flat traffic delineator, keep right sign, traffic cone or traffic pyramid shall be placed so as to guide traffic past the obstruction.*

*(5) A traffic sign referred to in column (2) of an item in the table below may be placed only if the conditions specified in column (3) of the item are complied with.*

*Table*

| *(1) Item* | *(2) Traffic sign* | *(3) Conditions* |
|---|---|---|
| *1.* | *Flat traffic delineator* | *1. At least three other flat traffic delineators must also be placed in relation to the osbstruction.*<br>*2. Each flat traffic delineator must be so placed as to face traffic approaching the obstruction from the side of the obstruction on which it is placed.* |
| *2.* | *Road vehicle sign* | *1. It must be placed to face traffic approaching the stationary vehicle from the front, rear or side of the vehicle on which it is placed.*<br>*2. It must be securely fixed to the stationary vehicle.*<br>*3. It must not obscure any registration plate, lamps or reflectors of the stationary vehicle.* |
| *3.* | *Traffic cone* | *At least three other traffic pyramids must also be placed in relation to the obstruction.* |
| *4.* | *Traffic pyramid* | *At least three other traffic pyramids must also be placed in relation to the obstruction.* |
| *5.* | *Traffic triangle* | *1. A traffic triangle must be placed at least 45 metres away from the obstruction.*<br>*2. A traffic triangle must be so placed as to face traffic approaching the obstruction from the side of the obstruction on which it is placed.* |
| *6.* | *Warning lamp* | *1. A warning lamp may be used only in conjunction with another traffic sign lawfully placed in accordance with these Regulations being—*<br>*(a) a flat traffic delineator;*<br>*(b) a keep right sign;*<br>*(c) a road vehicle sign;*<br>*(d) a traffic cone;*<br>*(e) a traffic pyramid; or*<br>*(f) a traffic triangle*<br>*and shall be so placed as not to obscure that other traffic sign from the view of approaching traffic.*<br>*2. Not more than one warning lamp shall be placed in conjunction with each such other traffic sign.* |

**Keynote**

A 'flat traffic delineator' is described at sch. 12 to the 1994 Regulations. It is the type of sign used to mark off a temporary traffic lane on roads.

## Temporary Traffic Signs

Part II of the 1997 Regulations provides that:

***4.**—(1) In addition to the requirement conveyed by the sign shown in diagram 610 of the 1994 Regulations in accordance with those Regulations, a keep right sign shall convey to vehicular traffic a warning of a temporary obstruction.*

*(2) Section 36 of the Road Traffic Act 1988 shall apply to the keep right sign.*

***5.** In addition to indicating the edge of a route for vehicular traffic through or past a temporary obstruction, in accordance with the 1994 Regulations, a traffic cone and a flat delineator shall each convey to such traffic on a road a warning of an obstruction in the road.*

*6. A road vehicle sign shall convey to vehicular traffic using a road a warning of a temporary obstruction in the road caused by a stationary vehicle.*

*7. A traffic pyramid, a traffic triangle and a warning lamp shall each convey to vehicular traffic using a road a warning of a temporary obstruction in the road, other than an obstruction caused by the carrying out of works.*

Part III sets out the requirements for the dimensions of certain traffic signs, including:

- 'Keep Right' signs
- Flat traffic delineators
- Road vehicle signs
- Traffic cones, pyramids and triangles
- Warning lamps

Diagrams showing the requirements for road vehicle signs, pyramids and triangles can be found in schs 1–3 of the 1997 Regulations.

## 10.3 Failing to Comply with Traffic Sign

Depending on the sign involved, failure to comply with a traffic sign can be divided into three categories:

1. Failing to comply with statutory restrictions or requirements (that is, under public or local Acts as opposed to Orders or Regulations. These cases are punishable under s. 36 of the Road Traffic Act 1988.
2. Failing to comply with signs where s. 36 of the Road Traffic Act 1988 is specifically referred to as applying to them (e.g. those listed in reg. 10 of the Traffic Signs Regulations and General Directions 1994, as amended).
3. Failing to comply with other 'authorised signs'. These cases are punishable under s. 91 of the Road Traffic Offenders Act 1988.

Those offences where s. 36 of the Road Traffic Act 1988 applies are subject to the Notice of Intended Prosecution procedure (**see chapter 3**).

The following signs are among those listed in reg. 10 of the Traffic Signs Regulations and General Directions 1994:

- 'STOP' signs
- 'GIVE WAY' signs at junctions and open level crossings
- 'KEEP LEFT/RIGHT' signs
- NO 'U' TURN signs
- 'NO ENTRY' signs

- 'STOP' board, operated manually on lengths of road where one-way working is necessary
- Signs prohibiting vehicles of a certain height
- Signs indicating bus or pedal cycle route
- Red traffic light signals
- Green traffic light filter signals
- Double white line systems.

### Offence — Failing to Comply with a Traffic Sign — Road Traffic Act 1988, s. 36(1)

*Triable summarily. Fine. Discretionary disqualification under certain circumstances.*
***(No specific power of arrest)***

The Road Traffic Act 1988, s. 36 states:

*(1) Where a traffic sign, being a sign—*
*(a) of the prescribed size, colour and type, or*
*(b) of another character authorised by the Secretary of State under the provisions in that behalf of the Road Traffic Regulation Act 1984,*
*has been lawfully placed on or near a road, a person driving or propelling a vehicle who fails to comply with the indication given by the sign is guilty of an offence.*

**Keynote**

This offence only applies to failure to comply with those signs listed at categories 1. and 2. above.

Section 36(3) states:

*(3) For the purposes of this section a traffic sign placed on or near a road shall be deemed—*
*(a) to be of the prescribed size, colour and type, or of another character authorised by the Secretary of State under the provisions in that behalf of the Road Traffic Regulation Act 1984, and*
*(b) (subject to subsection (2) . . .) to have been lawfully so placed unless the contrary is proved.*

### Offence — Failing to Comply with Other Traffic Sign — Road Traffic Offenders Act 1988, s. 91

*Triable summarily. Fine.*
***(No specific power of arrest)***

The Road Traffic Offenders Act 1988, s. 91 states:

*If a person acts in contravention of or fails to comply with—*
*(a) any regulations made by the Secretary of State under the Road Traffic Act 1988 other than regulations made under section 31, 45 or 132,*
*(b) any regulations made by the Secretary of State under the Road Traffic Regulation Act 1984, other than regulations made under section 28, Schedule 4, Part III of Schedule 9 or Schedule 12,*
*and the contravention or failure to comply is not made an offence under any other provision of the Traffic Acts, he shall for each offence be liable . . .*

**Keynote**

If the sign which a driver contravenes is not covered by s. 36 of the Road Traffic Act 1988 (e.g. failing to conform to an 'amber' traffic light), the appropriate charge would be under this Act and section.

**Offence — Failing to Comply with Traffic Directions of Constable — Road Traffic Act 1988, s. 35(1)**
*Triable summarily. Fine.*
***(No specific power of arrest)***

The Road Traffic Act 1988, s. 35 states:

> *(1) Where a constable is for the time being engaged in the regulation of traffic in a road, a person driving or propelling a vehicle who neglects or refuses—*
> *(a) to stop the vehicle, or*
> *(b) to make it proceed in, or keep to, a particular lane of traffic,*
> *when directed to do so by the constable in the execution of his duty is guilty of an offence.*

**Keynote**

This power applies to 'a vehicle' and is not limited to a motor, or even a mechanically propelled, vehicle.

'Neglecting' would appear to have a similar meaning to 'failing' (see e.g. *Pontin* v *Price* (1933) 97 JP 315).

Once the driver has stopped, he/she may commit this offence by moving off again in defiance of an order by the officer to stay put (see *Kentesber* v *Waumsley* [1980] Crim LR 383).

For a person to commit this offence, the constable must be engaged in the regulation of traffic.

If the constable was not so engaged and the direction given was to stop the vehicle, the appropriate charge would be under s. 163 of the Road Traffic Act 1988 (see below).

Unlike s. 163 however, there is no need for the constable to be in uniform but, if he/she is not, you would need to show that the defendant knew him/her to be a police officer.

Section 35 also applies to traffic wardens, **see para. 10.4.2**.

Section 35(2) provides a police power to direct traffic into a census area for the purpose of a traffic survey. That power must not be used in such a way as to cause unnecessary delay to someone who indicates that they are unwilling to provide information for the purposes of the survey (s. 35(3)).

## 10.4 Powers to Stop and Direct Traffic

### 10.4.1 Power to Stop Vehicles

Section 163(1) and (2) of the Road Traffic Act 1988 provide that:

*(1) A person driving a mechanically propelled vehicle on a road must stop the vehicle on being required to do so by a constable in uniform.*

*(2) A person riding a cycle on a road must stop the cycle on being required to do so by a constable in uniform.*

**Offence — Failing to Stop when Required — Road Traffic Act 1988, s. 163(3)**
*Triable summarily. Fine.*
**(*No specific power of arrest*)**

The Road Traffic Act 1988, s. 163 states:

*If a person fails to comply with this section he is guilty of an offence.*

**Keynote**

The exercise of powers to carry out road checks under Part I of the Police and Criminal Evidence Act 1984 is covered by s. 163, that is, if a driver fails to stop when required by a constable in uniform at such a road check, he/she will commit this offence (for a discussion of this and other powers relating to the stopping of motor vehicles, **see General Police Duties, chapter 2**).

The lawful exercise of police powers to stop people going about their business within the community can be a significant source of friction. The manner or frequency of the use of power such as the power to stop vehicles on a road might be perceived by the community as a source of oppression and discrimination, leading to a reduction in confidence in the police and the creation of an atmosphere of distrust. As with stop and search powers generally (**see General Police Duties, chapter 2**), this was highlighted in the Stephen Lawrence inquiry (CM 4262–I), see para. 46.31 and recommendation 61.

'Stop' means bringing the vehicle to a halt and remaining at rest for long enough for the officer (or traffic warden; **see para. 10.4.2**) to exercise whatever additional powers may be appropriate (see *Lodwick* v *Sanders* [1985] 1 All ER 577).

Unlike the power under s. 35(1) above, this power is confined to 'mechanically propelled vehicles' (**see chapter 1**) or cycles.

Use of this power by police officers to detect drink/driving offences was endorsed in *Chief Constable of Gwent* v *Dash* [1986] RTR 41.

## 10.4.2 Pedestrians Contravening Directions

**Offence — Pedestrians Failing to Comply with Directions of Constable — Road Traffic Act 1988, s. 37**
*Triable summarily. Fine.*
**(*No specific power of arrest*)**

The Road Traffic Act 1988, s. 37 states:

*Where a constable in uniform is for the time being engaged in the regulation of vehicular traffic in a road, a person on foot who proceeds across or along the carriageway in contravention of a direction to stop given by the constable in the execution of his duty, either to persons on foot or to persons on foot and other traffic, is guilty of an offence.*

## Offence — Failing to Provide Name and Address — Road Traffic Act 1988, s. 169

*Triable summarily. Fine.*

**(*No specific power of arrest*)**

The Road Traffic Act 1988, s. 169 states:

> *A constable may require a person committing an offence under section 37 of this Act to give his name and address, and if that person fails to do so he is guilty of an offence.*

### Keynote

The requirement here is for the person to state his/her own name and address. However, given the decision in *R* v *McCarthy*, *The Times*, 8 January 1999, under a similar provision relating to the duty following an accident (**see para. 4.2**), it is uncertain whether the furnishing of some other address such as that of the defendant's solicitor would be enough to meet the requirement.

### Traffic Wardens

By virtue of the Functions of Traffic Wardens Order 1970 (SI 1970 No. 1958) and s. 96 of the Road Traffic Regulation Act 1984, ss. 35 and 37 above also apply to directions given by traffic wardens. Traffic wardens can also demand the name and address of any person committing an offence under s. 37.

## CHAPTER ELEVEN

# DRIVER LICENSING

### 11.1 Introduction

The law regulating driver licensing was greatly simplified by the introduction of the Motor Vehicles (Driving Licences) Regulations 1996 (SI 1996 No. 2824). As with most statutory instruments in the area of road traffic, these principal Regulations have themselves been amended many times and it is important to refer to the most up to date list of such amendments when dealing with licensing matters. In cases of any doubt, the DVLA are generally the best source of information.

The government has recently signalled its intention to allow driving licences to be revoked for non-offence matters (e.g. by the Child Support Agency) and this area of the subject may change in the near future.

Most of the relevant legislation governing the licensing of drivers to drive motor vehicles can be found in the 1996 Regulations, together with:

- Part III of the Road Traffic Act 1988
- the Road Traffic (Driver Licensing and Information Systems) Act 1989
- the Road Traffic (New Drivers) Act 1995.

The 1996 Regulations, which have consolidated many of their predecessors, are complex and their exact wording should be consulted when considering offences or entitlements to drive. Infringement is generally charged under the Road Traffic Offenders Act 1988, s. 91.

### 11.2 Driving Otherwise than in Accordance with Licence

Since the implementation of the EC directive on driving licences (Council Directive 91/439/EEC) the categories of vehicles for the purposes of driving licences has been altered. The current categories are to be found in sch. 2 to the 1996 Regulations (**see appendix 6**).

**Offence — Driving Otherwise than in Accordance with Licence — Road Traffic Act 1988, s. 87**

*Triable summarily. Fine. Discretionary disqualification for s. 87(1) under specified circumstances.*

**(*No specific power of arrest*)**

The Road Traffic Act 1988, s. 87 states:

*(1) It is an offence for a person to drive on a road a motor vehicle of any class otherwise than in accordance with a licence authorising him to drive a motor vehicle of that class.*

*(2) It is an offence for a person to cause or permit another person to drive on a road a motor vehicle of any class otherwise than in accordance with a licence authorising that other person to drive a motor vehicle of that class.*

**Keynote**

This offence will apply where a person has a particular licence and has failed to abide by any conditions attached to it, or where a person does not hold a licence at all. In proving such an offence, you must show that the defendant drove a motor vehicle on a road (for the definitions of which, see **chapter 1**); it is then for the defendant to show that he/she had a licence to do so (see *John* v *Humphreys* [1955] 1 All ER 793).

Section 88 provides a long list of exceptions to the general prohibition imposed by s. 87. Those exemptions include:

- Drivers who have had their licence revoked on disqualification and who have re-applied for another.
- Drivers who have a 'qualifying application' lodged with the Secretary of State.
- Drivers from overseas becoming resident in Great Britain.

For the elements required in 'causing' and 'permitting', **see chapter 1**. Section 88 sets out a number of exemptions to the requirements of s. 87.

For overseas drivers, **see para. 11.6.3**.

For offences in relation to the supervision of learner drivers, **see para. 11.6.1**.

## 11.3 The Licence

A driving licence must be issued in the form prescribed by the Secretary of State under s. 98 of the Road Traffic Act 1988. From July 1998 a new photocard driving licence has been introduced as part of the harmonisation process between our domestic road traffic legislation and that of the rest of the European Union (see the Driving Licences (Community Driving Licence) Regulations 1998 (SI 1998 No. 1420)). Although the existing paper licences are still valid, the intention is to phase them out over time and current holders of such licences may exchange them for a new photocard licence. In addition to the photocard licence, there will be a paper counterpart which contains much of the same detail as the plastic card but not the holder's photograph.

Photocard licences are *pink* for full licence holders and *green* for provisional licence holders and need to be renewed every ten years until the holder is 70 years old. Licences held by drivers in Wales are printed in both Welsh and English.

Photocard licences are the same size as a credit card and contain the holder's:

- name
- address
- date of birth
- driver number
- driving entitlement
- photograph
- electronically-copied signature
- information codes showing any restrictions that apply to the holder.

The information codes, which appear in section 12 of the licence are reproduced in **appendix 10**. They can be of particular practical importance and will indicate, for instance, whether the driver is supposed to be wearing spectacles or some other form of visual correction. (For the power to require a driver to take an eyesight test, **see para. 11.6.4**).

Licences will *generally* last until the holder's 70th birthday or for three years, whichever is the longer (see s. 99 of the Road Traffic Act 1988). On reaching 70, a driver may renew his/her licence every three years. This applies to full driving licences and most provisional licences. As noted above the new photocard licence is renewable every 10 years.

Large goods vehicles and passenger carrying vehicles licences last until the drivers' 45th birthday or five years, whichever is the longer. If the driver is between 45 and 65 they last for five years or until the 66th birthday, whichever is the *shorter*. After the driver has reached 65 the licence must be renewed annually (**see chapter 13**).

Group A and A1 provisional licences (covering motor bicycles) generally last for two years (reg. 14). If a Group A provisional licence holder wants to 'pause' the two-year period (e.g. while he/she is out of the country), he/she may surrender the licence and continue with the rest of the two-year period once he/she gets the licence back.

Full licences can act as provisional licences in many cases (except e.g. motor cycles over 125cc) and you should refer to the licence itself, together with the Regulations and the provisions of s. 97 in establishing whether a particular licence does entitle the holder to drive other vehicles as a provisional licence holder.

The holder of a driving licence must sign it; failing to do so is an offence under reg. 18 and the Road Traffic Offenders Act 1988. Provisions have also been made for signing a document to allow the electronic reproduction of the driver's signature on the new photocard licence (**see para. 11.3.2**).

A licence holder must surrender his/her licence to the Secretary of State on changing name or address and failure to do so is a summary offence under s. 99(5) of the Road Traffic Act 1988. The Secretary of State may also revoke driving licences under certain conditions (see e.g. s. 93 of the 1988 Act).

## 11.3.1 Police Powers

### Power to Demand Production of Driving Licence

Section 164 of the Road Traffic Act 1988 states:

*(1) Any of the following persons—*
*(a) a person driving a motor vehicle on a road,*

*(b) a person whom a constable or vehicle examiner has reasonable cause to believe to have been the driver of a motor vehicle at a time when an accident occurred owing to its presence on a road,*

*(c) a person whom a constable or vehicle examiner has reasonable cause to believe to have committed an offence in relation to the use of a motor vehicle on a road, or*

*(d) a person—*

*(i) who supervises the holder of a provisional licence while the holder is driving a motor vehicle on a road, or*

*(ii) whom a constable or vehicle examiner has reasonable cause to believe was supervising the holder of a provisional licence while driving, at a time when an accident occurred owing to the presence of the vehicle on a road or at a time when an offence is suspected of having been committed by the holder of the provisional licence in relation to the use of the vehicle on a road,*

*must, on being so required by a constable or vehicle examiner, produce his licence and its counterpart for examination, so as to enable the constable or vehicle examiner to ascertain the name and address of the holder of the licence, the date of issue, and the authority by which they were issued.*

### Keynote

In order to have met with the requirement to 'produce' a licence — or other documentation — the person must allow the constable (or vehicle examiner) a reasonable time to check the name and address of the holder, the date of issue and the authority under which the licence was issued (*Tremelling* v *Martin* [1971] RTR 196). Therefore simply flashing the licence at a police officer or waving it under his/her nose would not discharge the requirements of s. 164.

The requirement under s. 164(1)(a) is worded in the present tense. Therefore the power to require a licence under this subsection ceases when the driver ceases 'driving' (as to which, **see chapter 1**) (*Boyce* v *Absolam* [1974] RTR 248). Unfortunately the legislators did not use the same wording when drafting s. 164(1)(d)(i) in relation to supervisors of learner drivers. It is submitted, however, that the same restrictions would apply and that the power under this section would only apply if the relevant person were still supervising a learner at the time of the demand.

Clearly if a driver is reasonably believed to *have been* driving under the circumstances described in s. 164(1)(b), (c) and (d)(i) then the power to demand the relevant licence would not be restricted to the present tense.

Note that the requirement is to produce both the driving licence *and* its counterpart (**see para. 11.3**). It also applies to community licences (s. 164(11)).

A vehicle examiner is an examiner appointed under s. 66A of the 1988 Act (s. 164(11)).

Unlike some other driving documents (e.g. an insurance certificate, **see chapter 6**) driving licences must be produced in person (s. 164(8)).

Failing to produce a licence and its counterpart when lawfully required is a summary offence under s. 164(6).

### Power to Demand Date of Birth

Section 164(2) of the Road Traffic Act 1988 states:

*(2) A person required by a constable under subsection (1) above to produce his licence must in prescribed circumstances, on being so required by the constable, state his date of birth.*

**Keynote**

The 'prescribed circumstances' are set out under reg. 77 of the Motor Vehicles (Driving Licences) Regulations 1996 and are:

- where the person *fails* to produce the licence *forthwith* (although the regulation says nothing about the *counterpart*); *or*
- where the person *produces* a licence which the police officer has reason to suspect
  - was not granted to that person
  - was granted to that person in error
  - contains an alteration made with intent to deceive; or
  - in which the driver number has been altered, removed or defaced; *or*
- where the person is/was a supervisor of a learner driver as specified under s. 164(1)(d) *and* the police officer has reason to suspect that he/she is under 21 years of age.

Making an alteration with intent to deceive may also amount to a more serious offence of deception/forgery (**see Crime, chapter 13**) or falsification of documents (**see chapter 16**). There does not need to be an 'intent to deceive'; simply reason for the officer to suspect such a motive.

Failing to state one's date of birth when lawfully required is a summary offence under s. 164(6).

Where a person does state his/her date of birth as required, the Secretary of State may serve a written notice on that person requiring him/her to provide evidence verifying that date of birth. If the person's name differs from his/her name at birth, the Secretary of State may also serve a similar notice requiring a statement from the person as to his/her name when born (s. 164(9)). Knowingly failing to do so is a summary offence (s. 164(9)).

## Other Powers

Where a police officer has reasonable cause to believe that the holder of a driving licence has knowingly made a false statement for obtaining it, the officer may require the production of that licence and its counterpart (s. 164(4)). Failing to do so is a summary offence under s. 164(6).

Where the rider of a motor bicycle (**see chapter 1**) produces a provisional driving licence to a police officer and that officer has reasonable cause to believe that the holder was not driving the motor bicycle as part of the training on an approved course, he/she may require the production of a prescribed certificate in relation to the completion of such a course (s. 164(4A)). Failing to produce such a certificate when lawfully required is a summary offence under s. 164(6).

## Licence Revoked

Where a person has had his/her licence revoked in relation to a disability or because it has expired and he/she fails to deliver the licence to the DVLA, a police officer or vehicle examiner may require the licence to be produced and may then seize it (s. 164(3)). Similar powers apply where the licence holder has been ordered to produce his/her licence to a court (s. 164(5)). Failing to do so is a summary offence under s. 164(6).

### Licences Surrendered under Fixed Penalty Procedure

If a person has surrendered his/her licence and its counterpart to a police officer in connection with a fixed penalty offence (**see chapter 14**) he/she cannot produce it if required under s. 164. Therefore s. 164(7) provides that, if such a person produces:

- a *current* receipt (under s. 56 of the Road Traffic Offenders Act 1988) to that effect (either then and there or within seven days) and
- *if required to do so*, produces the licence and counterpart on his/her return to a police station

he/she does not commit an offence under s. 164(6).

### Defence

Section 164(8) states:

> *(8) In proceedings against any person for the offence of failing to produce a licence and its counterpart it shall be a defence for him to show that—*
> *(a) within seven days after the production of his licence and its counterpart was required he produced them in person at a police station that was specified by him at the time their production was required, or*
> *(b) he produced them in person there as soon as was reasonably practicable, or*
> *(c) it was not reasonably practicable for him to produce them there before the day on which the proceedings were commenced,*
> *and for the purposes of this subsection the laying of the information . . . shall be treated as the commencement of the proceedings.*

### Keynote

This general defence allows for the issuing of an HORT/1 in respect of driving licences and counterparts; it also applies to the certificate showing that a licence holder has completed his/her compulsory training in relation to motor bicycles (s. 164(8A)). Section 164(8) and (8A) also allow for occasions where the production of the relevant documents is not possible at the time.

## 11.3.2 Offence

It is a summary offence — under reg. 18(b) of the Motor Vehicles (Driving Licences) Regulations 1996 and s. 91 of the Road Traffic Offenders Act 1988 — to fail to sign a driving licence immediately it is received by the holder. Holders of the new photocard licence (**see para 11.3**) are required to provide a signature on the relevant form in order that the DVLA can reproduce his/her signature electronically on that photocard and reg. 18 has been amended accordingly.

## 11.3.3 Categories and Ages

Section 87 of the Road Traffic Act 1988 requires that any person driving a motor vehicle on a road does so in accordance with a licence authorising him/her to drive a motor vehicle *of that class* (**see para. 11.2 and appendix 6**).

The classification of vehicles is created by virtue of reg. 4 of the Motor Vehicles (Driving Licences) Regulations 1996 (SI 1996 No. 2824) and sch. 2 to those Regulations. Schedule 2 is set out at **appendix 6**. In relation to licences granted before 1 January 1997, provisions for the change from the 'old' categories to the new ones are to be found in reg. 70.

Regulation 6 of the 1996 Regulations sets out the categories of vehicle that a driver will be deemed as competent to drive by virtue of holding a licence. This regulation restricts drivers who passed tests in relation to certain restricted classes of vehicle (e.g. those with an automatic transmission) to vehicles falling within that category or sub-category. Similar provisions apply under reg. 6 to drivers having adaptations in relation to a disability. The categories of vehicle that a licence holder is entitled to drive will be clearly marked on his/her licence and its counterpart and any relevant restrictions will appear in the information codes in section 12 (**see appendix 10**).

The ages at which a person may drive the relevant category are generally to be found in the Road Traffic Act 1988, s. 101 — although, confusingly, some of the restrictions on additional categories under reg. 6 above also include references to minimum ages. The table under s. 101 is set out at **appendix 1**.

That table is amended in certain cases by the provisions of reg. 7 of the 1996 Regulations. Those amendments are principally in the areas of:

- Large motor bicycles (**see chapter 1**) where, under certain circumstances, the age is raised to 21 years (unless the person has passed a relevant test or the vehicle is owned by the Secretary of State for Defence/is being used for military purposes by a member of the armed forces).
- Some small agricultural and forestry tractors without trailers or with smaller trailers, where the limit is lowered to 16 years.
- Small vehicles (**see chapter 1**) without trailers driven by someone in receipt of certain disability allowances where the limit is lowered to 16 years.
- Medium-sized goods vehicles (**see chapter 1**) drawing a trailer where the maximum authorised mass of the combination exceeds 7.5 tonnes where the limit is raised to 21 years.
- Large goods and large passenger carrying vehicles (**see chapter 1**) driven under certain circumstances in relation to NHS ambulances, training scheme employees and holders of provisional or full PSV licences operating under a PSV operators' licence (**see chapter 13**). In the specified circumstances, the limit is lowered to 18 years.
- Some vehicles owned or operated by the armed forces and some road rollers.

These amendments are very detailed and are frequently updated. Therefore reference should be made to the Regulations themselves wherever possible and again the DVLA are probably the best source of up-to-date information in this respect.

## 11.4 Driving Tests

Sections 89 and 89A of the Road Traffic Act 1988 impose the need to pass a driving test before being granted a licence, while Part III of the Motor Vehicles (Driving Licences) Regulations 1996 makes provisions for those driving tests.

The 1996 Regulations set out the requirements for the testing of drivers for specific categories of vehicle and introduce a two-part test (similar to that taken by car drivers) for drivers wishing to drive medium and large goods/passenger vehicles. Schedules 7 and 8 contain the syllabus for those tests. Schedule 13 contains elements for approved training courses for motor cycles.

Schedule 6 requires driving test candidates to produce proof of identity before taking their test. Regulation 34 makes provision for the testing of drivers coming to the UK and requires them to have been resident here for at least 185 days in the 12-month period before the test appointment.

## 11.5 Disqualified Drivers

**Offence — Driving while Disqualified — Road Traffic Act 1988, s. 103(1)(b)**
*Triable summarily. Six months' imprisonment and/or a fine. Discretionary disqualification.*
***(Statutory power of arrest)***

The Road Traffic Act 1988, s. 103 states:

> *(1) A person is guilty of an offence if, while disqualified for holding or obtaining a licence, he—*
> *(a) . . .*
> *(b) drives a motor vehicle on a road.*

**Offence — Obtaining Licence while Disqualified — Road Traffic Act 1988, s. 103(1)(a)**
*Triable summarily. Fine.*
***(No specific power of arrest)***

The Road Traffic Act 1988, s. 103 states:

> *(1) A person is guilty of an offence if, while disqualified for holding or obtaining a licence, he—*
> *(a) obtains a licence . . .*

**Keynote**

Most disqualifications are imposed by the courts under Part II of the Road Traffic Offenders Act 1988. Some special provisions exist in relation to the disqualification of holders of large goods or passenger-carrying vehicles (see the Road Traffic Act 1988, s. 115 and the Driving Licences (Community Driving Licence) Regulations 1998 (SI 1998 No. 1420)).

A licence obtained by a person who is disqualified is of no effect (s. 103(2)).

A constable in uniform may arrest without warrant any person driving a motor vehicle on a road whom he/she has reasonable cause to suspect of being disqualified.

The power of arrest is not so wide as to include someone who 'has been' driving (*James* v *DPP*; *Chorley* v *DPP* [1997] Crim LR 831).

If the person is disqualified *by reason of age* (under s. 101), neither this offence *nor the power of arrest* will apply; the relevant offence would be under s. 87(1) (**see para. 11.4**).

The offence of driving while disqualified is one of strict liability (**see Crime, chapter 1**) and there is no need to show that the driver knew of the disqualification (*Taylor* v *Kenyon* [1952] 2 All ER 726).

You must *prove* that the person who was driving the motor vehicle was in fact disqualified. The latter requirement has occasionally been overlooked causing problems at trial (*R* v *Derwentside Justices, ex parte Heaviside* [1996] RTR 384), and it may be that fingerprint evidence, admission by the defendant or evidence from someone present at the time the defendant was disqualified will be necessary (see, however, *R* v *Mansfield* [1997] RTR 96). However, an admission made to the arresting officer by a driver who said he was disqualified has also been held to be sufficient grounds upon which the court may satisfy itself that a person was in fact disqualified (*DPP* v *Mooney* [1997] RTR 434).

A person may still commit the offence(s) above even if the disqualification is later quashed on appeal; the offence is complete as long as he/she was disqualified at the relevant time (*R* v *Lynn* [1971] RTR 369).

The elements of 'driving', 'motor vehicle' and 'road' are set out in **chapter 1**.

The power of arrest (which is 'preserved' by s. 26 of the Police and Criminal Evidence Act 1984) is applicable only to an officer in uniform and that officer must have 'reasonable cause to suspect'; for the meaning of both expressions, **see chapter 5**.

There is no offence of 'attempting to drive while disqualified' and therefore no power of arrest (see s. 37 of the Criminal Justice Act 1988), a result which somewhat reduces the preventive nature of the legislation and almost forces officers to wait until a defendant who is under observation actually begins to drive. A similar practical problem arises under the offence of taking a conveyance without the owner's consent (**see Crime, chapter 12**).

If a passenger genuinely believes that the driver is entitled to drive the vehicle in which they are both found, that belief will prevent him/her being charged with 'aiding and abetting' the offence under s. 103(1)(b) (*Bateman* v *Evans* (1964) 108 SJ 522). In the case of someone supervising a 'learner driver' who turns out to be disqualified, it seems reasonable to expect a supervisor to establish that the driver under his/her supervision has a current and valid licence before venturing out onto the road.

The general and growing defence of 'duress of circumstances' (**see chapter 2 and Crime, chapter 4**) applies to the offence under s. 103(b).

### 11.5.1 Disqualification until Test is Passed

Section 36 of the Road Traffic Offenders Act 1988 provides that:

*(1) Where this subsection applies to a person the court must order him to be disqualified until he passes the appropriate driving test.*

*(2) Subsection (1) above applies to a person who is disqualified under section 34 of this Act on conviction of—*

*(a) manslaughter, or in Scotland culpable homicide, by the driver of a motor vehicle, or*

*(b) an offence under section 1 (causing death by dangerous driving) or section 2 (dangerous driving) of the Road Traffic Act 1988.*

*(3) Subsection (1) above also applies—*

*(a) to a person who is qualified under section 34 or 35 of this Act in such circumstances or for such period as the Secretary of State may by order prescribe, or*

*(b) to such other persons convicted of such offences involving obligatory endorsement as may be so prescribed.*

*(4) Where a person to whom subsection (1) above does not apply is convicted of an offence involving obligatory endorsement, the court may order him to be disqualified until he passes the appropriate driving test (whether or not he has previously passed any test).*

*(5) In this section—*

*'appropriate driving test' means—*

*(a) an extended driving test, where a person is convicted of an offence involving obligatory disqualification or is disqualified under section 35 of this Act,*

*(b) a test of competence to drive, other than an extended driving test, in any other case,*

*'extended test' means a test of competence to drive prescribed for the purposes of this section, and 'test of competence to drive' means a test prescribed by virtue of section 89(3) of the Road Traffic Act 1988.*

**Keynote**

Section 36 gives the court the power to disqualify a person from holding or obtaining a licence (s. 98(1)) until the person passes an 'appropriate' test. If the person is disqualified under the provisions for 'totting up' penalty points (see s. 35) or is found guilty of an offence involving obligatory disqualification (see s. 34), the 'appropriate' test is an *extended* tests as defined at s. 36(5)(b). In other cases the 'appropriate' test will be a regular driving test under s. 89(3) of the Road Traffic Act 1988.

Where a person is convicted of an offence involving obligatory disqualification that is not covered by s. 36(1) and (2) (e.g. an offence under s. 4(1) of the Road Traffic Act 1988; **see para. 5.2**), the court *may* order disqualification until that person passes an appropriate driving test (s. 36(4)). Here the appropriate test will generally be the regular driving test (unless the disqualification involves 'totting up'). In determining whether or not to disqualify a person in such a case, the court must have regard to the safety of road users (s. 36(6)).

Section 36(7) to (13) make provisions for the extent and effect of a disqualification until a test is passed and also provides for tests of competence in certain other European countries to be treated as meeting the requirements of s. 36.

A person who has been disqualified until he/she has passed a test can apply for a provisional licence and can drive in accordance with the conditions of such a licence (s. 37(3)). After all, it is the purpose of such a disqualification that the offender be required to prove their competence to drive, rather than simply removing them from the road.

Where a person so disqualified obtains a provisional licence and then drives without supervision or 'L' plates, he/she commits the offence of driving while disqualified under s. 103 of the Road Traffic Act 1988 above (*Scott* v *Jelf* [1974] RTR 256).

The courts have a power to impose an interim disqualification under certain conditions. Where a defendant has been convicted of an endorsable offence and the magistrates' court commits him/her to the Crown Court *for sentence*, the court may order an interim disqualification (see s. 26(1) of the Road Traffic Offenders Act 1988 and s. 56 of the Criminal Justice Act 1967). The magistrates' court may also impose an interim disqualification when:

- remitting the person to another magistrates' court (under s. 39 of the Magistrates' Courts Act 1980);
- deferring passing a sentence on the person; or

- adjourning after convicting the person but before dealing with him/her for the offence.

A magistrates' court cannot impose an interim disqualification when committing a defendant *for trial*.

### 11.5.2 After Disqualification has Expired

- Once a period of disqualification ends, the person may apply for another licence.
- On application for another licence the person falls within the category of someone who 'has held and is entitled to obtain' a licence under s. 88 of the Road Traffic Act 1988.
- Section 88 provides an exemption to the offence of driving otherwise than in accordance with a licence (s. 87) (**see para. 11.3.3**).
- The person can begin to drive again as soon as a proper application has been received by the Driver and Vehicle Licensing Agency.

If a person drives before applying for a new licence he/she commits the offence under s. 87 (**see para 11.3.3**).

A person disqualified until he/she passes a driving test may (or arguably *must*) apply for a provisional licence. On application he/she may begin to drive in accordance with the conditions below.

It should be noted that ss. 39 and 40 of the Crime (Sentences) Act 1997 give the court the power to disqualify a defendant following his/her conviction for *any* offence. The power extends to fine defaulters who may be disqualified for a period of up to 12 months under certain circumstances. These sections were brought into force, subject to transitional provisions and savings, by the Crime (Sentences) Act 1997 (Commencement No. 2 and Transitional Provisions) Order 1997 (SI 1997 No. 2200).

## 11.6 Learner Drivers

Learner drivers are generally required to hold provisional licences (**see para. 11.3**). The granting of provisional licences is governed by s. 97(3) of the Road Traffic Act 1988 which provides that:

> *(3) A provisional licence—*
>
> *(a) shall be granted subject to prescribed conditions,*
>
> *(b) shall, in any cases prescribed for the purposes of this paragraph, be restricted so as to authorise only the driving of vehicles of the classes so prescribed,*
>
> *(c) may, in the case of a person appearing to the Secretary of State to be suffering from a relevant disability or a prospective disability, be restricted so as to authorise only the driving of vehicles of a particular construction, or design specified in the licence.*

**Keynote**

Drivers — or potential drivers — may apply for provisional licences specifically to drive certain categories of vehicles or they may be able to use a licence that they already hold.

The type of provisional entitlement that each category of vehicle requires is governed by s. 97 of the Road Traffic Act 1988 and reg. 9 of the Motor Vehicles (Driving Licences) Regulations 1996.

Some sub-categories of vehicle can only be driven by certain learner drivers who hold a full licence in another, specified category. These categories are set out in the table found under reg. 9 (**see appendix 6**). Regulation 9 makes exemptions in relation to full-time members of the armed forces.

Further provision is made (by s. 98(2) of the Road Traffic Act 1988) to allow full licences in some categories to count as provisional licences for others. These categories are set out in the table found under reg. 17 (**see appendix 6**).

### Motor Bicycles and Mopeds

Section 97 of the Road Traffic Act 1988 goes on to state that a provisional licence:

*(3) . . .*

*(d) shall not authorise a person under the age of 21 years, before he has passed a test of competence to drive a motor bicycle,—*

*(i) to drive a motor bicycle without a side-car unless it is a learner motor bicycle (as defined in subsection (5) below) or its first use (as defined in regulations) occurred before January 1, 1982 and the cylinder capacity of its engine does not exceed 125 cubic centimetres, or*

*(ii) to drive a motor bicycle with a side-car unless its power to weight ratio is less than or equal to 0.16 kilowatts per kilogram.*

*(e) except as provided under subsection (3B) below, shall not authorise a person, before he has passed a test of competence to drive, to drive on a road a motor bicycle or moped except where he has successfully completed an approved training course for motor cyclists or is undergoing training on such a course and is driving the motor bicycle or moped on the road as part of the training.*

*(3A) Regulations may make provision as respects the training in the driving of motor bicycles and mopeds of persons wishing to obtain licences authorising the driving of such motor bicycles and mopeds by means of courses of training provided in accordance with the regulations; and the regulations may in particular make provision with respect to—*

*(a) the nature of the courses of training;*

*(b) the approval by the Secretary of State of the persons providing the courses and the withdrawal of his approval;*

*(c) the maximum amount of any charges payable by persons undergoing the training;*

*(d) certificates evidencing the successful completion by persons of a course of training and the supply by the Secretary of State of the forms which are to be used for such certificates; and*

*(e) the making, in connection with the supply of forms of certificates, of reasonable charges for the discharge of the functions of the Secretary of State under the regulations;*

*and different provision may be made for training in different classes of motor bicycles and mopeds.*

#### Keynote

The restrictions at s. 97(3)(d)(i) and (ii) apply to motor bicycles — which includes a sidecar combination. Therefore learner riders are generally restricted to using 'learner motor bicycles', motor *cycles* (i.e. mainly those having more than two wheels) and older motor bicycles first used before 1 January 1982 whose engine capacity does not exceed 125 cc. For the respective definitions, **see chapter 1**.

Unless a driver is exempted by the Regulations, he/she may not drive a motor bicycle or moped (**see chapter 1**) on a road before passing an approved training course or while on such a course as part of that training (s. 97(3)(e)). The regulation of approved training courses (also known as compulsory basic training — 'CBT') for riders of motor bicycles is governed by Part V of the 1996 Regulations. Among the other qualifications that such a person must have, an approved CBT instructor must show the Secretary of State that he/she is a 'fit and proper person'. (For the situation regarding the provision of driver instruction generally, **see para. 11.6.2.**)

As with other provisional licence holders, learner riders will be subject to the conditions set out in reg. 15 (**see below**). The requirement to have a qualified driver supervising him/her on the vehicle does not apply when the licence holder is riding a moped, or motor bicycle with or without a sidecar (reg. 15(2)(b)).

Regulation 15(5) provides that the holder of a provisional licence authorising the driving of a moped, or motor bicycle with or without a sidecar, shall not drive such a vehicle while carrying another person. This creates an absolute ban on passengers, qualified or otherwise, on such vehicles being driven by provisional licence holders. Holders of provisional licences authorising the driving of motor bicycles other than learner motor bicycles must abide by the requirements of reg. 17(5). These relate to:

- the presence of and supervision by an authorised direct access instructor;
- the availability of a non hand-held radio system for communicating with that instructor; and
- the wearing of apparel which is fluorescent or, if during the hours of darkness, fluorescent or reflective.

There is a specific requirement in relation to the riding of mopeds under a provisional licence. Such riders must, unless exempt, hold a valid certificate (issued by an authorised instructor under reg. 63) showing that he/she has completed an approved training course (reg. 15(6)).

### Full Licences used as Provisional

As mentioned above, s. 98(2) of the Road Traffic Act 1988 provides that a person holding a full licence for certain classes of vehicle may drive motor vehicles of other classes as if authorised by a provisional licence for those other classes. However, reg. 17(3) of the 1996 Regulations modifies the effect of s. 98(2) in relation to motor bicycles. In the case of a licence that authorises the driving only of learner or standard motor bicycles, s. 98(2) will not apply so as to authorise the driving of a large motor bicycle by a person under the age of 21. Therefore a person who holds a licence for a learner or standard motor bicycle but who is under the age of 21 cannot use that licence as a provisional licence for a large motor bicycle.

### General Requirements for Provisional Licence Holders

Holders of provisional licences must not drive or ride a motor vehicle of a class authorised by the licence unless he/she is under the supervision of a 'qualified driver' (**see below**) (reg. 15(1)(a) of the 1996 Regulations). He/she must also display the 'distinguishing mark' (L plate **see appendix** 7) in the form set out at part 1 to sch. 4 in such a manner that it is clearly visible to other persons using the road from within a reasonable distance from the front and back of the vehicle (reg. 15(1)(b)). Provisional licence holders driving a motor vehicle on a road in Wales may display the alternative distinguishing mark (a 'D' plate, signifying *dysgwr* or 'learner' (reg. 15(3)).

The requirement to have a qualified driver supervising him/her on the vehicle does not apply to invalid carriages or vehicles in certain categories that are constructed or adapted to carry only one person (reg. 15(2)(a)), neither does it apply to motor bicycles or mopeds (**see above**).

Provisional licence holders are generally prohibited from drawing trailers although certain classes of vehicles are exempt from this provision (reg. 15(1)(c)).

If a person is disqualified until he/she passes another test and then fails to abide by the provisions of the new provisional licence, he/she commits the offence of driving while disqualified (under s. 103 of the Road Traffic Act 1988), **see para. 11.5**.

If a person is a 'new driver' and has his/her licence revoked after accumulating six penalty points (under s. 3 of the Road Traffic (New Drivers) Act 1995, **see para. 11.8**), he/she will not be counted as 'disqualified' but will revert to the position of a learner driver.

If a provisional licence holder fails to observe these conditions, he/she commits an offence under s. 91 of the Road Traffic Offenders Act 1988 (i.e. breaching the Regulations); if the person does *not have* a provisional licence he/she commits the offence under s. 87 of driving otherwise than in accordance with a licence (**see para. 11.3.3**).

**Between Driving Test and Issue of Licence**

Regulation 15(10) of the 1996 Regulations makes provision for the situation where a provisional licence holder has been issued the relevant certificate stating that he/she has passed a driving test but has not yet received his/her full licence. In such cases, the requirements to display 'L' (or 'D') plates and to be supervised, together with the restrictions on the carrying of passengers are removed.

### 11.6.1 Supervision of Learner Drivers

There is only one acceptable minimum standard of driving and all drivers, including learners, must observe it; if not, they commit the offence of careless driving (*McCrone* v *Riding* [1938] 1 All ER 157). (**See also chapter 2**.)

A supervisor of a learner driver is required, not to provide tuition to the learner, but to 'supervise'. That means doing whatever might reasonably be expected to prevent the learner driver from acting carelessly or endangering others (see *Rubie* v *Faulkner* [1940] 1 All ER 285). The duty includes being in a position to take control of the vehicle in an emergency. If the supervisor is not able to do this, either because of his/her physical state (e.g. drunk) or their being out of the vehicle (e.g. giving directions), the condition will not have been fulfilled.

Whether or not a supervisor fulfilled his/her duty will be a question of fact for a court to determine in each case. If it can be shown that the qualified person was not actually 'supervising' the driver then the requirement under reg. 15 above will not have been observed and the offence (under s. 91 of the Road Traffic Offenders Act 1988) will be committed. That offence will be aided and abetted (**see Crime, chapter 1**) by the so-called supervisor.

A 'supervisor' can also be convicted of aiding and abetting where the learner driver is over the prescribed limit or unfit through drink or drugs (*Crampton* v *Fish* (1969) 113 SJ 1003). (**See also chapter 5**.)

The duties of a supervisor extend to ensuring compliance with other legislative requirements made of drivers such as remaining at the scene of an accident (*Bentley* v *Mullen* [1986] RTR 7). (**See also chapter 4**.)

The supervisor must be a 'qualified driver' under reg. 13A of the 1996 Regulations which now states:

*(1) Subject to paragraph (3), a person is a qualified driver for the purposes of regulation 15 if he—*

*(a) is 21 years old,*

*(b) holds a relevant licence,*

*(c) has the relevant driving experience and*

*(d) in the case of a disabled driver, he is supervising a provisional licence holder who is driving the vehicle of a class included in category B and would in an emergency be able to take control of the steering and braking functions of the vehicle . . .*

**Keynote**

This definition was amended by the Motor Vehicles (Driving Licences) (Amendment) (No. 2) Regulations 1999 (SI 1999/617). A 'relevant licence' means a full licence (including a Northern Ireland or Community licence) authorising the driving of vehicles of the same class as the vehicle being driven by the provisional licence holder — reg. 13A(2)(c). In the case of disabled drivers it means a full licence authorising the driving of a class of vehicles in category B other than invalid carriages. The reference to paragraph (3) is to people who are members of the armed forces acting in the course of their duties. 'Relevant driving experience' is defined at reg. 13A(2)(d). *Generally* a person will have relevant driving experience if they have held the relevant full licence for a continuous or aggregate period of not less than three years.

### Offence — Supervisor of Learner Driver Failing to Give Details — Road Traffic Act 1988, s. 165(5)

*Triable summarily. Fine.*

***(No specific power of arrest)***

The Road Traffic Act 1988, s. 165 states:

*(5) A person—*

*(a) who supervises the holder of a provisional licence granted under Part III of this Act while the holder is driving on a road a motor vehicle (other than an invalid carriage), or*

*(b) whom a constable or vehicle examiner has reasonable cause to believe was supervising the holder of such a licence while driving, at a time when an accident occurred owing to the presence of the vehicle on a road or at a time when an offence is suspected of having been committed by the holder of the provisional licence in relation to the use of the vehicle on a road,*

*must, on being so required by a constable or vehicle examiner, give his name and address and the name and address of the owner of the vehicle.*

**Keynote**

Regulation 74 allows certain holders of foreign licences to be treated as holders of full driving licences under Part III of the Road Traffic Act 1988 after they have been resident in Great Britain for 12 months. These requirements only apply in relation to the requirements of s. 87(1) (driving otherwise than in accordance with a licence (**see para. 11.3.3**)) and therefore do not entitle such licence holders to supervise learner drivers.

### 11.6.2 Instruction of Learner Drivers

Anyone is able to give driving lessons provided they do not charge money or money's worth in return. If a person wants to give driving instruction for payment, he/she must be registered in accordance with the provisions of Part V of the Road Traffic Act 1988 (see s. 123). The purpose of the regulation of driving instructors was examined in *Mahmood* v *Vehicle Inspectorate* (1998) 18 WRTLB. There it was held by the Divisional Court that notions of contractual payment under civil law were not particularly helpful or relevant. What mattered was whether or not the defendant (instructor) had some sort of arrangement with the learner driver and that the arrangement had a 'commercial flavour'.

Free driving lessons offered by someone in the business of buying and selling cars will be deemed to be given for payment if they are given in connection with the supply of a vehicle (s. 132(3)).

Police driving instructors are exempt from this requirement (s. 124 and reg. 21 of the 1996 Regulations).

These restrictions only apply to 'motor cars' as specifically designed for this purpose (**see chapter 1**) therefore it would not prevent someone charging for driving lessons on motor cycles or other vehicles falling outside the definition (for motor bicycles, **see chapter 1**).

The relevant conditions for registered driving instructors can be found in the Motor Cars (Driving Instruction) Regulations 1996 (SI 1996 No. 1983).

The Road Traffic (Driving Instruction by Disabled Persons) Act 1993 introduced provisions for driving lessons to be provided by disabled people and those provisions can be found in ss. 125A and 125B and ss. 133A–133D of the Road Traffic Act 1988.

### 11.6.3 Drivers from Other Countries

Regulation 74 of the Motor Vehicles (Driving Licences) Regulations 1996 allow some people who become resident in Great Britain to use their foreign driving permit to drive here for the first 12 months. That permit allows the holder to take a driving test in that 12 month period. If they do not do so successfully then they will need a GB provisional licence. The permit does not allow them to supervise learner drivers (**see para. 11.6.1**).

Visitors and new residents holding a valid driving licence may also use that licence during the first 12 months and, if they apply for a GB provisional licence during that period, they will be exempt from the conditions imposed on provisional licence holders (reg. 16).

Members of visiting forces and their dependants are covered by the Motor Vehicles (International Circulation) Order 1975, as amended (Article 3).

The former requirement for drivers from EU member States to exchange their licences within one year of becoming a resident in Great Britain has been removed. The law governing such drivers can now be found in the Driving Licences (Community Driving Licence) Regulations 1996 (SI 1996 No. 1974).

Drivers from member States must meet the fitness requirements of British drivers (**see para. 11.6.4**) and, provided they are not disqualified, drivers meeting those physical requirements may exchange their licence for a Part III licence if they have become normally resident in Great Britain (s. 89 of the Road Traffic Act 1988).

The 1988 Act also makes provision for the exchange of other licences from some non-EU countries.

### 11.6.4 Physical Fitness and Disability

Section 92 of the Road Traffic Act 1988 provides that:

*(1) An application for the grant of a licence must include a declaration by the applicant, in such form as the Secretary of State may require, stating whether he is suffering or has at any time (or, if a period is prescribed for the purposes of this subsection, has during that period) suffered from any relevant disability or any prospective disability.*

*(2) In this Part of this Act—*

*'disability' includes disease and the persistent misuse of drugs or alcohol, whether or not such misuse amounts to dependency,*

*'relevant disability' in relation to any person means—*

*(a) any prescribed disability, and*

*(b) any other disability likely to cause the driving of a vehicle by him in pursuance of a licence to be a source of danger to the public, and*

*'prospective disability' in relation to any person means any other disability which—*

*(a) at the time of the application for the grant of a licence or, as the case may be, the material time for the purposes of the provision in which the expression is used, is not of such a kind that it is a relevant disability, but*

*(b) by virtue of the intermittent or progressive nature of the disability or otherwise, may become a relevant disability in course of time.*

*(3) If it appears from the applicant's declaration, or if on inquiry the Secretary of State is satisfied from other information, that the applicant is suffering from a relevant disability, the Secretary of State must, subject to the following provisions of this section, refuse to grant the licence.*

**Keynote**

Part 6 of the Motor Vehicle (Driving Licences) Regulations 1996 set out the specific requirements as to the physical fitness of drivers and include the standard of eyesight demanded of drivers of different vehicle groups.

**Offence — Driving with Uncorrected Defective Eyesight — Road Traffic Act 1988, s. 96(1)**
*Triable summarily. Fine.*
**(*No specific power of arrest*)**

The Road Traffic Act 1988, s. 96 states:

*(1) If a person drives a motor vehicle on a road while his eyesight is such (whether through a defect which cannot be or one which is not for the time being sufficiently corrected) that he cannot*

*comply with any requirement as to eyesight prescribed under this Part of this Act for the purposes of tests of competence to drive, he is guilty of an offence.*

**Keynote**

Under s. 96(2) a constable having reason to suspect that a person driving a motor vehicle may be guilty of this offence may require him/her to submit to an eyesight test. Refusing to do so is a further offence under s. 96(3).

The specific requirements as to eyesight are set out at sch. 8 to the Motor Vehicles (Driving Licences) Regulations 1996 (SI 1996 No. 2824). These require a potential driver to be able to read letters and figures on a registration mark at 20.5 metres 'in good daylight (with the aid of corrective lenses if worn)'. For this reason it would seem that an eyesight test under s. 96(2) ought to be carried out under the same conditions, though there is no direct authority on the point. If the intention of parliament in passing s. 96(2) was to improve road safety, it would perhaps have been more useful to have a power to test a driver's ability to see clearly under the conditions which prevailed when he/she was found to be driving (e.g. at night).

One source of a police officer's 'reasonable suspicion' under s. 96(2) might be the information code on the driver's photocard licence which will state whether the holder has any eyesight correction (**see para. 11.3**).

The 1996 Regulations also set out the conditions under which the Secretary of State may require (under s. 94) an applicant for a licence to undergo a medical examination if he/she has convictions for drink/driving offences (for which, **see chapter 5**).

Regulation 67(2) makes special provision for drivers who suffer from epilepsy who may obtain a Group 1 licence as long as they have been free from an attack over the preceding 12 months or have only suffered from those attacks while asleep.

A person refused a licence may appeal against that decision under s. 100.

A court has a duty to notify the Secretary of State if it appears that a person has a relevant disease or disability (s. 22 of the Road Traffic Offenders Act 1988).

The Secretary of State may attach conditions to a licence in light of any disability of the holder. If the holder does not observe those conditions, he/she commits the offence under s. 87(1) (**see para. 11.3.3**).

Section 94 imposes a requirement for a licence holder to notify the Secretary of State *in writing*, of any relevant disability which has either not been disclosed in the past or which has become more acute since the licence was granted.

**Offences — Failing to Give Notification of Relevant Disability — Road Traffic Act 1988, s. 94(3)**
*Triable summarily. Fine.*
**(*No specific power of arrest*)**

The Road Traffic Act 1988, s. 94 states:

*(3) A person who fails without reasonable excuse to notify the Secretary of State as required by subsection (1) above is guilty of an offence.*

**Offence — Driving Motor Vehicle before Giving Notification of Disability — Road Traffic Act 1988, s. 94(3A)**
*Triable summarily. Fine. Discretionary disqualification.*
***(No specific power of arrest)***

The Road Traffic Act 1988, s. 94 states:

> *(3A) A person who holds a licence authorising him to drive a motor vehicle of any class and who drives a motor vehicle of that class on a road is guilty of an offence if at any earlier time while the licence was in force he was required by subsection (1) above to notify the Secretary of State but has failed without reasonable excuse to do so.*

**Offence — Driving Motor Vehicle after Refusal or Revocation — Road Traffic Act 1988, s. 94A**
*Triable summarily. Six months' imprisonment and/or a fine. Discretionary disqualification.*
***(No specific power of arrest)***

The Road Traffic Act 1988, s. 94A states:

> *(1) A person who drives a motor vehicle of any class on a road otherwise than in accordance with a licence authorising him to drive a motor vehicle of that class is guilty of an offence if—*
> *(a) at any earlier time the Secretary of State—*
> *(i) has in accordance with section 92(3) of this Act refused to grant such a licence,*
> *(ii) has under section 93(1) or (2) of this Act revoked such a licence, or*
> *(iii) has served notice on that person in pursuance of section 99C(1) or (2) of this Act requiring him to deliver to the Secretary of State a Community licence authorising him to drive a motor vehicle of that or a corresponding class, and*
> *(b) since that earlier time he has not been granted—*
> *(i) a licence under this Part of this Act, or*
> *(ii) a Community licence,*
> *authorising him to drive a motor vehicle of that or a corresponding class.*

## 11.7 The Road Traffic (Driver Licensing and Information Systems) Act 1989

The purpose of this Act is to provide a unified information system about and for drivers, under the authority of the Secretary of State.

Part I of the 1989 Act introduces a unified licensing system, abolishing the former special licences for heavy goods vehicles (HGV) and public service vehicles (PSV).

The Act provides for the licensing of drivers of such vehicles and sets out the requirements of those drivers, including their suitability to hold the relevant licence.

The Act provides the Secretary of State with powers to refuse driving licences to some applicants or to revoke existing licences on grounds of physical unfitness.

Part II of the Act provides for the introduction of driver information systems which will collect, store, process and transmit data on 'driver information'. Such systems are intended to help drivers in relation to traffic routes, congestion etc. The systems are to be provided by operators licensed to do so by the Secretary of State. Operating an unlicensed system is an offence (s. 9).

## 11.8 New Drivers

The Road Traffic (New Drivers) Act 1995 places additional requirements on those who have recently 'qualified' as drivers. It sets out a 'probationary' period of two years and if, during that period, a driver receives six or more penalty points on his/her licence, the full entitlement to drive will be lost (s. 2). The driver concerned must then pass a further test of competence in the category of vehicle which he/she was entitled to drive.

# CHAPTER TWELVE

# EXCISE AND REGISTRATION

## 12.1 Introduction

The law regulating the registration of vehicles and the charging of excise duty on them was largely consolidated in the Vehicle Excise and Registration Act 1994. As with most other areas of road traffic law however, the main Act is supported by a substantial number of statutory instruments making further regulations.

In addition, as one of the purposes behind the legislation is to generate income, the law is regularly extended and amended by the various Finance Acts which should be consulted in each case.

## 12.2 Categories and Exemptions

### 12.2.1 Rates of Duty

The relevant rate of excise duty must be paid by anyone using or keeping a mechanically propelled vehicle on a public road unless the vehicle is exempt. The relevant rates of duty can be found in sch. 1 to the Vehicle Excise and Registration Act 1994 and also in the latest Finance Act.

The 1994 Act provides for vehicles to be 'taxed' at different rates according to their category and it sets out many different categories of vehicle, each of which is defined within s. 62 and sch.1.

### 12.2.2 Exemptions

Certain vehicles are exempt from excise duty. These are set out in sch. 2, as amended, and include:

- vehicles used for police, ambulance or fire brigade purposes
- mines rescue and lifeboat haulage vehicles
- certain vehicles used for the carriage of disabled people

- electrically assisted pedal cycles
- vehicles neither made nor adapted to carry the driver or passengers
- some agricultural or forestry vehicles
- certain vehicles when being tested
- vehicles temporarily in the country or to be exported.

Vehicles which are more than 25 years old may qualify as 'exempt' from excise duty provided they were constructed before 1 January 1973 (see the Finance Act 1998, s. 17).

### 12.2.3 The Offences

**Offence — Using or Keeping an Unlicensed Vehicle on a Public Road — Vehicle Excise and Registration Act 1994, s. 29**
*Triable summarily. Fine plus back duty.*
***(No specific power of arrest)***

The Vehicle Excise and Registration Act 1994, s. 29 states:

*(1) If a person uses, or keeps, on a public road a vehicle (not being an exempt vehicle) which is unlicensed he is guilty of an offence.*
*(2) For the purposes of subsection (1) a vehicle is unlicensed if no vehicle licence or trade licence is in force for or in respect of the vehicle.*

**Keynote**

'Public roads' are roads maintained at the public expense, a much narrower definition than that of 'road' generally (**see para. 1.2.7**).

'Exempt' vehicles may be issued with a 'nil' licence under the Finance Act 1997; if so, using or keeping them without such a licence being in force will be an offence under the specific offence created under s. 43A of the 1994 Act and not the above offence.

A keeper of a vehicle may make a statutory declaration under s. 22 to the effect that a vehicle will not be used or kept on a public road during a specified period. This declaration is known as a Statutory Off-Road Notification (SORN) and particulars for such a notification can be demanded by the Secretary of State from keepers of vehicles who do not renew their licences.

Proceedings under s. 29 may only be brought by the Secretary of State or by the police with his or her approval (s. 47(1)). A certificate in the approved form giving that authority is sufficient proof of that authority being given (s. 47(4)).

Under sch. 2A the Secretary of State may provide for the wheel-clamping, removal and disposal of vehicles where an offence under s. 29(1) above is being committed (see the Vehicle Excise Duty (Immobilisation, Removal and Disposal of Vehicles) Regulations 1997 (SI 1997 No. 2439)).

The 1997 Regulations empower 'authorised persons' (who may be employed by local authorities, members of a police force or any other person authorised by the Secretary of State (reg. 3) to clamp certain vehicles. Generally, clamping may take place when the authorised person has reason to believe that an offence under s. 29 of the Vehicle Excise and Registration Act 1994 involving a vehicle which is stationary on a public road is being committed (reg. 5).

The vehicle may be clamped where it is at the time or it may be moved to another place on a public road and clamped there.

The Regulations go on to provide a number of summary offences in relation to the unauthorised removal of, or interference with immobilisation notices and devices (reg. 7). Regulations 8, 13 and 15 create either way offences, punishable with a maximum of two years' imprisonment on indictment for making false declarations to secure the release of a clamped vehicle or to show that such a vehicle is 'exempt' (**see below**).

### Exemptions

Under reg. 4 the following vehicles are generally exempt from the provisions of the 1997 Regulations when being used on a public road:

- Vehicles displaying a **current** disabled person's badge **C**
- Vehicles stationary at a time when **less** than 24 hours have elapsed since their release from immobilisation/removal **L**
- Vehicles that appear to have been **abandoned** **A**
- Vehicles displaying a British **Medical** Association car badge **M**
- **PS**Vs being used for the carriage of **p**assengers; vehicles being used by a **p**ublic utility or the **p**ost office **P**
- Vehicles **exempt** from excise duty **displaying** nil licences **E** **D**

The above list is a summary of the exemptions. For the specific conditions under which exemption is granted see reg. 4.

A defendant may be required to pay up to five times the annual rate of duty applicable to the particular type of vehicle (s. 29(3)) and must pay any back duty.

The offence is committed at the time at which the vehicle is shown to have been used or kept on a public road. The practice of allowing 14 days' grace does not affect that situation, neither does the fact that a defendant buys a licence immediately afterwards (see *Wharton* v *Taylor* (1965) 109 SJ 475).

The fact that 'the cheque is in the post' will not save a defendant from the provisions of s. 29 either (*Nattrass* v *Gibson* (1968) 112 SJ 866).

The burden of proof in relation to the character, weight or cylinder capacity of the vehicle used, or of the purpose to which the vehicle was being put lies with the defendant for this offence (s. 53).

### Offence — Failing to Display Licence — Vehicle Excise and Registration Act 1994, s. 33(1) and (1A)

*Triable summarily. Fine.*

***(No specific power of arrest)***

The Vehicle Excise and Registration Act 1994, s. 33 states:

*(1) A person is guilty of an offence if—*

*(a) he uses, or keeps, on a public road a vehicle in respect of which vehicle excise duty is chargeable, and*

*(b) there is not fixed to and exhibited on the vehicle in the manner prescribed by regulations made by the Secretary of State a licence for, or in respect of, the vehicle which is for the time being in force.*

*(1A) A person is guilty of an offence if—*

*(a) he uses, or keeps, on a public road an exempt vehicle,*

*(b) that vehicle is one in respect of which regulations under this Act require a nil licence to be in force, and*

*(c) there is not fixed to and exhibited in the vehicle in the manner prescribed by regulations made by the Secretary of State a nil licence for that vehicle which is for the time being in force.*

**Keynote**

Although it is not common practice to prosecute both offences in full, there is no reason why both failing to display a current licence and using/keeping a vehicle without having such a licence in force cannot be charged together (*Pilgram* v *Dean* [1974] RTR 299).

The 'manner prescribed' is set out in reg. 16 of the Road Vehicles (Registration and Licensing) Regulations 1971 (SI 1971 No. 450) (clearly visible in the windscreen of the vehicle so that it can be read from the nearside in daylight).

Regulation 16(1) of the 1971 Regulations allows for a very limited defence where the person removes the licence at a post office to take the old one out and replace it.

The offence appears to be an 'absolute' liability offence (**see Crime, chapter 1**), and no guilty state of mind is needed; it may even be committed if someone else removes the licence from the vehicle (see *Strowger* v *John* [1974] RTR 124).

The Secretary of State may also make regulations prohibiting a person from exhibiting on a vehicle which is kept on a public road anything that is intended to be, or that could reasonably be mistaken for a current licence (s. 33(4)).

### Offence — Not Paying Duty Chargeable at Higher Rate — Vehicle Excise and Registration Act 1994, s. 37(1)

*Triable summarily. Fine.*

***(No specific power of arrest)***

The Vehicle Excise and Registration Act 1994, s. 37 states:

*(1) Where—*

*(a) a vehicle licence has been taken out for a vehicle at any rate of vehicle excise duty,*

*(b) at any time while the licence is in force the vehicle is so used that duty at a higher rate becomes chargeable in respect of the licence for the vehicle under section 15, and*

*(c) duty at that higher rate was not paid before the vehicle was so used, the person so using the vehicle is guilty of an offence.*

**Keynote**

If a vehicle is taxed at a certain rate and is then used in a way that attracts a higher rate, the higher duty becomes payable (s. 15). Failing to pay that higher rate is an offence which can be punished by a penalty of five times the difference between the rate paid and the annual higher rate. Using a vehicle in breach of certain conditions attached to a low rate licence would be an example of where this might happen.

As with the offences of failing to display the correct excise licence (above), the burden of proof in relation to the character, weight or cylinder capacity of the vehicle used, or of the purpose to which the vehicle was being put lies with the defendant for this offence (s. 53).

## 12.3 Notification of Changes in Ownership or Address

Under the Road Vehicles (Registration and Licensing) Regulations 1971 (SI 1971 No. 450), the owner of a vehicle has certain obligations to notify the Secretary of State.

One such obligation is where there is any alteration to the vehicle that makes any of the details on its registration document incorrect (e.g. significant changes in the vehicle's appearance) (reg. 10). Another obligation is made in relation to changes of ownership, under reg. 12 (where the registration book was issued before 24 March 1997) and reg. 12A (where the registration document was issued on or after that date). On a change of ownership the previous owner must pass the relevant registration document to the new owner and must notify the Secretary of State of the name and address of the new owner in writing forthwith. Similarly, the new owner is under an obligation to notify the Secretary of State that he/she is the new owner of the vehicle. The new owner must also give notification if he/she does not intend to keep the vehicle on a public road.

If the owner of a vehicle changes his/her address or sends the vehicle for destruction or export, he/she must notify the Secretary of State (regs 13 and 14).

## 12.4 Trade Licences

Motor traders and vehicle testers may apply for trade licences which exempt them, under certain circumstances, from the rates of duty applicable above (s. 11 of the Vehicle Excise and Registration Act 1994).

A *motor trader* is a person who:

- manufactures
- repairs or
- deals in vehicles; or
- anyone else carrying on a prescribed business of modifying or valeting vehicles (as set out in the Road Vehicles (Registration and Licensing) Regulations 1971.

'Dealing' includes those whose business is wholly or mainly concerned with collecting or delivering vehicles (s. 62(1)).

A *vehicle tester* is a person other than a motor trader who regularly in the course of his/her business tests vehicles belonging to other people on roads (s. 62(1)).

Motor traders' and vehicle testers' licences ('trade plates') carry different conditions.

A motor trader's licence will cover:

- all vehicles temporarily in his/her possession *in the course of his/her business* as a motor trader;

- all vehicles kept and used solely for research and development *in the course of the trader's business* as a manufacturer; and
- all vehicles received from other manufacturers for testing on roads *in the course of the trader's business* as a manufacturer.

A vehicle testers' licence will cover all vehicles which are from time to time submitted to the tester for testing *in the course of his/her business.*

The italicised references to the course of the trader's/tester's business are important. If the relevant holder uses the trade plates on a vehicle for a purpose other than a business purpose, he/she commits an offence under reg. 34(1) of the 1971 Regulations.

The vehicles used under a trade licence must not carry loads other than those set out in s. 12 of the 1994 Act (which generally covers things which are permanently attached to the vehicle or which are needed in order to test it, or loads which are themselves 'vehicles'). There are also very strict provisions as to which *passengers* may be carried in a vehicle using trade plates (see reg. 40 of the 1971 Regulations).

Trade licences can apply for a year or for part of a year (under certain conditions).

When a vehicle is being used under a trade licence, trade plates must be fixed and displayed and illuminated in a way which complies with regs 18 and 19 of the 1971 Regulations — that is, they must be clearly displayed on the front and the back of the vehicle.

Each holder of a trade licence will be issued a pair of trade plates which will contain a registration mark assigned to the holder. One of the plates will be designed to display the trade licence (reg. 31(1) of the 1971 Regulations). Trade plates remain the property of the Secretary of State (reg. 31(2)).

It is summary offence to alter, deface or add anything to a trade plate (reg. 32(1)). It is also an offence to exhibit:

- a trade plate that has been so altered or defaced,
- a trade plate that is illegible, or
- anything that could be mistaken for a trade plate

on a mechanically propelled vehicle (reg. 32(1) and (2)). Strangely, reg. 32(2) does not specify that the vehicle must be on a public road — or any other road for that matter.

### Offence — Improper Use of Trade Licence — Vehicle Excise and Registration Act 1994, s.34(1)

*Triable summarily. Fine.*

***(No specific power of arrest)***

The Vehicle Excise and Registration Act 1994, s. 34 states:

> *(1) A person holding a trade licence or trade licences is guilty of an offence if he—*
>
> *(a) uses at any one time on a public road a greater number of vehicles (not being vehicles for which vehicle licences are for the time being in force) than he is authorised to use by virtue of the trade licence or licences,*
>
> *(b) uses a vehicle (not being a vehicle for which a vehicle licence is for the time being in force) on a public road for any purpose other than a purpose which has been prescribed under section 12(2)(b), or*
>
> *(c) uses the trade licence, or any of the trade licences, for the purposes of keeping on a public road in any circumstances other than circumstances which have been prescribed under section 12(1)(c) a vehicle which is not being used on that road.*

**Keynote**

Section 34 creates three different offences.

A licence holder may be required to pay up to five times the duty payable on the particular class of vehicle concerned.

Only one vehicle may be used on one licence at a time but a person may hold more than one trade licence.

The burden of proof in relation to the character, weight or cylinder capacity of the vehicle used, the number of vehicles used or of the purpose to which the vehicle was being put lies with the defendant for this offence (s. 53).

### 12.4.1 Dishonoured Cheques

Vehicle licences and trade licences may be paid for by cheque (s. 19A(1) of the 1994 Act). If a cheque used to pay for either type of licence is subsequently dishonoured, the Secretary of State (through the DVLA) may send a notice to the licence holder informing him/her that the licence is void as from the time it was granted (s. 19A(2)). Where such a notice is sent, the licence holder may also be required to deliver up that licence. If the licence holder fails to do so, he/she commits a summary offence punishable by a fine or an amount equal to five times the duty payable on that vehicle (s. 35A). The court must also impose a requirement to pay any outstanding duty owed on the vehicle since the application was made or since it was due to take effect (s. 36).

## 12.5 Furnishing Information

Section 46 of the Vehicle Excise and Registration Act 1994 provides that:

*(1) Where it is alleged that a vehicle has been used on a road in contravention of section 29, 34 or 37—*

*(a) the person keeping the vehicle shall give such information as he may be required to give in accordance with subsection (7) as to the identity of the driver of the vehicle or any person who used the vehicle, and*

*(b) any other person shall give such information as it is in his power to give and which may lead to the identification of the driver of the vehicle or any person who used the vehicle if he is required to do so in accordance with subsection (7).*

*(2) Where it is alleged that a vehicle has been kept on a road in contravention of section 29—*

*(a) the person keeping the vehicle shall give such information as he may be required to give in accordance with subsection (7) as to the identity of the person who kept the vehicle on the road, and*

*(b) any other person shall give such information as it is in his power to give and which may lead to the identification of the person who kept the vehicle on the road if he is required to do so in accordance with subsection (7).*

*(3) Where it is alleged that a vehicle has at any time been used on a road in contravention of section 29, the person who is alleged to have so used the vehicle shall give such information as it is in his power to give as to the identity of the person who was keeping the vehicle at that time if he is required to do so in accordance with subsection (7).*

**Offence — Failing to Give Information — Vehicle Excise and Registration Act 1994, s. 46(4)**
*Triable summarily. Fine.*
**(*No specific power of arrest*)**

The Vehicle Excise and Registration Act 1994, s. 46 states:

*(4) A person who fails to comply with subsection (1), (2) or (3) is guilty of an offence.*

**Keynote**

The requirement for information to be given must come on behalf of a chief officer of police or the Secretary of State (s. 46(7)).

The obligation to furnish the required information, in relation to section 46(1)(a) and (2)(a), applies to the person who is the keeper *at the time of the requirement*, even if they were not the keeper at the time of the alleged offence (*Hateley* v *Greenough* [1962] Crim LR 329).

Section 46A goes on to make further provisions for the Secretary of State to require information leading to the identity of a person who is keeping or who has sold or disposed of a vehicle in contravention of the regulations relating to the registration of vehicles (i.e. under s. 22). Failing to comply with a notice under s. 46A is an offence similar to that under s. 46(4) above.

This offence also applies to the offence relating to 'nil licences' under s. 43A (**see para. 12.2.3**).

Evidence that a person has been served with a notice requiring the relevant information is admissible in proving the listed offences (s. 51), so too is evidence held by the Secretary of State (DVLA) in official records (s. 52).

Section 45 creates a number of offences concerned with the making of false or misleading statements made in connection with just about any transaction, application or duty to furnish information under the Act.

### 12.5.1 Defence

Section 46(6) provides that:

> *(6) If a person is charged with an offence under subsection (4) consisting of failing to comply with subsection (1)(a) or (2)(a), it is a defence for him to show to the satisfaction of the court that he did not know, and could not with reasonable diligence have ascertained, the identity of the person or persons concerned.*

## 12.6 Registration Marks

Sections 21 to 28 of the Vehicle Excise and Registration Act 1994, as amended, contain the provisions relating to the registration of vehicles.

Section 21 makes detailed provision for the requirements to provide information when registering, selling and disposing of vehicles. It also places certain obligations on people who surrender vehicle licences or who do not renew them (see s. 22(1C), (1D) and (1E)). The applicable regulations governing these aspects of registration are:

- The Road Vehicles (Registration and Licencing) Regulations 1971 (SI 1971 No. 450).
- The Vehicle Registration (Sale of Information) Regulations 1996 (SI 1996 No. 2800).
- The Road Vehicles (Statutory Off-road Notification) Regulations 1997 (SI 1997 No. 3025).

Under s. 23, the Secretary of State must assign a registration mark to a vehicle when it is registered.

The Road Vehicles (Registration and Licensing) Regulations 1971 with their many amendments, impose conditions as to the manner and form in which registration plates must be exhibited (regs 17 to 23). They make further conditions such as the need to notify the DVLA when buying, selling or altering a vehicle, or when changing address (see regs 10, 12 to 15).

Schedules 2 and 3 to the 1971 Regulations set the colours and specifications for registration plates. The increasingly common use of stylised lettering on number plates is not provided for in the Regulations and the computer-generated italicised writing on some plates does not appear to be unlawful. Regulation 18(3) requires the registration mark to be fixed and displayed so that the letters and figures are easily legible in normal daylight. If the writing on the plate is not 'easily legible' (a question of fact for a court to decide) or there are figures which look like numbers (or vice versa), reg. 18 would appear to be breached. Provided that the dimensions set out in paras 9–18 of sch. 2 to the Road Vehicles (Registration and Licensing) Regulations 1971 are complied with, number plates need only be 'easily legible'.

Although the practice of buying and displaying 'cherished' or personalised numbers is not only permitted, but is also condoned (see Sale of Registration Marks Regulations 1995 (SI 1995 No. 2880)), some drivers and owners are extremely creative in trying to fashion words, letters, acronyms etc. on their existing plates. Where owners of vehicles move bolts holding the number plates on or where they move letters/numbers apart in this way, they often commit the offence under s. 42(1) below.

### 12.6.1 Lighting

The requirements to light the rear registration plate on a vehicle is covered under the Road Vehicles Lighting Regulations 1989 (**see chapter 9**).

Under the Road Vehicles (Registration and Licensing) Regulations 1971 however, there is also an offence of using, or causing or permitting the use of a vehicle on a road during the hours of darkness unless all letters and numbers are illuminated in a way that makes them clearly legible (reg. 19(1)).

### 12.6.2 Other Offences

**Offence — Not Fixing Registration Mark — Vehicle Excise and Registration Act 1994, s. 42(1)**
*Triable summarily. Fine.*
***(No specific power of arrest)***

The Vehicle Excise and Registration Act 1994, s. 42 states:

*(1) If a registration mark is not fixed on a vehicle as required by virtue of section 23, the relevant person is guilty of an offence.*
*(2) . . .*
*(3) In subsection (1) 'the relevant person' means the person driving the vehicle or, where it is not being driven, the person keeping it.*

**Offence — Obscured Registration Mark — Vehicle Excise and Registration Act 1994, s. 43(1)**
*Triable summarily. Fine.*
**(*No specific power of arrest*)**

The Vehicle Excise and Registration Act 1994, s. 43 states:

*(1) If a registration mark fixed on a vehicle as required by virtue of section 23 is in any way—*
*(a) obscured, or*
*(b) rendered, or allowed to become, not easily distinguishable, the relevant person is guilty of an offence.*

**Keynote**

The offence under each section is committed by the 'relevant' person; that is, the person *driving* the vehicle (**see chapter 1**) or, if the vehicle is not being driven, the keeper (s. 42(3)). A person is the 'keeper' if he/she causes the vehicle to be on a public road for any period, *however short*, when it is not in use there (s. 62(2)).

If the person can show that he/she had no reasonable opportunity to register the vehicle and that the vehicle was being driven for the purpose of it being so registered, he/she has a defence to a charge under s. 42(1); not fixing a registration mark (s. 42(4)). The burden of proof is upon the defendant.

In answer to a charge under s. 43(1) (obscured registration marks), the person has a defence if he/she can show that he/she took all steps which were reasonably practicable to prevent the mark being obscured or not easily distinguishable (s. 43(4)).

**Offence — Failing to have Nil Licence for Exempt Vehicle — Vehicle Excise and Registration Act 1994, s. 43A**
*Triable summarily. Fine.*
**(*No specific power of arrest*)**

The Vehicle Excise and Registration Act 1994, s. 43A states:

*(1) A person is guilty of an offence if—*
*(a) he uses, or keeps, on a public road an exempt vehicle,*
*(b) that vehicle is one in respect of which regulations under this Act require a nil licence to be in force, and*
*(c) a nil licence is not for the time being in force in respect of the vehicle.*

**Keynote**

This offence came into effect on 1 April 1998.

A 'nil licence' means a document which is in the form of a vehicle licence and is issued by the Secretary of State in respect of an 'exempt vehicle' (s. 62).

## 12.6.3 Overseas Vehicles

The Motor Vehicles (International Circulation) Regulations 1985 (SI 1985 No. 610), as amended, govern the use of vehicles from abroad while in Great Britain.

Anyone who is resident outside Great Britain bringing a vehicle into the country must produce any registration card or document in respect of the vehicle to a police officer (or authorised person) on request at any reasonable time (reg. 4).

# CHAPTER THIRTEEN

# GOODS AND PASSENGER VEHICLES

## 13.1 Introduction

The law regulating the use of goods and passenger vehicles is notoriously complex, not least because of the need to achieve a common transport policy in line with the UK's membership of the European Union.

The use and operation of goods and passenger vehicles, particularly in the course of a business, presents many opportunities for the creation of risk and danger to the community and is therefore seen as an area which requires fairly stringent legal provision. This chapter is intended as a summary of some of the more relevant of those provisions. The legislation which follows relies heavily on certain documents being held or produced by the relevant people; for the offences involving fraudulent use of such documents, **see chapter 16**.

## 13.2 Large Goods Vehicles and Passenger Carrying Vehicles

### 13.2.1 Large Goods Vehicles

A large goods vehicle (LGV) is:

- a motor vehicle (not being a medium-sized goods vehicle)
- which is constructed or adapted
- to carry or haul goods
- having a permissible maximum weight over 7.5 tonnes

(Road Traffic Act 1988, s. 121).

### 13.2.2 Passenger Carrying Vehicles

A passenger-carrying vehicle (PCV) is either:

- a vehicle used for carrying passengers
- which is constructed or adapted
- to carry more than 16 passengers (a 'large PCV')

*or*

- a vehicle used for carrying passengers *for hire or reward*
- which is constructed or adapted
- to carry more than 8 but not more than 16 passengers (a 'small PCV')

(Road Traffic Act 1988, s. 121).

## 13.2.3 LGV and PCV Licences

The driving licences under Part III of the Road Traffic Act 1988 (**see chapter 11**) are needed to drive large goods vehicles and passenger carrying vehicles. However, in order to drive such vehicles, a person must also hold an LGV or PCV licence granted under s. 110 of the 1988 Act.

If a person is granted an LGV or PCV licence, it is an offence to fail to comply with the conditions attached to it.

**Offence — Conditions of LGV or PCV Licence — Road Traffic Act 1988, s. 114**
*Triable summarily. Fine.*
***(No specific power of arrest)***

The Road Traffic Act 1988, s. 114 states:

*(1) The following licences, that is to say—*
*(a) a large goods vehicle or passenger-carrying vehicle driver's licence issued as a provisional licence,*
*(b) a full large goods vehicle or passenger-carrying vehicle driver's licence granted to a person under the age of 21, and*
*(c) a LGV Community licence held by a person under the age of 21 who is normally resident in Great Britain,*
*shall be subject to the prescribed conditions, and if the holder of the licence fails, without reasonable excuse, to comply with any of the conditions he is guilty of an offence.*
*(2) It is an offence for a person knowingly to cause or permit another person who is under the age of 21 to drive a large goods vehicle of any class or a passenger-carrying vehicle of any class in contravention of the prescribed conditions to which that other person's licence is subject.*

**Keynote**

If a person drives an LGV or a PCV on a road without such a licence, they commit the offence under s. 87(1) of driving otherwise than in accordance with a licence (**see chapter 11**).

A person may not be granted such a licence unless the Secretary of State is satisfied that he/she is, in relation to his/her conduct, a fit person to hold such a licence (s. 112). A person may appeal against any refusal under s. 119.

Part IV of the 1988 Act provides for the revocation of these licences and the disqualification of holders.

Application for an LGV or PCV licence is made under the Motor Vehicles (Driving Licences) Regulations 1996 (SI 1996 No. 2824). Those Regulations set out the requirements for the relevant tests which much be passed, together with the requirements of provisional licences and learner drivers.

### 13.2.4 Disqualification

Where a person is disqualified by a court (**see chapter 11**) from driving, that person may also have his/her LGV/PCV licence revoked for such a period as the licensing authority thinks fit (reg. 53 of the 1996 Regulations).

If the holder of an LGV licence is under 21 years of age and he/she accumulates more than three penalty points (or is disqualified) that person *must* be disqualified from holding an LGV licence:

- indefinitely *or*
- at least until reaching the age of 21

(s. 115(1)(a) of the Road Traffic Act 1988 and reg. 52 of the 1996 Regulations).

Large goods vehicles and passenger carrying vehicles licences last until the drivers' 45th birthday or five years, whichever is the longer. If the driver is aged between 45 and 65 they last for five years or until the 66th birthday, whichever is the *shorter*. After the driver has reached 65 the licence must be renewed annually (s. 99(1A)(a)). (Contrast ordinary licences; **see chapter 11**.)

### 13.2.5 Exemptions

Regulations 47 and 48 of the 1996 Regulations exempt certain classes of vehicle which would otherwise require LGV or PCV licences. These include some agricultural, forestry and road-rolling vehicles, together with steam-driven vehicles and industrial plant.

If a small PCV (**see para. 13.2.2**) is driven for purposes other than hire or reward, there is no need for a PCV licence. The driver must however be over the age of 21 and have held an ordinary licence for at least two years (reg. 6).

Regulation 6 also makes provision for certain people to drive passenger carrying vehicles for the purposes of repair or testing.

## 13.3 Licences

### 13.3.1 Operators' Licences

In addition to the need for drivers to hold certain specialised driving licences, there are also requirements for those who wish to *use* goods vehicles in the course of their business.

The use of goods vehicles for business purposes is governed by the Goods Vehicles (Licensing of Operators) Act 1995 and the similarly-named Regulations (SI 1995 No. 2869).

If a person wishes to use a goods vehicle on a road for hire or reward or in connection with his/her trade or business, he/she will need an 'operators' licence' (s. 2).

Such a licence is very different from a driving licence and amounts to an authority to operate a number of goods vehicles.

In line with an EC Directive (96/26/EC, 23 May 1996), there are two types of operators' licence; standard and restricted.

**Standard Operators' Licence**

Vehicles under this licence may be used for:

- hire or reward *or*
- in connection with the holder's trade or business.

Standard operators' licences are divided into those which allow the above activities to be carried out internationally and those which may only be used nationally.

**Restricted Operators' Licence**

Vehicles under this licence may be used:

- in connection with the holder's trade or business *other than the carriage of goods for hire or reward.*

Whether or not a goods vehicle is being used for hire or reward will be a matter of fact for a court to determine (for guidance, see *Albert* v *Motor Insurers' Bureau* [1971] 2 All ER 1345).

Given the much wider effect of the standard operators' licence, holders of them are subject to much more stringent control than those with restricted licences.

**Operators' Licence Generally**

Under the 1995 Regulations, applicants for operators' licences have to demonstrate that they are of good repute, that they are professionally competent and that they have the appropriate financial standing.

In determining these matters, and the fitness of applicants for LGV/PCV licences, the traffic commissioners have a significant role to play (see s. 111 of the Road Traffic Act 1988).

The 1995 Regulations, together with the provisions of the 1995 Act itself, set out requirements for:

- the specification of vehicles which an operator can use
- the operating centre at which the vehicles are kept and despatched
- environmental controls on operating centres
- conditions attached to the operators' licence.

Regulation 23 requires a disc to be displayed on the vehicle stating, among other things, what type of licence the holder has. In the case of a standard (national) licence, the disc is blue, for a standard (international) licence the disc is green and a restricted licence the disc is orange.

## Offence — Using Vehicle without Operators' Licence — Goods Vehicles (Licensing of Operators) Act 1995, s. 2

*Triable summarily. Fine.*

***(No specific power of arrest)***

The Goods Vehicles (Licensing of Operators) Act 1995, s. 2 states:

*(1) Subject to subsection (2) and section 4, no person shall use a goods vehicle on a road for the carriage of goods—*

*(a) for hire or reward, or*

*(b) for or in connection with any trade or business carried on by him, except under a licence issued under this Act; and in this Act such a licence is referred to as an 'operator's licence'.*

*(2) Subsection (1) does not apply to—*

*(a) the use of a small goods vehicle within the meaning given in Schedule 1;*

*(b) the use of a goods vehicle for international carriage by a haulier established in a member State other than the United Kingdom and not established in the United Kingdom;*

*(c) the use of a goods vehicle for international carriage by a haulier established in Northern Ireland and not established in Great Britain; or*

*(d) the use of a vehicle of any class specified in regulations.*

*(3) . . .*

*(4) It is hereby declared that, for the purposes of this Act the performance by a local or public authority of their functions constitutes the carrying on of a business.*

**Keynote**

For an explanation of 'using' a vehicle, **see chapter 1**.

It would appear that it is necessary to prove that the vehicle was actually carrying goods at the relevant time (see *Robertson* v *Crew* [1977] RTR 141).

The duty to furnish information in relation to the identity of the driver at the time of an alleged offence under this section is to be found in the Road Traffic Act *1960* (s. 232).

## Offence — Contravening Condition of Operators' Licence — Goods Vehicles (Licensing of Operators) Act 1995, s. 22(6)

*Triable summarily. Fine.*

***(No specific power of arrest)***

The Goods Vehicles (Licensing of Operators) Act 1995, s. 22 states:

*(6) Any person who contravenes any condition attached under this section to a licence of which he is the holder is guilty of an offence . . .*

**Keynote**

One of the conditions which must be attached to the licence is a duty to report any changes to the traffic commissioners. Such changes will usually include any convictions of the holder or the transport manager or any changes in their financial standing, good repute etc. above. Such notification must be made within 28 days of the event (or of the event coming to the knowledge of a transport manager).

### 13.3.2 Exemptions

Section 2(2) of the 1995 Act sets out exemptions for 'small' goods vehicles and for vehicles being used by a haulier established in Northern Ireland or a European Union member State.

Small goods vehicle includes a vehicle with a 'plated' weight of 3.5 tonnes or less or, if there is no plated weight, then an unladen weight of 1,525kgs. There are further calculations to be made if trailers are involved and sch. 1 to the 1995 Act should be consulted.

Other exempted vehicles include emergency services vehicles, vehicles being used for the provision of emergency supplies by utilities companies, funeral vehicles and 'showman's vehicles'.

Vehicles temporarily in Great Britain are covered by the obviously-named Goods Vehicles (Licensing of Operators) (Temporary Use in Great Britain) Regulations 1996 (SI 1996 No. 2186). The Regulations are extremely detailed and should be consulted in full.

If a vehicle is brought into the country frequently enough, it may cease to be 'temporary' (*BRS* v *Wurzal* [1971] 3 All ER 480).

## 13.4 Public Service Vehicles

The operation of public service vehicles (PSVs) is contained in the Public Passenger Vehicles Act 1981, as amended, and the Transport Act 1985.

The legislation is very detailed and what follows is a brief outline of some of the relevant features.

Like the operation of goods vehicles, the use of PSVs is closely controlled although one aim of the Transport Act 1985 was to deregulate controls on local services.

Under s. 1 of the Public Passenger Vehicles Act 1981 a public service vehicle is:

> *(1) a motor vehicle (other than a tramcar) which—*
> *(a) being a vehicle adapted to carry more than eight passengers, is used for carrying passengers for hire or reward; or*
> *(b) being a vehicle not so adapted, is used for carrying passengers for hire or reward at separate fares in the course of a business of carrying passengers.*

**Keynote**

The use that is made of the particular PSV and the payment by passengers is important in determining whether the legislation applies or not:

- 'Stage carriages' are PSVs being used for local services, that is, used for carrying passengers for hire or reward on specified short journeys.
- 'Express carriages' are PSVs being used for carrying passengers for hire or reward at separate fares, other than on local services.
- 'Contract carriages' are PSVs being used for carrying passengers for hire or reward other than at separate fares.

Local or 'stage' services differ from 'express' services in the length of journey being made. If the passengers are picked up and dropped off within a relatively short distance (as with a traditional bus service), each paying the relevant fare, the service is likely to be a 'stage' service using 'stage carriages'.

If the passengers are taken 15 miles or more (e.g. from one part of the country to another), the service is likely to be an 'express' service and the PSV an 'express' carriage.

'Hire or reward' does not only mean a service provided under some contractual arrangement. It will include a provision of a transport facility amounting to a business activity that goes beyond simple kindness (see *DPP* v *Sikondar* [1993] RTR 90).

Hotel courtesy buses have been held to be PSVs on the basis that the service was part of the overall hotel 'service', the cost of which was included in the price or a room or meal (*Rout* v *Swallow Hotels Ltd* [1993] RTR 80).

If a person hires an entire PSV for a particular journey or journeys (e.g. a club outing or a 'hen' or 'stag' night), this is a 'contract' service using a 'contract carriage'.

Local or stage services must be registered with the relevant traffic commissioners (in London a special local service licence is required).

### 13.4.1 Operators' Licences

All PSVs being used on a road for hire or reward require an operators' licence, irrespective of the type of service being provided (s. 12(1) of the Public Passenger Vehicles Act 1981).

Operators' licences are obtained from the relevant traffic commissioners and are categorised in the same way as goods vehicles operators' licences, namely standard and restricted licences.

Again, operators must show that they are of good repute and financial standing in order to be granted an operators' licence. In the case of a standard licence, they must also demonstrate professional competence.

An operators' disc must be exhibited on the relevant vehicle(s) and the Public Service Vehicles (Operators' Licences) Regulations 1995 set out other conditions which must be followed by the holder of a licence.

Traffic commissioners are required to attach certain conditions to an operators' licence in relation to the numbers of vehicles covered by that licence; they may also attach other conditions as they think fit (s. 16 of the Public Passenger Vehicles Act 1981).

Conditions may also be attached under ss. 16, 26 and 27 of the Transport Act 1985.

Contravention of a condition of an operators' licence is an offence under s. 16(7) of the Public Passenger Vehicles Act 1981.

#### Standard PSV Operators' Licence

This licence authorises the use of any PSV for both national and international journeys.

#### Restricted PSV Operators' Licence

This licence authorises the use of certain smaller PSVs for both national and international journeys. Taxi licence-holders (**see para. 13.7**) may apply for a restricted licence under s. 12 of the Transport Act 1985 (referred to as a 'special licence').

### 13.4.2 Exemptions

There are many exemptions to the requirements for an operators' licence. These include education authorities using school buses, small PSVs being used privately and other vehicles being used for charitable purposes.

Some foreign PSVs are also exempt from these provisions.

### 13.4.3 Conduct of People on PSVs

The behaviour of drivers, conductors and passengers on PSVs is regulated by statutory instrument.

Most of the conditions are contained in the Public Service Vehicles (Conduct of Drivers, Inspectors, Conductors and Passengers) Regulations 1990 (SI 1990 No. 1020), as amended.

Regulations are made under the two Acts referred to above. Regulations 4–5 address the behaviour prohibited from bus crews generally and impose certain duties upon them (e.g. taking all reasonable precautions to ensure passenger safety).

Regulations 6–7 make requirements of passengers in relation to the payment of fares, altering tickets, and general anti-social or dangerous behaviour (including the playing of things such as personal stereos to the annoyance of other passengers — reg. 6(1)).

Clearly, in more serious cases, offences under the Public Order Act 1986 or the Protection from Harassment Act 1997 might be considered (see **General Police Duties, chapter 3**).

Under regs 8 and 9 passengers can be required to give their name and address to a driver, inspector or conductor if those people reasonably suspect the passenger to have contravened one of the regulations.

## 13.5 Community Buses and Trams

### 13.5.1 Community Buses

Sections 22 and 23 of the Transport Act 1985 make provision for the operation of 'Community bus services' which are services provided for the social and welfare needs of one or more communities.

Drivers of 'community buses' may hold a community bus permit which exempts them from the need for a PCV licence and the conditions relating to such a permit can be found in the Community Bus Regulations 1978 (SI 1978 No. 1313) and 1986 (SI 1986 No. 1254) (as amended in each case).

Under the 1978 Regulations, community buses must display appropriate discs on the inside of the vehicle but where they can be read easily from outside the vehicle.

Community bus services are subject to the conditions laid down in the Transport Act 1985, which also creates a number of offences.

### 13.5.2 Tramcars

Under s. 193A of the Road Traffic Act 1988, the Secretary of State may make amendments to various Acts so that they include tram and trolley vehicles.

Under this power the Tramcars and Trolley Vehicles (Modification of Enactments) Regulations 1992 (SI 1992 No. 1217) have been made. Many local variations exist in the regulation of tram and trolley services (e.g. the Stage Carriages Act 1832 still applies to trams in Blackpool), and reference should be made to those local regulations in each case.

In addition, the Transport and Works Act 1992 provides for certain offences (including drink/driving (see Part II of the Act)) committed by people employed in guided transport systems (which also include railways) — **see General Police Duties, chapter 13**.

## 13.6 Drivers' Hours

Drivers of goods vehicles or passenger carrying vehicles have, in the past, come under considerable commercial pressure to drive for long distances or for long hours. In order to reduce the increased risk which is presented to the public by drivers of those vehicles who are suffering from fatigue, the Transport Act 1968 (Part VI) introduced a system for the recording and monitoring of the hours which some drivers work.

This was achieved by setting out maximum periods of driving, together with minimum rest periods in between and by requiring certain vehicles to have tachographs (**see paras 13.6.3 and 13.6.4**) fitted and maintained.

The law has been extended — and considerably complicated — by the effects of EC legislation and is now a highly complex area of road traffic law. The many 'Community rules' (see s. 96 of the Transport Act 1968) and exemptions should be consulted, and expert assistance sought in each case.

What follows here is a *very brief overview* of the legal regulation of drivers' hours.

### 13.6.1 Type of Vehicle

The provisions of Part VI of the Transport Act 1968 apply generally to:

- **Passenger vehicles** — PSVs and other motor vehicles constructed or adapted to carry more than 12 passengers.

- **Goods vehicles** — locomotives, motor tractors, any motor vehicle constructed so that it may be used as an articulated vehicle and other motor vehicles constructed or adapted to carry goods other than passengers' effects.

As the purpose of the legislation is to exercise control over working hours a number of exemptions are provided for. These essentially refer to vehicles used for the conveyance of passengers for short distances, public service and public utility vehicles, ambulances etc., types of tractors, showmens' goods vehicles and some breakdown vehicles. Most of the exempted vehicles are controlled by public authorities or public utilities.

## GOODS AND PASSENGER VEHICLES

The rules and restrictions vary according to the type of *vehicle*; they also vary according to the type of *journey* being made by that vehicle.

### 13.6.2 Type of Journey

The relevant types of journey or work are:

- international journeys
- national journeys
- domestic journeys
- mixed (i.e. a combination of some of the above).

As ever, there are many exemptions to the requirements for observing and recording drivers' hours and these generally appear in the particular rules.

**Community Legislation**

Most journeys will be covered by:

- Regulation 85/3820 (in relation to drivers' hours); and
- Regulation 85/3821, as amended (in relation to tachograph records).

### 13.6.3 Drivers' Hours

The following is a brief résumé of the regulations in relation to drivers' hours.

**Driving Periods**

- Normally 9 hours daily driving period but 10 hours not more than twice a week.
- Generally 4.5 hours continuous driving period.
- The total period of driving in any one week must not exceed 56 hours.
- The total period of driving in any one fortnight must not exceed 90 hours.

These figures are an aggregation of the various prescribed driving and rest periods found within the relevant articles.

**Rest Breaks**

- At least 45 minutes rest break unless the driver is beginning a daily or weekly rest period.
- Rest breaks may be replaced by rest periods of at least 15 minutes each totalling 45 minutes distributed within the continuous driving period or immediately after it.
- Rest breaks must not be taken as part of a daily rest period.

**Rest Periods**

- After 6 daily driving periods drivers must take a weekly rest period.

- The weekly rest period may be postponed until the end of the sixth day if the total driving time over the 6 days does not exceed the maximum corresponding to 6 daily driving periods.
- In the case of national and international carriage of passengers other than on regular services (i.e. coach tours) it is 12 and not 6 daily driving periods.
- Drivers must have a daily rest period of at least 11 consecutive hours in each period of 24 hours.
- The rest period may be reduced to at least 9 consecutive hours not more than three times a week. This applies provided that an equivalent period is granted as compensation before the end of the following week.
- Where there is no reduction in hours, daily rest periods may be taken in two or three separate periods during a 24-hour period but one of these must be at least 8 consecutive hours.
- Where there is a reduction in hours, the minimum length of rest for that day must be increased to 12 hours.
- Daily rest periods may be taken in a vehicle as long as it is fitted with a bunk and is stationary.
- During each period of 30 hours when a vehicle is manned by at least two drivers each shall have a rest period of not less than 8 consecutive hours.
- In the course of each week one of the rest periods shall be extended by way of weekly rest to a total of 45 consecutive hours.
- Weekly rest may be reduced to 36 hours if it is taken at a vehicle base or driver base or to a minimum of 24 hours if taken elsewhere. If this is done there will be compensation by an equivalent rest taken en bloc before the end of the third week following the week in question.
- A weekly rest period which begins in one week and continues into the following week may be attached to either of these weeks.

'Driver' for the purpose of the regulations is any person who drives a vehicle, even for a short period, or who is in the vehicle in order to be available for driving if necessary.

The term 'week' means the period between 00.00 hours on Monday and 24.00 hours on Sunday.

A 'day' means successive periods of 24 hours beginning with the resumption of driving after the last weekly rest period.

'Rest' means any uninterrupted period of at least one hour during which the driver may freely dispose of his/her time. To 'freely dispose of his/her time' means that the employer cannot direct the driver to engage in doing some other type of work.

The relevant 'daily working period' will include the time spent by a driver taking the vehicle to and from their home address before and after work (*DPP* v *Guy* [1998] RTR 82).

### Offences

Section 96 of the Transport Act 1968 states:

> *(11) It is an offence for the requirements of the domestic drivers' code as to hours of work to be contravened and a driver or any other person (being that driver's employer or a person to whose orders that driver was subject) who caused or permitted the contravention will be liable.*
> *(11A) It is an offence for any requirement of the applicable Community rules as to periods of driving, or distance driven, or periods on or off duty, to be contravened and the driver and any other person (being that driver's employer or a person to whose orders that driver was subject) who caused or permitted the contravention will be liable.*

## 13.6.4 Tachographs

Tachographs (referred to in the legislation as 'recording equipment') are really a combination of a speedometer, a odometer and a clock.

**TACHOS** must measure:

- **T**imes of driving
- **A**ny breaks taken in a journey
- **C**ases housing the tachograph being opened (and any interruption to their power supply)
- **H**ours of work or availability
- **O**verall distances travelled
- **S**peed.

The regulations require that a tachograph must be installed and used in vehicles which are registered in a member State of the EU and are used for the carriage of goods or passengers by road.

Tachographs may only be fitted and repaired by approved fitters or workshops at which time the tachograph is sealed and marked.

Employers must ensure that sufficient tachograph sheets are issued to each driver. These record sheets are circular discs upon which the tachograph records certain information. It is the responsibility of each driver to operate switches on the device which separately cause records to be made of driving time, other work or attendance duties, breaks and rest periods.

Completed discs must be retained by an employer for at least one year and produced to an authorised inspector on request. An 'authorised inspector' includes a constable. If in uniform a constable does not need to produce a form of authority.

The following must be entered on the tachograph record sheet by each driver:

- full name
- date and place where the use of the sheet starts and ends
- registration number of the vehicle and of any other vehicle used during the driver's duties
- odometer reading at the start of the first, and at the end of the last, journey recorded on the sheet and, if applicable, for any other vehicle used, and
- the time any change of vehicle takes place.

Drivers must be able to produce record sheets for the current week and in any case for the last day of the previous week on which they drove. Employed drivers must return completed record sheets to their employer within 21 days.

The Divisional Court has held that employers are under a duty to conduct periodic checks of tachograph charts even though there is no reason to suspect any breach (*Vehicle Inspectorate* v *Nuttall* [1998] RTR 321).

### Offences

Section 97 of the Transport Act 1968 states:

> *(1) It is an offence for a person to use, or cause or permit to be used, a vehicle to which this section applies unless there is recording equipment in the vehicle which complies with the Community Recording Equipment Regulation.*

Section 97A of the Transport Act 1968 states:

> *It is an offence for an employed driver to fail without reasonable excuse to return any record sheet which relates to him to his employer within 21 days of completing it; or where he has two or more employers by whom he is employed as a driver of such a vehicle, to notify each of them of the name and address of the other or others of them.*

Section 97AA of the Transport Act 1968 states:

> *(1) It is an offence for a person, with intent to deceive, to forge, alter or use any seal on recording equipment installed in or designed for installation in, a vehicle to which s. 97 applies.*

Section 98 of the Transport Act 1968 states:

> *(4) It is an offence for any person to contravene any regulations made or any requirements as to books, records or documents.*

Section 99 of the Transport Act 1968 states:

> *(4) It is an offence for any person to fail to comply with any requirement to allow the inspection of records or to obstruct an officer in the exercise of his powers under s. 99.*

## 13.6.5 Police Powers

Under s. 99(1) of the Transport Act 1968, a constable may require any person to produce and permit him/her to inspect and copy any book or register which the person is required by regulations under s. 98 of the 1968 Act to carry or have in his/her possession for the purpose of making in it:

- any entry required by those regulations or which is required to be carried on any vehicle of which that person is the driver;
- any book or register which that person is required to preserve;
- any record sheet which that person is required by Article 14(2) of the Community Recording Equipment Regulation to retain or to be able to produce (Article 15(7) of the Regulation);

- if that person is the owner of a vehicle to which the Transport Act 1968 applies, any other document of that person which the officer may reasonably require to inspect for the purpose of ascertaining whether the provisions of the Act, or of regulations made thereunder, have been complied with;

- any book, register or document required by the applicable Community rules or which the officer may reasonably require to inspect for the purpose of ascertaining whether the requirements of the applicable Community rules have been complied with;

- and that record sheet, book, register or document shall, if the officer so requires by notice in writing served on that person, be produced at the office of the traffic commissioner specified not less than 10 days from the service of the notice.

For the purpose of exercising these powers an officer may detain the vehicle in question during such time as is required for the exercise of that power.

These powers are also available to examiners authorised under s. 66A or Part IV of the Road Traffic Act 1988 or authorised by the traffic commissioners (s. 99(2)), provided that, in each case, the examiner produces the requisite authority.

There is a requirement for a person 'keeping' a vehicle involved in an alleged offence under s. 99 to provide details leading to the identification of the driver when required to do so by police (Road Traffic Act 1960, s. 232).

### 13.6.6 AETR Agreement

Foreign vehicles operating in the UK and UK vehicles making certain overseas journeys may also be subject to the provisions of the European Agreement concerning the Work of Crews of Vehicles engaged in International Road Transport, known as the AETR Agreement (Cmnd 7401).

## 13.7 Taxis

The law regulating the use of taxis and hackney carriages is mainly provided for in three statutes:

- the Town Police Clauses Act 1847
- the Local Government (Miscellaneous Provisions) Act 1976
- the Metropolitan Public Carriage Act 1869.

(However, the Private Hire Vehicles (London) Act 1998 has received Royal Assent. When this Act *comes into force* it will regulate the operation of private hire vehicles in London. It will not extend to licensed taxis, public service vehicles or private hire vehicles used only for weddings and funerals.)

Taxis — vehicles which ply for hire — are generally referred to in the relevant legislation as hackney carriages; those which do not ply for hire are referred to as private hire vehicles.

What follows is a brief review of some of the relevant legislation in this area.

## 13.7.1 Licensing System

Under the Town Police Clauses Act 1847 local authorities are empowered to provide a licensing system for hackney carriages to ply for hire as taxis (s. 37). In England and Wales that licensing system is to apply throughout the whole of a district council area (s. 15 of the Transport Act 1985).

References to licences in Part II of the Local Government (Miscellaneous Provisions) Act 1976 are to licences issued by a particular district. The effect of this is that each operator, driver and vehicle will require a valid licence in respect of each district area in which they work.

Under s. 16 the council can limit the number of hackney carriage licences it issues, provided that it is satisfied that there is no significant demand for those services (see *Ghafoor* v *Wakefield Metropolitan District Council* [1990] RTR 389).

In London the system for hackney carriages and private hire vehicles is provided under the Metropolitan Public Carriage Act 1869. Both the 1869 and 1976 Acts create offences and regulatory provisions in relation to the licensing and use of such vehicles.

## 13.7.2 Application

An applicant for a licence must satisfy the granting authority that he/she is a fit and proper person. The authority may decide against the application on the civil law standard of a 'balance of probabilities', even where it is considering the applicant's acquittal for a criminal offence (see *R* v *Maidstone Crown Court, ex parte Olson*, *The Times,* 21 May 1992).

In arriving at its decision, the authority may seek the advice of the local police (see s. 47 of the Road Traffic Act 1991).

The main relevant licences are:

- Taxi drivers' licences granted under the Town Police Clauses Act 1847 and the Metropolitan Public Carriage Act 1869.
- Private hire drivers' licences granted under s. 51 of the Local Government (Miscellaneous Provisions) Act 1976.
- Private hire proprietors' licences granted under s. 48 of the 1976 Act.
- Private hire operators' licences granted under s. 55 of the 1976 Act.

There are summary offences of operating, driving or plying for hire without the relevant licence.

Taxi and private hire licences (under the Town Police Clauses Act 1847 and the Local Government (Miscellaneous Provisions) Act 1976) remain in force for any time up to three years and must be produced on request to a police officer or authorised officer of the council (s. 53(3) of the Local Government (Miscellaneous Provisions) Act 1976). Failure to do so will not be an offence if it is produced within seven days.

A council may attach such conditions as it considers reasonably necessary to the licences it issues, including the markings and appearance of the vehicle (s. 47 of the Local Government (Miscellaneous Provisions) Act 1976). However, each of the many licensing provisions is open to an appeal process to a magistrates' court (see *R* v *Blackpool Borough Council, ex parte Red Cab Taxis Ltd* [1994] RTR 402).

If a vehicle is licensed as a hackney carriage in one district, it can also be licensed as a private hire vehicle in another district (*Kingston-upon-Hull City Council* v *Wilson, The Times*, 25 July 1995).

If a licensed hackney carriage gives the appearance of such it cannot be used without a current licence, even in a private capacity as a family motor car by the owner (*Darlington Borough Council* v *Thain* (23 November 1994, unreported)).

Licence plates are issued under s. 35 of the Local Government (Miscellaneous Provisions) Act 1976 and remain the property of the issuing council. Using or permitting the use of a private hire vehicle without displaying such a plate is a summary offence (s. 48).

### 13.7.3 Exemptions

The legislation allows for a number of exemptions to the licensing provisions (see s. 75 of the 1976 Act). These include the use of hire vehicles for funerals and weddings and for contractual hire periods of at least seven days. In such cases, the onus is on the defendant to establish that he/she falls within one of the exemptions (*Leeds City Council* v *Azam* [1989] RTR 66).

# CHAPTER FOURTEEN

# FIXED PENALTY SYSTEM

## 14.1 Introduction

Originally introduced by the Transport Act 1982 the fixed penalty system is intended to speed up the administrative procedure for the prosecution of certain road traffic offences. The process is initiated by serving a person with a fixed penalty notice, attaching such a notice to a stationary vehicle or through the 'conditional offer' system.

The main elements of the first two of these processes are set out briefly below. However reference should be made to the legislation itself for a full explanation of the procedure to be followed in each case. The 'conditional offer' is dealt with at the end of this chapter.

## 14.2 Extended Fixed Penalty System

The law governing the extended fixed penalty system is to be found under Part III of the Road Traffic Offenders Act 1988.

The 'fixed penalty' itself is determined by s. 53 which allows for the setting of the level of any penalty to be imposed under the system.

The purpose of the system is to avoid court hearings for the listed offences but, at the same time, to ensure that those committing them receive the appropriate punishment including the endorsement of their licence. The definition of a 'fixed penalty notice', under s. 52 sums up the essence of the system:

> *(1) 'A 'fixed penalty notice' means a notice offering the opportunity of the discharge of any liability to conviction of the offence to which the notice relates by payment of a fixed penalty . . .*

Where a fixed penalty offence (see below) has been committed, the system allows for a procedure other than prosecution to be followed during a specified period. This period, known as the 'suspended enforcement period' (s. 52(3)(a)), is at least 21 days following the date of the fixed penalty notice or such longer period as may be specified in it.

## 14.3 Fixed Penalty Offences

The offences to which the system applies are set out in sch. 3 to the Road Traffic Offenders Act 1988 (**see appendix 3**).

Section 51(2) of the 1988 Act, however, provides that an offence specified in the schedule is not a fixed penalty offence if it is committed by *causing* or *permitting* a vehicle to be used by another in contravention of any statutory provision, restriction or prohibition. Effectively this means that defendants reported for causing or permitting offences may not enjoy the administrative provisions made under the fixed penalty system.

Further offences may be added or removed from the system by s. 51(3).

The Road Traffic (Vehicle Emissions) (Fixed Penalty) Regulations 1997 (SI 1997 No. 3058), provide for certain specified local authorities to issue fixed penalty notices to vehicle users who contravene regs 61 and 98 of the Road Vehicles (Construction and Use) Regulations 1986 (**see chapter 9**) in relation to the emission of smoke and fumes.

## 14.4 Fixed Penalty Procedure

As mentioned above, the fixed penalty procedure envisages two situations; where the driver is present and where there is a stationary vehicle to which a notice can be fixed. Where the relevant offence is endorsable, the procedure makes provision for the submission by a driver of his/her licence. This is to allow the clerk at the relevant court to record the endorsement on the licence.

The procedure in each case has been briefly summarised in **appendix 9, diagrams 1 to 3**.

Proof of the service of fixed penalty notices by police officers is provided for under s. 79 of the 1988 Act.

### 14.4.1 Procedure Where Driver is Present

Section 54 of the Road Traffic Offenders Act 1988 provides that:

*(1) This section applies where in England and Wales on any occasion a constable in uniform has reason to believe that a person he finds is committing or has on that occasion committed a fixed penalty offence.*

*(2) Subject to subsection (3) below, the constable may give him a fixed penalty notice in respect of the offence.*

*(3) Where the offence appears to the constable to involve obligatory endorsement, the constable may only give him a fixed penalty notice under subsection (2) above in respect of the offence if—*

*(a) he produces his licence and its counterpart for inspection by the constable,*

*(b) the constable is satisfied, on inspecting the licence and its counterpart, that he would not be liable to be disqualified under section 35 of this Act if he were convicted of that offence, and*

*(c) he surrenders his licence and its counterpart to the constable to be retained and dealt with in accordance with this Part of this Act.*

*(4) Where—*

*(a) the offence appears to the constable to involve obligatory endorsement, and*

*(b) the person concerned does not produce his licence and its counterpart for inspection by the constable,*

*the constable may give him a notice stating that if, within seven days after the notice is given, he produces the notice together with his licence and its counterpart in person to a constable or authorised person at the police station specified in the notice (being a police station chosen by the person concerned) and the requirements of subsection (5)(a) and (b) below are met he will then be given a fixed penalty notice in respect of the offence.*

*(5) If a person to whom a notice has been given under subsection (4) above produces the notice together with his licence and its counterpart in person to a constable or authorised person at the police station specified in the notice within seven days after the notice was so given to him and the following requirements are met, that is—*

*(a) the constable or authorised person is satisfied, on inspecting the licence and its counterpart, that he would not be liable to be disqualified under section 35 of this Act if he were convicted of the offence, and*

*(b) he surrenders his licence and its counterpart to the constable or authorised person to be retained and dealt with in accordance with this Part of this Act,*

*the constable or authorised person must give him a fixed penalty notice in respect of the offence to which the notice under subsection (4) above relates.*

*(6) A notice under subsection (4) above shall give such particulars of the circumstances alleged to constitute the offence to which it relates as are necessary for giving reasonable information about the alleged offence.*

*(7) A licence and a counterpart of a licence surrendered in accordance with this section must be sent to the fixed penalty clerk.*

## Keynote

The constable must be in uniform in order to give the fixed penalty notice. If the offence is endorsable (**see appendix 9, diagram 2**) the notice can only be given if the person surrenders his/her licence and the penalty incurred will not take him/her up to 12 points or beyond.

If he/she does not produce his/her licence, the person may be issued with a notice to be produced, together with the licence, within seven days at a police station.

If a person surrenders his/her licence and a notice issued under s. 54(4) at the police station within seven days, he/she must be given a fixed penalty notice so long as the total number of points on the licence will not then reach 12 or more (s. 54(5)).

If the person has not paid the fixed penalty, or given notice requesting a court hearing (under s. 55(2)), by the end of the suspended enforcement period, the police can register a sum equal to 1.5 times the amount of the penalty for enforcement against that person (s. 55(3)). Where this happens, the justices' clerk for the area where the person lives will notify the person to that effect (s. 71(6)).

If a person receives such a notification he/she can serve a statutory declaration to the effect that either:

- he/she was not the person who was given the fixed penalty notice, or
- he/she has given notice requesting a court hearing under s. 55(2).

In either case he/she must make and serve this notice within 21 days of receiving the notification from the clerk.

Under the Functions of Traffic Wardens (Amendment) Order 1986 (SI 1986 No. 1328), traffic wardens may exercise the functions conferred upon constables by Part III of the 1988 Act for certain offences under the fixed penalty system.

### 14.4.2 Where the Driver is Not Present

Section 62 of the Road Traffic Offenders Act 1988 provides that:

*(1) Where on any occasion a constable has reason to believe in the case of any stationary vehicle that a fixed penalty offence is being or has on that occasion been committed in respect of it, he may fix a fixed penalty notice in respect of the offence to the vehicle unless the offence appears to him to involve obligatory endorsement.*

#### Keynote

Again a person may give notice during the suspended enforcement period, requesting a court hearing (s. 63(3)).

If no such notice has been given and the penalty has not been paid by the end of the suspended enforcement period, the police may serve a 'notice to owner' on the person who appears to be the owner of the vehicle (s. 63(2)).

If there is no response to the 'notice to owner', the police may register a sum equal to 1.5 times the amount of the penalty for enforcement against the person (s. 64(2)).

As in the above case where the person is present, the appropriate justices' clerk must notify the person that this has been done. The recipient can then make a statutory declaration (under sch. 4) to the effect that:

- he/she did not know of the fixed penalty notice until he/she received notification from the clerk, or
- he/she was not the owner of the vehicle at the time, or
- he/she gave notice requesting a court hearing.

If the person served with the 'notice to owner' was not in fact the owner he/she will not be liable if he/she can provide a statutory statement of ownership in relation to the vehicle (s. 64(4)).

#### Traffic Wardens

Under the Functions of Traffic Wardens (Amendment) Order 1986 (SI 1986 No. 1328), traffic wardens may exercise the functions conferred upon constables by Part III of the 1988 Act for certain offences under the fixed penalty system.

### 14.4.3 The Offences

**Offence — Making False Statements in Relation to Notice to Owner — Road Traffic Offenders Act 1988, s. 67**

*Triable summarily. Fine.*

***(No specific power of arrest)***

The Road Traffic Offenders Act 1988, s. 67 states:

*A person who, in response to a notice to owner, provides a statement which is false in a material particular and does so recklessly or knowing it to be false in that particular is guilty of an offence.*

#### Keynote

The statement made must be false in a 'material particular', that is, in relation to some matter which is directly relevant to the information required in the notice to owner.

For the meaning of 'recklessly' and 'knowing', see **Crime, chapter 1**.

**Offence — Removing or Interfering with Fixed Penalty Notice on Vehicle — Road Traffic Offenders Act 1988, s. 62(2)**

*Triable summarily. Fine.*

***(No specific power of arrest)***

The Road Traffic Offenders Act 1988, s. 62 states:

*(2) A person is guilty of an offence if he removes or interferes with any notice fixed to a vehicle under this section, unless he does so by or under the authority of the driver or person in charge of the vehicle or the person liable for the fixed penalty offence in question.*

**Keynote**

Clearly if the person removing the notice can show that he/she did so on behalf of the owner or person liable for the offence, he/she would not commit this offence.

Given the procedure set out in the 1988 Act, the removal of a notice would not impede the effect of the fixed penalty system; its service can be proved by the officer under s. 79 and the notification of registration by the justices' clerk allows a defendant time to contest the allegation of the particular offence.

## 14.5 Conditional Offers

The introduction of automatic devices for detecting speeding and traffic signal offences (by the Road Traffic Act 1991) created the need for a method of issuing fixed penalty notices where neither of the previous circumstances applied, namely the presence of the defendant or his/her vehicle. The result was the introduction of the 'conditional offer' system.

Section 75 of the Road Traffic Offenders Act 1988 provides that:

*(1) Where . . .*

*(a) a constable has reason to believe that a fixed penalty offence has been committed, and*

*(b) no fixed penalty notice in respect of the offence has been given under section 54 of this Act or fixed to a vehicle under section 62 of this Act,*

*a notice under this section may be sent to the alleged offender by or on behalf of the chief officer of police.*

*. . .*

*(6) Where a person issues [such a notice] he must notify the justices' clerk specified in it of its issue and its terms; . . .*

*(7) A conditional offer must—*

*(a) give such particulars of the circumstances alleged to constitute the offence to which it relates as are necessary for giving reasonable information about the alleged offence,*

*(b) state the amount of the fixed penalty for that offence, and*

*(c) state that proceedings against the alleged offender cannot be commenced in respect of that offence until the end of the period of twenty-eight days following the date on which the conditional offer was issued or such longer period as may be specified in the conditional offer.*

*(8) A conditional offer must indicate that if the following conditions are fulfilled, that is—*

*(a) within the period of twenty-eight days following the date on which the offer was issued, or such longer period as may be specified in the offer, the alleged offender—*

*(i) makes payment of the fixed penalty to the fixed penalty clerk, and*

*(ii) where the offence to which the offer relates is an offence involving obligatory endorsement, at the same time delivers his licence and its counterpart to that clerk, and*

*(b) where his licence and its counterpart are so delivered, that clerk is satisfied on inspecting them that, if the alleged offender were convicted of the offence, he would not be liable to be disqualified under section 35 of this Act,*

*any liability to conviction of the offence shall be discharged.*

**Keynote**

A conditional offer can be sent through the post but it can only be issued where the defendant has neither been served with a fixed penalty notice in person, nor had such a notice fixed to his/her vehicle.

The offer must state that, if payment is made and — where the offence is endorsable — the defendant's licence surrendered within the specified time, any liability to conviction for the offence(s) shall be discharged.

If the defendant fails to pay the fixed penalty and, where appropriate, surrender his/her licence, the police will be notified (s. 76(5)).

If the defendant is liable to disqualification, the payment and the licence will be returned and the police notified (s. 76(4)).

# CHAPTER FIFTEEN

# PEDAL CYCLES

## 15.1 Introduction

Although many provisions under road traffic legislation apply only to motor vehicles, there are a number of offences and restrictions which apply specifically to pedal cycles. Many offences have been drafted to include pedal cycles and, as mentioned in the introduction to **chapter 1**, it is important to check the exact definition of each offence or provision in every case.

For the offences of dangerous, careless and inconsiderate cycling on a road, **see chapter 2**.

This chapter sets out the more commonly-encountered legislation which applies particularly to pedal cycles.

## 15.2 Construction and Use

The Pedal Cycles (Construction and Use) Regulations 1983 (SI 1983 No. 1176) make provision for the construction and use of all pedal cycles including electrically assisted pedal cycles. The Regulations are treated as having been made under s. 81 of the Road Traffic Act 1988.

Breaches of the Regulations are an offence under s. 91 of the Road Traffic Offenders Act 1988.

### 15.2.1 Electrically Assisted Pedal Cycles

Electrically assisted pedal cycles are cycles which do not exceed 40kg kerbside weight (60kg if a tandem) and which have an electric motor that is incapable of propelling the cycle once it has reached a speed of 15 miles per hour. The best example of such a contraption is the Sinclair C5. These cycles are not motor vehicles for the purposes of the Road Traffic Act 1988 and the only qualification or authority to ride one on a road is that you are 14 years old or over (see s. 32 of the Road Traffic Act 1988.)

Electrically assisted pedal cycles must, under the 1983 Regulations, be fitted with a plate showing details about the cycle and its motor; they must have a battery which does not leak, a braking system as set out in the Regulations and a device to control the motor. All of these features must be in efficient working order.

### 15.2.2 Pedal Cycles

Other conventional pedal cycles are subject to some of the provisions of the 1983 Regulations.

All must have a braking system which complies with reg. 7 or 8 (reg. 6). That is, they must have at least one braking system unless they are fixed-wheel cycles or cycles temporarily used in Great Britain by a visitor.

Pedal cycles with a saddle height over 635mm made on or after 1 August 1984 are required to have:

- Two independent braking systems with one acting on the front wheel(s) and one on the rear if the cycle is a free wheel cycle.

- One braking system acting on the front wheel(s) if the cycle is a fixed-wheel cycle.

Cycles made before 1 August 1984 are categorised for the purposes of their brake systems by their wheel size, with those having wheels larger than 460mm in diameter requiring similar braking systems to those above.

A constable in uniform may test a pedal cycle to ensure conformity with these requirements:

- on a road; or
- if the cycle has been involved in an accident within 48 hours before the test, on any premises provided the owner of the premises consents (reg. 11).

**Selling or Supplying Unsound Pedal Cycle**

It is a summary offence, under s. 81(6) of the Road Traffic Act 1988 to sell or supply (or offer to do so), a pedal cycle in such a condition that use of it on a road would contravene the 1983 Regulations.

## 15.3 Riding a Pedal Cycle While Unfit

**Offence — Riding Cycle While Unfit — Road Traffic Act 1988, s. 30(1)**
*Triable summarily. Fine.*
***(No specific power of arrest)***

The Road Traffic Act 1988, s. 30 states:

> *(1) A person who, when riding a cycle on a road or other public place, is unfit to ride through drink or drugs (that is to say, is under the influence of drink or a drug to such an extent as to be incapable of having proper control of the cycle) is guilty of an offence.*

**Keynote**

There are no parallel provisions to those provided in respect of motorists for the requirement of a breath specimen.

There may be occasions where the person is wheeling, rather than 'riding' the cycle. In such cases the appropriate charge may be under s. 12 of the Licensing Act 1872, which creates an offence of 'being in charge of any carriage, horse or cattle on any public highway or other public place when drunk'. This offence — which carries a fine or one month's imprisonment — has been held to apply to cyclists (*Corkery* v *Carpenter* [1951] 1 KB 102). Although an ancient one, the offence is acknowledged in s. 5 of the Road Traffic Offenders Act 1988, which provides an exemption for people charged with other drink/drug related driving offences.

## 15.4 Cycle Racing

**Offence — Cycle Racing on Public Highway — Road Traffic Act 1988, s. 31(1)**

*Triable summarily. Fine.*

***(No specific power of arrest)***

The Road Traffic Act 1988, s. 31 states:

*(1) A person who promotes or takes part in a race or trial of speed on a public way between cycles is guilty of an offence, unless the race or trial—*
*(a) is authorised, and*
*(b) is conducted in accordance with any conditions imposed,*
*by or under regulations under this section.*

**Keynote**

'Public way' means a highway (s. 31(6)); **see chapter 1**.

Section 31(4) states:

*Without prejudice to any other powers exercisable in that behalf, the chief officer of police may give directions with respect to the movement of, or the route to be followed by, vehicular traffic during any period, being directions which it is necessary or expedient to give in relation to that period to prevent or mitigate—*
*(a) congestion or obstruction of traffic, or*
*(b) danger to or from traffic,*
*in consequence of the holding of a race or trial of speed authorised by or under regulations under this section.*

**Keynote**

If injury is caused to a person by a cyclist racing or driving 'furiously' the offence under s. 35 of the Offences Against the Person Act 1861 may apply (**see chapter 2**).

There is also a specific offence of driving on footways that applies to cycles under the Highways Act 1835, s. 72.

# CHAPTER SIXTEEN

# FORGERY AND FALSIFICATION OF DOCUMENTS

## 16.1 Introduction

Much of the law regulating road traffic depends on the production and examination of documents. This chapter deals with occasions where a defendant has, or uses false documentation. When dealing with such occasions, it is important to consider the overlapping legislation which deals with deception, forgery and fraud generally (**see Crime, chapter 13**).

## 16.2 The Offences

**Offence — Forgery of Documents — Road Traffic Act 1988, s. 173**
*Triable either way. Two years' imprisonment and/or a fine on indictment; fine summarily.*
***(No specific power of arrest)***

The Road Traffic Act 1988, s. 173 states:

> *(1) A person who, with intent to deceive—*
> *(a) forges, alters or uses a document or other thing to which this section applies, or*
> *(b) lends to, or allows to be used by, any other person a document or other thing to which this section applies, or*
> *(c) makes or has in his possession any document or other thing so closely resembling a document or other thing to which this section applies as to be calculated to deceive,*
> *is guilty of an offence.*

**Keynote**

'Forges' for this purpose means making a false document or other thing in order that it may be used as genuine (s. 173(3)).

In each of the circumstances set out in s. 173(1)(a) to (c) you must show an intention to deceive, making this a crime of 'specific intent' (**see Crime, chapter 1**).

## FORGERY AND FALSIFICATION OF DOCUMENTS

The documents to which these offences apply are set out in s. 173(2) and include:

- licences
- test certificates
- certificates of insurance
- certificates exempting the wearing of seat belts
- international road haulage permits
- goods vehicle plates.

'Calculated to deceive' (s. 173(1)(c)) means likely to deceive. Where a defendant produces a certificate of insurance issued under a policy which has since been cancelled, this offence may be made out (see *R* v *Cleghorn* [1938] 3 All ER 398).

Although the offences under s. 173 carry no specific power of arrest, the more general offences of forgery and possessing false instruments (**see Crime, chapter 13**) are *arrestable offences* and can be considered in such cases. See also the power of seizure below.

### Offences — False Statements and Withholding Information — Road Traffic Act 1988, s. 174

*Triable summarily. Fine.*

***(No specific power of arrest)***

The Road Traffic Act 1988, s. 174 states:

*(1) A person who knowingly makes a false statement for the purpose—*
*(a) of obtaining the grant of a licence under any Part of this Act to himself or any other person, or*
*(b) of preventing the grant of any such licence, or*
*(c) of procuring the imposition of a condition or limitation in relation to any such licence, or*
*(d) of securing the entry or retention of the name of any person in the register of approved instructors maintained under Part V of this Act, or*
*(dd) of obtaining the grant to any person of a certificate under section 133A of this Act, or*
*(e) of obtaining the grant of an international road haulage permit to himself or any other person,*
*is guilty of an offence.*
*(2) A person who, in supplying information or producing documents for the purposes either of sections 53 to 60 and 63 of this Act or of regulations made under sections 49 to 51, 61, 62 and 66(3) of this Act—*
*(a) makes a statement which he knows to be false in a material particular or recklessly makes a statement which is false in a material particular, or*
*(b) produces, provides, sends or otherwise makes use of a document which he knows to be false in a material particular or recklessly produces, provides, sends or otherwise makes use of a document which is false in a material particular,*
*is guilty of an offence.*
*(3) A person who—*
*(a) knowingly produces false evidence for the purposes of regulations under section 66(1) of this Act, or*
*(b) knowingly makes a false statement in a declaration required to be made by the regulations,*
*is guilty of an offence.*
*(4) A person who—*
*(a) wilfully makes a false entry in any record required to be made or kept by regulations under section 74 of this Act, or*
*(b) with intent to deceive, makes use of any such entry which he knows to be false,*
*is guilty of an offence.*
*(5) A person who makes a false statement or withholds any material information for the purpose of obtaining the issue—*

*(a) of a certificate of insurance or certificate of security under Part VI of this Act, or*
*(b) of any document issued under regulations made by the Secretary of State in pursuance of his power under section 165(2)(a) of this Act to prescribe evidence which may be produced in lieu of a certificate of insurance or a certificate of security,*
*is guilty of an offence.*

**Keynote**

There is no need to show that, in making the false statements above, the person actually gained anything or brought about the desired consequence (see e.g. *Jones* v *Meatyard* [1939] 1 All ER 140). For the interpretation of 'knowingly', 'recklessly', 'wilfully' etc., **see Crime, chapter 1**.

The offence under s. 174(4)(b) is an offence of specific intent (**see Crime, chapter 1**).

**Offence — Issue of False Documents — Road Traffic Act 1988, s. 175**
*Triable summarily. Fine.*
***(No specific power of arrest)***

The Road Traffic Act 1988, s. 175 states:

*If a person issues—*
*(a) any such document as is referred to in section 174(5)(a) or (b) of this Act, or*
*(b) a test certificate or certificate of conformity (within the meaning of Part II of this Act),*
*and the document or certificate so issued is to his knowledge false in a material particular, he is guilty of an offence.*

**Keynote**

In proving this offence you must show that the person issuing the documents knew that they were false (see *Ocean Accident etc. Co.* v *Cole* (1932) 96 JP 191).

Again it is useful to consider the offences of forgery in cases involving the issue of false documents.

Test certificates bearing a false stamp or ones which have been backdated are 'false in a material particular' (see *Murphy* v *Griffiths* [1967] 1 All ER 424).

### 16.2.1 Police Powers

Section 176 of the Road Traffic Act 1988 provides:

*(1) If a constable has reasonable cause to believe that a document produced to him—*
*(a) in pursuance of section 137 of this Act, or*
*(b) in pursuance of any of the preceding provisions of this Part of this Act, is a document in relation to which an offence has been committed under section 173, 174 or 175 or this Act or under section 115 of the Road Traffic Regulation Act 1984, he may seize the document.*
*(1A) Where a licence to drive or a counterpart of any such licence or of any Community licence may be seized by a constable under subsection (1) above, he may also seize the counterpart, the licence to drive or the Community licence (as the case may be) produced with it.*
*(2) When a document is seized under subsection (1) above, the person from whom it was taken shall, unless—*
*(a) the document has been previously returned to him, or*
*(b) he has been previously charged with an offence under any of those sections,*
*be summoned before a magistrates' court . . . to account for his possession of the document.*

*(3) . . .*

*(4) If a constable, an examiner appointed under section 66A of this Act has reasonable cause to believe that a document or plate carried on a motor vehicle or by the driver of the vehicle is a document or plate to which this subsection applies, he may seize it.*

*For the purposes of this subsection the power to seize includes power to detach from a vehicle.*

*(5) Subsection (4) above applies to a document or plate in relation to which an offence has been committed under sections 173, 174 or 175 of this Act in so far as they apply—*

*(a) to documents evidencing the appointment of examiners under section 66A of this Act, or*

*(b) to goods vehicle test certificates, plating certificates, certificates of conformity or Minister's approval certificates (within the meaning of Part II of this Act), or*

*(c) to plates containing plated particulars (within the meaning of that Part) or containing other particulars required to be marked on goods vehicles by sections 54 to 58 of this Act or regulations made under them, or*

*(d) to records required to be kept by virtue of section 74 of this Act, or*

*(e) to international road haulage permits.*

*(6) When a document or plate is seized under subsection (4) above, either the driver or owner of the vehicle shall, if the document or plate is still detained and neither of them has previously been charged with an offence in relation to the document or plate under section 173, 174 or 175 of this Act, be summoned before a magistrates' court . . . to account for his possession of, or the presence on the vehicle of, the document or plate.*

**Keynote**

This extensive power also allows (where appropriate) for the items to be detached from the vehicle (s. 176(4)). The power under subsection (4) is restricted to officers who are authorised vehicle examiners.

The references in subsection (1) to s. 137 of the Act and s. 115 of the Road Traffic Regulation Act 1984 relate to the registration of driving instructors and the misuse of parking documents respectively.

## 16.3 Other Offences Involving False Records and Forgery

**Offence — Forging or Altering Registration Documents —
Vehicle Excise and Registration Act 1994, ss. 44 and 45**

*Triable either way. Two years' imprisonment and/or a fine on indictment; fine summarily.*
**(*No specific power of arrest*)**

The Vehicle Excise and Registration Act 1994, ss. 44 and 45 state:

***44.**—(1) A person is guilty of an offence if he forges, fraudulently alters, fraudulently uses, fraudulently lends or fraudulently allows to be used by another person anything to which subsection (2) applies.*

*(2) This subsection applies to—*

*(a) a vehicle licence,*

*(b) a trade licence,*

*(c) a document in the form of a licence which is issued in pursuance of regulations under this Act in respect of a vehicle which is an exempt vehicle under paragraph 19 of Schedule 2,*

*(d) a registration mark,*

*(e) a registration document, and*

*(f) a trade plate (including a replacement trade plate).*

***45.**—(1) A person who in connection with—*

*(a) an application for a vehicle licence or a trade licence,*

*(b) a claim for a rebate under section 20, or*

*(c) an application for an allocation of registration marks,*

*makes a declaration which to his knowledge is either false or in any material respect misleading is guilty of an offence.*

*(2) A person who makes a declaration which—*

*(a) is required by regulations under this Act to be made in respect of a vehicle which is an exempt vehicle under paragraph 19 of Schedule 2, and*

*(b) to his knowledge is either false or in any material respect misleading, is guilty of an offence.*

*(2A) A person who makes a declaration or statement which—*

*(a) is required to be made in respect of a vehicle by regulations under section 22, and*

*(b) to his knowledge is either false or in any material respect misleading, is guilty of an offence.*

*(3) A person who—*

*(a) is required by [virtue of] this Act to furnish particulars relating to, or to the keeper of, a vehicle, and*

*(b) furnishes particulars which to his knowledge are either false or in any material respect misleading,*

*is guilty of an offence.*

*(3A) A person who, in supplying information or producing documents for the purposes of any regulations made under section 61A—*

*(a) makes a statement which to his knowledge is false or in any material respect misleading or recklessly makes a statement which is false or in any material respect misleading, or*

*(b) produces or otherwise makes use of a document which to his knowledge is false or in any material respect misleading,*

*is guilty of an offence.*

*(3B) A person who—*

*(a) with intent to deceive, forges, alters or uses a certificate issued by virtue of section 61A;*

*(b) knowing or believing that it will be used for deception lends such a certificate to another or allows another to alter or use it; or*

*(c) without reasonable excuse makes or has in his possession any document so closely resembling such a certificate as to be calculated to deceive,*

*is guilty of an offence.*

**Keynote**

'Fraudulently' means dishonestly deceiving someone who has a public duty to examine and enforce items covered by the 1988 Act (including a police officer) and there is no need to prove any intent to cause economic loss (see *R* v *Terry* [1984] AC 374).

For the law governing excise and registration of vehicles generally, **see chapter 12**.

## Offence — Forgery of Documents Relating to Public Service Vehicles — Public Passenger Vehicles Act 1981, s. 65(2)

*Triable either way. Two years' imprisonment on indictment; fine summarily.*

**(*No specific power of arrest*)**

The Public Passenger Vehicles Act 1981, s. 65 states:

*(1) This section applies to the following documents and other things, namely—*

*(a) a licence under Part II of this Act;*

*(b) a certificate of initial fitness under section 6 of this Act;*

*(c) a certificate under section 10 of this Act that a vehicle conforms to a type vehicle;*

*(d) an operator's disc under section 18 of this Act;*

*(e) a certificate under section 21 of this Act as to the repute, financial standing or professional competence of any person.*

*(2) A person who, with intent to deceive—*

*(a) forges or alters, or uses or lends to, or allows to be used by, any other person, a document or other thing to which this section applies, or*

*(b) makes or has in his possession any document or other thing so closely resembling a document or other thing to which this section applies as to be calculated to deceive,*

*shall be liable . . .*

**Keynote**

'Forges' means making a false document or other thing in order that it may be used as genuine (s. 65(3)).

The expression 'calculated to deceive' means likely to do so (**see para. 16.2**).

For the legislation governing PSVs generally, **see chapter 13**.

### Offence — Forgery or Alteration of Documents Relating to Goods Vehicle Operators — Goods Vehicles (Licensing of Operators) Act 1995, s. 38

*Triable either way. Two years' imprisonment and/or a fine on indictment; fine summarily.*
***(No specific power of arrest)***

*(1) A person is guilty of an offence if, with intent to deceive, he—*
*(a) forges, alters or uses a document or other thing to which this section applies;*
*(b) lends to, or allows to be used by, any other person a document or other thing to which this sections applies; or*
*(c) makes or has in his possession any document or other thing so closely resembling a document or other thing to which this section applies as to be calculated to deceive.*
*(2) This section applies to the following documents and other things, namely—*
*(a) any operator's licence;*
*(b) any document, plate, mark or other thing by which, in pursuance of regulations, a vehicle is to be identified as being authorised to be used, or as being used, under an operator's licence;*
*(c) any document evidencing the authorisation of any person for the purposes of sections 40 and 41;*
*(d) any certificate of qualification under section 49; and*
*(e) any certificate or diploma such as is mentioned in paragraph 13(1) of Schedule 3.*

**Keynote**

'Forges' means making a false document or other thing in order that it may be used as genuine (s. 38(4)).

This offence requires proof of an intent to deceive, making it a crime of 'specific intent' (**see Crime, chapter 1**).

Section 41 of the 1995 Act gives a power of seizure to police officers.

For the law governing goods vehicle operators generally, **see chapter 13**.

### Offence — Misuse of Parking Documents and Apparatus — Road Traffic Regulation Act 1984, s. 115

*Triable either way. Two years' imprisonment and/or a fine on indictment; fine summarily.*
***(No specific power of arrest)***

The Road Traffic Regulation Act 1984, s. 115 states:

*(1) A person shall be guilty of an offence who, with intent to deceive—*
*(a) uses, or lends to, or allows to be used by, any other person,—*
*(i) any parking device or apparatus designed to be used in connection with parking devices;*
*(ii) any ticket issued by a parking meter, parking device or apparatus designed to be used in connection with parking devices;*
*(iii) any authorisation by way of such a certificate, other means of identification or device as is referred to in any of sections 4(2), 4(3), 7(2) and 7(3) of this Act; or*

*(iv) any such permit or token as is referred to in section 46(2)(i) of this Act;*

*(b) makes or has in his possession anything so closely resembling any such thing as is mentioned in paragraph (a) above as to be calculated to deceive; . . .*

*(2) A person who knowingly makes a false statement for the purpose of procuring the grant or issue to himself or any other person of any such authorisation as is mentioned in subsection (1) above shall be guilty of an offence.*

**Keynote**

For the general offence of 'going equipped', **see Crime, chapter 12**.

This is an offence of 'specific intent', **see Crime, chapter 1**.

# APPENDIX ONE

# ROAD TRAFFIC ACT 1988, SECTION 101

(1) A person is disqualified for holding or obtaining a licence to drive a motor vehicle of a class specified in the following Table if he is under the age specified in relation to it in the second column of the Table.

TABLE

| Class of motor vehicle | Age (in years) |
|---|---|
| 1. Invalid carriage | 16 |
| 2. Moped | 16 |
| 3. Motor bicycle | 17 |
| 4. Agricultural or forestry tractor | 17 |
| 5. Small vehicle | 17 |
| 6. Medium-sized goods vehicle | 18 |
| 7. Other motor vehicle | 21 |

(2) The Secretary of State may by regulations provide that subsection (1) above shall have effect as if for the classes of vehicles and the ages specified in the Table in that subsection there were substituted different classes of vehicles and ages or different classes of vehicles or different ages.

(3) Subject to subsection (4) below, the regulations may—

(a) apply to persons of a class specified in or under the regulations,

(b) apply in circumstances so specified,

(c) impose conditions or create exemptions or provide for the imposition of conditions or the creation of exemptions,

(d) contain such transitional and supplemental provisions (including provisions amending section 108, 120 or 183(5) of this Act) as the Secretary of State considers necessary or expedient.

(4) For the purpose of defining the class of persons to whom, the class of vehicles to which, the circumstances in which or the conditions subject to which regulations made by virtue of subsection (2) above are to apply where an approved proved training scheme for drivers is in force, it is sufficient for the regulations to refer to a document which embodies the terms (or any of the terms) of the scheme or to a document which is in force in pursuance of the scheme.

(5) In subsection (4) above—

'approved' means approved for the time being by the Secretary of State for the purpose of the regulations,

'training scheme for drivers' means a scheme for training persons to drive vehicles of a class in relation to which the age which is in force under this section (but apart from any such scheme) is 21 years,

but no approved training scheme for drivers shall be amended without the approval of the Secretary of State.

# APPENDIX TWO

# ROAD TRAFFIC REGULATION ACT 1984, SCHEDULE 6

SCHEDULE 6 SPEED LIMITS FOR VEHICLES OF CERTAIN CLASSES

PART I VEHICLES FITTED WITH PNEUMATIC TYRES ON ALL WHEELS
(see application provisions below the following Table)

TABLE

| 1 | 2 | | | |
|---|---|---|---|---|
| Item No. | Class of Vehicle | Maximum speed (in miles per hour) while vehicle is being driven on: | | |
| | | (a) Motorway | (b) Dual carriageway road not being a motorway | (c) Other road |
| 1. | A passenger vehicle, motor caravan or dual-purpose vehicle not drawing a trailer being a vehicle with an unladen weight exceeding 3.05 tonnes or adapted to carry more than 8 passengers: | | | |
| | (i) if not exceeding 12 metres in overall length | 70 | 60 | 50 |
| | (ii) if exceeding 12 metres in overall length | 60 | 60 | 50 |
| 2. | An invalid carriage | not applicable | 20 | 20 |
| 3. | A passenger vehicle, motor caravan, car-derived van or dual-purpose vehicle drawing one trailer | 60 | 60 | 50 |
| 4. | A passenger vehicle, motor caravan, car-derived van or dual-purpose vehicle drawing more than one trailer | 40 | 20 | 20 |

TABLE (continued)

| 1<br>Item No. | 2<br>Class of Vehicle | Maximum speed (in miles per hour) while vehicle is being driven on: (a) Motorway | (b) Dual carriageway road not being a motorway | (c) Other road |
|---|---|---|---|---|
| 5. | (1) A goods vehicle having a maximum laden weight not exceeding 7.5 tonnes and which is not—<br>(a) an articulated vehicle, or<br>(b) drawing a trailer, or<br>(c) a car-derived van | 70 | 60 | 50 |
| | (2) A goods vehicle which is—<br>(a) (i) an articulated vehicle having a maximum laden weight not exceeding 7.5 tonnes, or (ii) a motor vehicle, other than a car-derived van, which is drawing one trailer where the aggregate maximum laden weight of the motor vehicle and the trailer does not exceed 7.5 tonnes | 60 | 60 | 50 |
| | (b) (i) an articulated vehicle having a maximum laden weight exceeding 7.5 tonnes, (ii) a motor vehicle having a maximum laden weight exceeding 7.5 tonnes and not drawing a trailer, or (iii) a motor vehicle drawing one trailer where the aggregate maximum laden weight of the motor vehicle and the trailer exceeds 7.5 tonnes | 60 | 50 | 40 |
| | (c) a motor vehicle, other than a car-derived van, drawing more than one trailer | 40 | 20 | 20 |
| 6. | A motor tractor (other than an industrial tractor), a light locomotive or a heavy locomotive—<br>(a) if the provisions about springs and wings as specified in paragraph 3 of Part IV of this Schedule are complied with, and the vehicle is not drawing a trailer, or if those provisions are complied with and the vehicle is drawing one trailer, which also complies with those provisions | 40 | 30 | 30 |
| | (b) in any other case | 20 | 20 | 20 |
| 7. | A works truck | 18 | 18 | 18 |
| 8. | An industrial tractor | not applicable | 18 | 18 |
| 9. | An agricultural motor vehicle | 40 | 40 | 40 |

Application

This Part applies only to motor vehicles, not being track-laying vehicles, every wheel of which is fitted with a pneumatic tyre and to such vehicles drawing one or more trailers, not being track-laying vehicles, every wheel of which is fitted with a pneumatic tyre.

# APPENDIX THREE

# SCHEDULES 2 AND 3 TO THE ROAD TRAFFIC OFFENDERS ACT 1988

## Schedule 2 of the Road Traffic Offenders Act 1988

### SCHEDULE 2
### PROSECUTION AND PUNISHMENT OF OFFENCES

### PART I
### OFFENCES UNDER THE TRAFFIC ACTS

| (1) Provision creating offence | (2) General nature of offence | (3) Mode of prosecution | (4) Punishment | (5) Disqualification | (6) Endorsement | (7) Penalty points |
|---|---|---|---|---|---|---|
| | | | *Offences under the Road Traffic Regulation Act 1984* | | | |
| RTRA section 5 | Contravention of traffic regulation order. | Summarily. | Level 3 on the standard scale. | | | |
| RTRA section 8 | Contravention of order regulating traffic in Greater London. | Summarily. | Level 3 on the standard scale. | | | |
| RTRA section 11 | Contravention of experimental traffic order. | Summarily. | Level 3 on the standard scale. | | | |
| RTRA section 13 | Contravention of experimental traffic scheme in Greater London. | Summarily. | Level 3 on the standard scale. | | | |
| RTRA section 16(1) | Contravention of temporary prohibition or restriction. | Summarily. | Level 3 on the standard scale. | Discretionary if committed in respect of a speed restriction. | Obligatory if committed in respect of a a speed restriction. | 3–6 or 3 (fixed penalty). |
| RTRA section 16C(1) | Contravention of prohibition or restriction relating to relevant event. | Summarily. | Level 3 on the standard scale. | | | |

| (1) Provision creating offence | (2) General nature of offence | (3) Mode of prosecution | (4) Punishment | (5) Disqualification | (6) Endorsement | (7) Penalty points |
|---|---|---|---|---|---|---|
| | | *Offences under the Road Traffic Regulation Act 1984* | | | | |
| RTRA section 17(4) | Use of special road contrary to scheme or regulations. | Summarily. | Level 4 on the standard scale. | Discretionary if committed in respect of a motor vehicle otherwise than by unlawfully stopping or allowing the vehicle to remain at rest on a part of a special road on which vehicles are in certain circumstances permitted to remain at rest. | Obligatory if committed as mentioned in the entry in column 5. | 3–6 or 3 (fixed penalty) if committed in respect of a speed restriction, 3 in any other case. |
| RTRA section 18(3) | One-way traffic on trunk road. | Summarily. | Level 3 on the standard scale. | | | |
| RTRA section 20(5) | Contravention of prohibition or restriction for roads of certain classes. | Summarily. | Level 3 on the standard scale. | | | |
| RTRA section 25(5) | Contravention of pedestrian crossing regulations. | Summarily. | Level 3 on the standard scale. | Discretionary if committed in respect of a motor vehicle. | Obligatory if committed in respect of a motor vehicle. | 3 |
| RTRA section 28(3) | Not stopping at school crossing. | Summarily. | Level 3 on the standard scale. | Discretionary if committed in respect of a motor vehicle. | Obligatory if committed in respect of a motor vehicle. | 3 |
| RTRA section 29(3) | Contravention of order relating to street playground. | Summarily. | Level 3 on the standard scale. | Discretionary if committed in respect of a motor vehicle. | Obligatory if committed in respect of a motor vehicle. | 2 |
| RTRA section 35A(1) | Contravention of order as to use of parking place. | Summarily. | (a) Level 3 on the standard scale in the case of an offence committed by a person in a street parking place reserved for disabled persons' vehicles or in an off-street parking place reserved for such vehicles, where that person would not have been guilty of that offence if the motor vehicle in respect of which it was committed had been a disabled person's vehicle. (b) Level 2 on the standard scale in any other case. | | | |
| RTRA section 35A(2) | Misuse of apparatus for collecting charges or of parking device or connected apparatus. | Summarily. | Level 3 on the standard scale. | | | |
| RTRA section 35A(5) | Plying for hire in parking place. | Summarily. | Level 2 on the standard scale. | | | |
| RTRA section 43(5) | Unauthorised disclosure of information in respect of licensed parking place. | Summarily. | Level 3 on the standard scale. | | | |

| (1) Provision creating offence | (2) General nature of offence | (3) Mode of prosecution | (4) Punishment | (5) Disqualification | (6) Endorsement | (7) Penalty points |
|---|---|---|---|---|---|---|
| | | *Offences under the Road Traffic Regulation Act 1984* | | | | |
| RTRA section 43(10) | Failure to comply with term or conditions of licence to operate parking place. | Summarily. | Level 3 on the standard scale. | | | |
| RTRA section 43(12) | Operation of public off-street parking place without licence. | Summarily. | Level 5 on the standard scale. | | | |
| RTRA section 47(1) | Contraventions relating to designated parking places. | Summarily. | (a) Level 3 on the standard scale in the case of an offence committed by a person in a street parking place reserved for disabled persons' vehicles where that person would not have been guilty of the offence if the motor vehicle in respect of which it was committed had been a disabled person's vehicle. (b) Level 2 in any other case. | | | |
| RTRA section 47(3) | Tampering with parking meter. | Summarily. | Level 3 on the standard scale. | | | |
| RTRA section 52(1) | Misuse of parking device. | Summarily. | Level 2 on the standard scale. | | | |
| RTRA section 53(5) | Contravention of certain provisions of designation orders. | Summarily. | Level 3 on the standard scale. | | | |
| RTRA section 53(6) | Other contraventions of designation orders. | Summarily. | Level 2 on the standard scale. | | | |
| RTRA section 61(5) | Unauthorised use of loading area. | Summarily. | Level 3 on the standard scale. | | | |
| RTRA section 88(7) | Contravention of minimum speed limit. | Summarily. | Level 3 on the standard scale. | | | |
| RTRA section 89(1) | Exceeding speed limit. | Summarily. | Level 3 on the standard scale. | Discretionary. | Obligatory. | 3–6 or 3 (fixed penalty). |
| RTRA section 104(5) | Interference with notice as to immobilisation device. | Summarily. | Level 2 on the standard scale. | | | |
| RTRA section 104(6) | Interference with immobilisation device. | Summarily. | Level 3 on the standard scale. | | | |
| RTRA section 105(5) | Misuse of disabled person's badge (immobilisation devices). | Summarily. | Level 3 on the standard scale. | | | |
| RTRA section 108(2) (or that subsection as modified by section 109(2) and (3)). | Non-compliance with notice (excess charge). | Summarily. | Level 3 on the standard scale. | | | |
| RTRA section 108(3) (or that subsection as modified by section 109(2) and (3)). | False response to notice (excess charge). | Summarily. | Level 5 on the standard scale. | | | |
| RTRA section 112(4) | Failure to give information as to identity of driver. | Summarily. | Level 3 on the standard scale. | | | |
| RTRA section 115(1) | Mishandling or faking parking documents. | (a) Summarily. (b) On indictment. | (a) The statutory maximum. (b) 2 years. | | | |

## SCHEDULES 2 AND 3 TO THE ROAD TRAFFIC OFFENDERS ACT 1988

| (1) Provision creating offence | (2) General nature of offence | (3) Mode of prosecution | (4) Punishment | (5) Disqualification | (6) Endorsement | (7) Penalty points |
|---|---|---|---|---|---|---|
| | | | *Offences under the Road Traffic Regulation Act 1984* | | | |
| RTRA section 115(2) | False statement for procuring authorisation. | Summarily. | Level 4 on the standard scale. | | | |
| RTRA section 116(1) | Non-delivery of suspect document or article. | Summarily. | Level 3 on the standard scale. | | | |
| RTRA section 117 | Wrongful use of disabled person's badge. | Summarily. | Level 3 on the standard scale. | | | |
| RTRA section 129(3) | Failure to give evidence at inquiry. | Summarily. | Level 3 on the standard scale. | | | |
| | | | *Offences under the Road Traffic Act 1988* | | | |
| RTA section 1 | Causing death by dangerous driving. | On indictment. | 10 years. | Obligatory. | Obligatory. | 3–11 |
| RTA section 2 | Dangerous Driving. | (a) Summarily.<br>(b) On indictment. | (a) 6 months or the statutory maximum or both.<br>(b) 2 years or a fine or both. | Obligatory. | Obligatory. | 3–11 |
| RTA section 3 | Careless, and inconsiderate, driving. | Summarily. | Level 4 on the standard scale. | Discretionary. | Obligatory. | 3–9 |
| RTA section 3A | Causing death by careless driving when under influence of drink or drugs. | On indictment. | 10 years or a fine or both. | Obligatory. | Obligatory. | 3–11 |
| RTA section 4(1) | Driving or attempting to drive when unfit to drive through drink or drugs. | Summarily. | 6 months or level 5 on the standard scale or both. | Obligatory. | Obligatory. | 3–11 |
| RTA section 4(2) | Being in charge of a mechanically propelled vehicle when unfit to drive through drink or drugs. | Summarily. | 3 months or level 4 on the standard scale or both. | Discretionary. | Obligatory. | 10 |
| RTA section 5(1)(a) | Driving or attempting to drive with excess alcohol in breath, blood or urine. | Summarily. | 6 months or level 5 on the standard scale or both. | Obligatory. | Obligatory. | 3–11 |
| RTA section 5(1)(b) | Being in charge of a motor vehicle with excess alcohol in breath, blood or urine. | Summarily. | 3 months or level 4 on the standard scale or both. | Discretionary. | Obligatory. | 10 |
| RTA section 6 | Failing to provide a specimen of breath for a breath test. | Summarily. | Level 3 on the standard scale. | Discretionary. | Obligatory. | 4 |
| RTA section 7 | Failing to provide specimen for analysis or laboratory test. | Summarily. | (a) Where the specimen was required to ascertain ability to drive or proportion of alcohol at the time offender was driving or attempting to drive, 6 months or level 5 on the standard scale or both.<br>(b) In any other case, 3 months or level 4 on the standard scale or both. | (a) Obligatory in case mentioned in column 4(a).<br>(b) Discretionary in any other case. | Obligatory. | (a) 3–11 in case mentioned in column 4(a).<br>(b) 10 in any other case. |
| RTA section 12 | Motor racing and speed trials on public ways. | Summarily. | Level 4 on the standard scale. | Obligatory. | Obligatory. | 3–11 |
| RTA section 13 | Other unauthorised or irregular competitions or trials on public ways. | Summarily. | Level 3 on the standard scale. | | | |
| RTA section 14 | Driving or riding in a motor vehicle in contravention of regulations requiring wearing of seat belts. | Summarily. | Level 2 on the standard scale. | | | |

# SCHEDULES 2 AND 3 TO THE ROAD TRAFFIC OFFENDERS ACT 1988

| (1) Provision creating offence | (2) General nature of offence | (3) Mode of prosecution | (4) Punishment | (5) Disqualification | (6) Endorsement | (7) Penalty points |
|---|---|---|---|---|---|---|
| | | | *Offences under the Road Traffic Act 1988* | | | |
| RTA section 15(2) | Driving motor vehicle with child not wearing seat belt. | Summarily. | Level 2 on the standard scale. | | | |
| RTA section 15A(3) or (4) | Selling etc. in certain circumstances equipment as conducive to the safety of children in motor vehicles. | Summarily. | Level 3 on the standard scale. | | | |
| RTA section 16 | Driving or riding motor cycles in contravention of regulations requiring wearing of protective headgear. | Summarily. | Level 2 on the standard scale. | | | |
| RTA section 17 | Selling, etc., helmet not of the prescribed type as helmet for affording protection for motor cyclists. | Summarily. | Level 3 on the standard scale. | | | |
| RTA section 18(3) | Contravention of regulations with respect to use of head-worn appliances on motor cycles. | Summarily. | Level 2 on the standard scale. | | | |
| RTA section 18(4) | Selling, etc., appliance not of prescribed type as approved for use on motor cycles. | Summarily. | Level 3 on the standard scale. | | | |
| RTA section 19 | Prohibition of parking of heavy commercial vehicles on verges, etc. | Summarily. | Level 3 on the standard scale. | | | |
| RTA section 21 | Driving or parking on cycle track. | Summarily. | Level 3 on the standard scale. | | | |
| RTA section 22 | Leaving vehicles in dangerous positions. | Summarily. | Level 3 on the standard scale. | Discretionary if committed in respect of a motor vehicle. | Obligatory if committed in respect of a motor vehicle. | 3 |
| RTA section 22A | Causing danger to road users. | (a) Summarily.<br>(b) On indictment. | (a) 6 months or the statutory maximum or both.<br>(b) 7 years or a fine or both. | | | |
| RTA section 23 | Carrying passenger on motor-cycle contrary to section 23. | Summarily. | Level 3 on the standard scale. | Discretionary. | Obligatory. | 3 |
| RTA section 24 | Carrying passenger on bicycle contrary to section 24. | Summarily. | Level 1 on the standard scale. | | | |
| RTA section 25 | Tampering with motor vehicles. | Summarily. | Level 3 on the standard scale. | | | |
| RTA section 26 | Holding or getting on to vehicle, etc., in order to be towed or carried. | Summarily. | Level 1 on the standard scale. | | | |
| RTA section 27 | Dogs on designated roads without being held on lead. | Summarily. | Level 1 on the standard scale. | | | |
| RTA section 28 | Dangerous cycling. | Summarily. | Level 4 on the standard scale. | | | |
| RTA section 29 | Careless, and inconsiderate, cycling. | Summarily. | Level 3 on the standard scale. | | | |
| RTA section 30 | Cycling when unfit through drink or drugs. | Summarily. | Level 3 on the standard scale. | | | |
| RTA section 31 | Unauthorised or irregular cycle racing or trials of speed on public ways. | Summarily. | Level 1 on the standard scale. | | | |
| RTA section 32 | Contravening prohibition on persons under 14 driving electrically assisted pedal cycles. | Summarily. | Level 2 on the standard scale. | | | |
| RTA section 33 | Unauthorised motor vehicle trial on footpaths or bridleways. | Summarily. | Level 3 on the standard scale. | | | |

| (1) Provision creating offence | (2) General nature of offence | (3) Mode of prosecution | (4) Punishment | (5) Disqualification | (6) Endorsement | (7) Penalty points |
|---|---|---|---|---|---|---|
| | | | *Offences under the Road Traffic Act 1988* | | | |
| RTA section 34 | Driving motor vehicles elsewhere than on roads. | Summarily. | Level 3 on the standard scale. | | | |
| RTA section 35 | Failing to comply with traffic directions. | Summarily. | Level 3 on the standard scale. | Discretionary, if committed in respect of a motor vehicle by failure to comply with a direction of a constable or traffic warden. | Obligatory if committed as described in column 5. | 3 |
| RTA section 36 | Failing to comply with traffic signs. | Summarily. | Level 3 on the standard scale. | Discretionary, if committed in respect of a motor vehicle by failure to comply with an indication given by a sign specified for the purposes of this paragraph in regulations under RTA section 36. | Obligatory if committted as described in column 5. | 3 |
| RTA section 37 | Pedestrian failing to stop when directed by constable regulating traffic. | Summarily. | Level 3 on the standard scale. | | | |
| RTA section 40A | Using vehicle in dangerous condition etc. | Summarily. | (a) Level 5 on the standard scale if committed in respect of a goods vehicle or a vehicle adapted to carry more than eight passengers.<br>(b) Level 4 on the standard scale in any other case. | Discretionary. | Obligatory. | 3 |
| RTA section 41A | Breach of requirement as to brakes, steering-gear or tyres. | Summarily. | (a) Level 5 on the standard scale if committed in respect of a goods vehicle or a vehicle adapted to carry more than eight passengers.<br>(b) Level 4 on the standard scale in any other case. | Discretionary. | Obligatory. | 3 |
| RTA section 41B | Breach of requirement as to weight: goods and passenger vehicles. | Summarily. | Level 5 on the standard scale. | | | |
| RTA section 42 | Breach of other construction and use requirements. | Summarily. | (a) Level 4 on the standard scale if committed in respect of a goods vehicle or a vehicle adapted to carry more than eight passengers.<br>(b) Level 3 on the standard scale in any other case. | | | |

| (1) Provision creating offence | (2) General nature of offence | (3) Mode of prosecution | (4) Punishment | (5) Disqualification | (6) Endorsement | (7) Penalty points |
|---|---|---|---|---|---|---|
| | | | *Offences under the Road Traffic Act 1988* | | | |
| RTA section 47 | Using, etc., vehicle without required test certificate being in force. | Summarily. | (a) Level 4 on the standard scale in the case of a vehicle adapted to carry more than eight passengers. (b) Level 3 on the standard scale in any other case. | | | |
| Regulations under RTA section 49 made by virtue of section 51(2) | Contravention of requirement of regulations (which is declared by regulations to be an offence) that driver of goods vehicle being tested be present throughout test or drive, etc., vehicle as and when directed. | Summarily. | Level 3 on the standard scale. | | | |
| RTA section 53(1) | Using, etc., goods vehicle without required plating certificate being in force. | Summarily. | Level 3 on the standard scale. | | | |
| RTA section 53(2) | Using, etc., goods vehicle without required goods vehicle test certificate being in force. | Summarily. | Level 4 on the standard scale. | | | |
| RTA section 53(3) | Using, etc., goods vehicle where Secretary of State is required by regulations under section 49 to be notified of an alteration to the vehicle or its equipment but has not been notified. | Summarily. | Level 3 on the standard scale. | | | |
| Regulations under RTA section 61 made by virtue of subsection (4) | Contravention of requirement of regulations (which is declared by regulations to be an offence) that driver of goods vehicle being tested after notifiable alteration be present throughout test and drive, etc., vehicle as and when directed. | Summarily. | Level 3 on the standard scale. | | | |
| RTA section 63(1) | Using, etc., goods vehicle without required certificate being in force showing that it complies with type approval requirements applicable to it. | Summarily. | Level 4 on the standard scale. | | | |
| RTA section 63(2) | Using, etc., certain goods vehicles for drawing trailer when plating certificate does not specify maximum laden weight for vehicle and trailer. | Summarily. | Level 3 on the standard scale. | | | |
| RTA section 63(3) | Using, etc., goods vehicle where Secretary of State is required to be notified under section 59 of alteration to it or its equipment but has not been notified. | Summarily. | Level 3 on the standard scale. | | | |

| (1) Provision creating offence | (2) General nature of offence | (3) Mode of prosecution | (4) Punishment | (5) Disqualification | (6) Endorsement | (7) Penalty points |
|---|---|---|---|---|---|---|
| | | *Offences under the Road Traffic Act 1988* | | | | |
| RTA section 64 | Using goods vehicle with unauthorised weights as well as authorised weights marked on it. | Summarily. | Level 3 on the standard scale. | | | |
| RTA section 64A | Failure to hold EC certificate of conformity for unregistered light passenger vehicle. | Summarily. | Level 3 on the standard scale. | | | |
| RTA section 65 | Supplying vehicle or vehicle part without required certificate being in force showing that it complies with type approval requirements applicable to it. | Summarily. | Level 5 on the standard scale. | | | |
| RTA section 65A | Light passenger vehicles not to be sold without EC certificate of conformity. | Summarily. | Level 5 on the standard scale. | | | |
| RTA section 67 | Obstructing testing of vehicle by examiner on road or failing to comply with requirements of RTA section 67 or schedule 2. | Summarily. | Level 3 on the standard scale. | | | |
| RTA section 67A (including application by section 67B(4)) | Failure of owner of apparently defective vehicle to give required certificate or declaration or failure of person in charge of vehicle being tested to give information. | Summarily. | Level 3 on the standard scale. | | | |
| RTA section 67B | Obstructing further testing of vehicle of Secretary of State's officer or failing to comply with requirements of RTA section 67B or paragraph 3 or 4 of Schedule 2. | Summarily. | Level 3 on the standard scale. | | | |
| RTA section 68 | Obstructing inspection, etc., of vehicle by examiner or failing to comply with requirement to take vehicle for inspection. | Summarily. | Level 3 on the standard scale. | | | |
| RTA section 71 | Driving, etc., vehicle in contravention of prohibition on driving it as being unfit for service, or refusing, neglecting or otherwise failing to comply with direction to remove a vehicle found overloaded. | Summarily. | Level 5 on the standard scale. | | | |
| RTA section 74 | Contravention of regulations requiring goods vehicle operator to inspect, and keep records of inspection of, goods vehicles. | Summarily. | Level 3 on the standard scale. | | | |
| RTA section 75 | Selling, etc., unroadworthy vehicle or trailer or altering vehicle or trailer so as to make it unroadworthy. | Summarily. | Level 5 on the standard scale. | | | |

| (1) Provision creating offence | (2) General nature of offence | (3) Mode of prosecution | (4) Punishment | (5) Disqualification | (6) Endorsement | (7) Penalty points |
|---|---|---|---|---|---|---|
| | | | *Offences under the Road Traffic Act 1988* | | | |
| RTA section 76(1) | Fitting of defective or unsuitable vehicle parts. | Summarily. | Level 5 on the standard scale. | | | |
| RTA section 76(3) | Supplying defective or unsuitable vehicle parts. | Summarily. | Level 4 on the standard scale. | | | |
| RTA section 76(8) | Obstructing examiner testing vehicles to ascertain whether defective or unsuitable part has been fitted, etc. | Summarily. | Level 3 on the standard scale. | | | |
| RTA section 77 | Obstructing examiner testing condition of used vehicle at sale rooms, etc. | Summarily. | Level 3 on the standard scale. | | | |
| RTA section 78 | Failing to comply with requirement about weighing motor vehicle or obstructing authorised person. | Summarily. | Level 5 on the standard scale. | | | |
| RTA section 81 | Selling, etc., pedal cycle in contravention of regulations as to brakes, bells, etc. | Summarily. | Level 3 on the standard scale. | | | |
| RTA section 83 | Selling, etc., wrongly made tail lamps or reflectors. | Summarily. | Level 5 on the standard scale. | | | |
| RTA section 87(1) | Driving otherwise than in accordance with a licence. | Summarily. | Level 3 on the standard scale. | Discretionary in a case where the offender's driving would not have been in accordance with any licence that could have been granted to him. | Obligatory in the case mentioned in column 5. | 3–6 |
| RTA section 87(2) | Causing or permitting a person to drive otherwise than in accordance with a licence. | Summarily. | Level 3 on the standard scale. | | | |
| RTA section 92(7C) | Failure to deliver licence revoked by virtue of section 92(7A) and counterpart to Secretary of State. | Summarily. | Level 3 on the standard scale. | | | |
| RTA section 92(10) | Driving after making false declaration as to physical fitness. | Summarily. | Level 4 on the standard scale. | Discretionary. | Obligatory. | 3–6 |
| RTA section 93(3) | Failure to deliver revoked licence and counterpart to Secretary of State. | Summarily. | Level 3 on the standard scale. | | | |
| RTA section 94(3) and that subsection as applied by RTA section 99D | Failure to notify Secretary of State of onset of, or deterioration in, relevant or prospective disability. | Summarily. | Level 3 on the standard scale. | | | |
| RTA section 94(3A) and that subsection as applied by RTA section 99D(b) | Driving after such a failure. | Summarily. | Level 3 on the standard scale. | Discretionary. | Obligatory. | 3–6 |
| RTA section 94A | Driving after refusal of licence under section 92(3), revocation under section 93 or service of a notice under section 99C. | Summarily. | 6 months or level 5 on the standard scale or both. | Discretionary. | Obligatory. | 3–6 |
| RTA section 96 | Driving with uncorrected defective eyesight, or refusing to submit to test of eyesight. | Summarily. | Level 3 on the standard scale. | Discretionary. | Obligatory. | 3 |

| (1) Provision creating offence | (2) General nature of offence | (3) Mode of prosecution | (4) Punishment | (5) Disqualification | (6) Endorsement | (7) Penalty points |
|---|---|---|---|---|---|---|
| | | *Offences under the Road Traffic Act 1988* | | | | |
| RTA section 99(5) | Driving licence holder failing, to surrender licence and counterpart. | Summarily. | Level 3 on the standard scale. | | | |
| RTA section 99B(11) | Driving after failure to comply with a requirement under section 99B(6), (7) or (10). | Summarily. | Level 3 on the standard scale. | | | |
| RTA section 99C(4) | Failure to deliver Community licence to Secretary of State when required by notice under section 99C. | Summarily. | Level 3 on the standard scale. | | | |
| RTA section 103(1)(a) | Obtaining driving licence while disqualified. | Summarily. | Level 3 on the standard scale. | | | |
| RTA section 103(1)(b) | Driving while disqualified. | (a) Summarily, in England and Wales.<br>(b) Summarily, in Scotland.<br>(c) On indictment, in Scotland. | (a) 6 months or level 5 on the standard scale or both.<br>(b) 6 months or the statutory maximum or both.<br>(c) 12 months or a fine or both. | Discretionary. | Obligatory. | 6 |
| RTA section 109 | Failing to produce to court Northern Ireland driving licence and its counterpart. | Summarily. | Level 3 on the standard scale. | | | |
| RTA section 114 | Failing to comply with conditions of LGV, PCV licence or LGV Community licence, or causing or permitting person under 21 to drive LGV or PCV in contravention of such conditions. | Summarily. | Level 3 on the standard scale. | | | |
| RTA section 115A(4) | Failure to deliver LGV or PCV Community licence when required by notice under section 115A. | Summarily. | Level 3 on the standard scale. | | | |
| RTA section 118 | Failing to surrender revoked or suspended LGV or PCV licence and counterpart. | Summarily. | Level 3 on the standard scale. | | | |
| Regulations made by virtue of RTA section 120(5) | Contravention of provision of regulations (which is declared by regulations to be an offence) about LGV or PCV drivers' licences or LGV or PCV Community licence. | Summarily. | Level 3 on the standard scale. | | | |
| RTA section 123(4) | Giving of paid driving instruction by unregistered and unlicensed persons or their employers. | Summarily. | Level 4 on the standard scale. | | | |

| (1) Provision creating offence | (2) General nature of offence | (3) Mode of prosecution | (4) Punishment | (5) Disqualification | (6) Endorsement | (7) Penalty points |
|---|---|---|---|---|---|---|
| | | *Offences under the Road Traffic Act 1988* | | | | |
| RTA section 123(6) | Giving of paid instruction without there being exhibited on the motor car a certificate of registration or a licence under RTA part V. | Summarily. | Level 3 on the standard scale. | | | |
| RTA section 125A(4) | Failure, on application for registration as disabled driving instructor, to notify Registrar of onset of, or deterioration in, relevant or prospective disability. | Summarily. | Level 3 on the standard scale. | | | |
| RTA section 133C(4) | Failure by registered or licensed disabled driving instructor to notify Registrar of onset of, or deterioration in, relevant or prospective disability. | Summarily. | Level 3 on the standard scale. | | | |
| RTA section 133D | Giving of paid driving instruction by disabled persons or their employers without emergency control certificate or in unauthorised motor car. | Summarily. | Level 3 on the standard scale. | | | |
| RTA section 135 | Unregistered instructor using title or displaying badge, etc., prescribed for registered instructor, or employer using such title, etc., in relation to his unregistered instructor or issuing misleading advertisement, etc. | Summarily. | Level 4 on the standard scale. | | | |
| RTA section 136 | Failure of instructor to surrender to Registrar certificate or licence. | Summarily. | Level 3 on the standard scale. | | | |
| RTA section 137 | Failing to produce certificate of registration or licence as driving instructor. | Summarily. | Level 3 on the standard scale. | | | |
| RTA section 143 | Using motor vehicle while uninsured or unsecured against third-party risks. | Summarily. | Level 5 on the standard scale. | Discretionary. | Obligatory. | 6–8 |
| RTA section 147 | Failing to surrender certificate of insurance or security to insurer on cancellation or to make statutory declaration of loss or destruction. | Summarily. | Level 3 on the standard scale. | | | |
| RTA section 154 | Failing to give information, or wilfully making a false statement, as to insurance or security when claim made. | Summarily. | Level 4 on the standard scale. | | | |
| RTA section 163 | Failing to stop motor vehicle or cycle when required by constable. | Summarily. | Level 3 on the standard scale. | | | |

| (1) Provision creating offence | (2) General nature of offence | (3) Mode of prosecution | (4) Punishment | (5) Disqualification | (6) Endorsement | (7) Penalty points |
|---|---|---|---|---|---|---|
| | | *Offences under the Road Traffic Act 1988* | | | | |
| RTA section 164 | Failing to produce driving licence and its counterpart or to state date of birth, or failing to provide the Secretary of State with evidence of date of birth, etc. | Summarily. | Level 3 on the standard scale. | | | |
| RTA section 165 | Failing to give certain names and addresses or to produce certain documents. | Summarily. | Level 3 on the standard scale. | | | |
| RTA section 168 | Refusing to give, or giving false, name and address in case of reckless, careless or inconsiderate driving or cycling. | Summarily. | Level 3 on the standard scale. | | | |
| RTA section 169 | Pedestrian failing to give constable his name and address after failing to stop when directed by constable controlling traffic. | Summarily. | Level 1 on the standard scale. | | | |
| RTA section 170(4) | Failing to stop after accident and give particulars or report accident. | Summarily. | Six months or level 5 on the standard scale or both. | Discretionary. | Obligatory. | 5–10 |
| RTA section 170(7) | Failure by driver, in case of accident involving injury to another, to produce evidence of insurance or security or to report accident. | Summarily. | Level 3 on the standard scale. | | | |
| RTA section 171 | Failure by owner of motor vehicle to give police information for verifying compliance with requirement of compulsory insurance or security. | Summarily. | Level 4 on the standard scale. | | | |
| RTA section 172 | Failure of person keeping vehicle and others to give police information as to identity of driver, etc., in the case of certain offences. | Summarily. | Level 3 on the standard scale. | Discretionary if committed otherwise than than by virtue of subsection (5) or (11). | Obligatory if committed otherwise than than by virtue of subsection (5) or (11). | 3 |
| RTA section 173 | Forgery, etc., of licences, counterparts of Community licences, certificates of insurance and other documents and things. | (a) Summarily. | (a) The statutory maximum. | | | |
| | | (b) On indictment. | (b) 2 years. | | | |
| RTA section 174 | Making certain false statements, etc., and withholding certain material information. | Summarily. | Level 4 on the standard scale. | | | |
| RTA section 175(1) | Issuing false documents. | Summarily. | Level 4 on the standard scale. | | | |
| RTA section 175(2) | Falsely amending certificate of conformity. | Summarily. | Level 4 on the standard scale. | | | |
| RTA section 177 | Impersonation of, or of person employed by, authorised examiner. | Summarily. | Level 3 on the standard scale. | | | |
| RTA section 178 | [Scotland.] | | | | | |
| RTA section 180 | Failing to attend, give evidence or produce documents to, inquiry held by Secretary of State, etc. | Summarily. | Level 3 on the standard scale. | | | |
| RTA section 181 | Obstructing inspection of vehicles after accident. | Summarily. | Level 3 on the standard scale. | | | |

# SCHEDULES 2 AND 3 TO THE ROAD TRAFFIC OFFENDERS ACT 1988

| (1) Provision creating offence | (2) General nature of offence | (3) Mode of prosecution | (4) Punishment | (5) Disqualification | (6) Endorsement | (7) Penalty points |
|---|---|---|---|---|---|---|
| | *Offences under the Road Traffic Act 1988* | | | | | |
| RTA schedule 1 paragraph 6 | Applying warranty to equipment, protective helmet, appliance or information in defending proceedings under RTA section 15A, 17 or 18(4) where no warranty given, or applying false warranty. | Summarily. | Level 3 on the standard scale. | | | |
| Section 25 of this Act. | Failing to give information as to date of birth or sex to court or to provide Secretary of State with evidence of date of birth, etc. | Summarily. | Level 3 on the standard scale. | | | |
| Section 26 of this Act. | Failing to produce driving licence and its counterpart to court making order for interim disqualification | Summarily. | Level 3 on the standard scale. | | | |
| Section 27 of this Act. | Failing to produce licence and its counterpart to court for endorsement on conviction of offence involving obligatory endorsement or on committal for sentence, etc., for offence involving obligatory or discretionary disqualification when no interim disqualification ordered. | Summarily. | Level 3 on the standard scale. | | | |
| Section 62 of this Act. | Removing fixed penalty notice fixed to vehicle. | Summarily. | Level 2 on the standard scale. | | | |
| Section 67 of this Act. | False statement in response to notice to owner. | Summarily. | Level 5 on the standard scale. | | | |
| | *Offences under the Road Traffic (Driver Licensing and Information Systems) Act 1989* | | | | | |
| RTA 1989 section 1(5) | Failure of holder of existing HGV or PSV driver's licence to surrender it upon revocation or surrender of his existing licence under part III of RTA. | Summarily. | Level 3 on the standard scale. | | | |
| RTA 1989 schedule 1, para. 3 | Failing to comply with conditions of existing HGV driver's licence, or causing or permitting a person under 21 to drive HGV in contravention of such conditions. | Summarily. | Level 3 on the standard scale. | | | |
| RTA 1989 schedule 1, para. 8(2) | Contravention of provision of regulations (which is declared by regulations to be an offence) about existing HGV or PSV drivers' licences. | Summarily. | Level 3 on the standard scale. | | | |
| RTA 1989 schedule 1, para. 10(4) | Taking PSV test before applying for licence or within prescribed period afterwards. | Summarily. | Level 3 on the standard scale. | | | |

| (1) Provision creating offence | (2) General nature of offence | (3) Mode of prosecution | (4) Punishment | (5) Disqualification | (6) Endorsement | (7) Penalty points |
|---|---|---|---|---|---|---|
| | *Offences under the Road Traffic (Driver Licensing and Information System) Act 1989* | | | | | |
| RTA 1989 schedule 1, para. 10(5) | Taking PSV test after refusal of a licence. | Summarily. | Level 3 on the standard scale. | | | |

## PART II
## OTHER OFFENCES

| (1) Offence | (2) Disqualification | (3) Endorsement | (4) Penalty points |
|---|---|---|---|
| Manslaughter or, in Scotland, culpable homicide by the driver of a motor vehicle. | Obligatory. | Obligatory. | 3–11 |
| An offence under section 12A of the Theft Act 1968 (aggravated vehicle-taking). | Obligatory. | Obligatory. | 3–11 |
| Stealing or attempting to steal a motor vehicle. | Discretionary. | | |
| An offence or attempt to commit an offence in respect of a motor vehicle under section 12 of the Theft Act 1968 (taking conveyance without consent of owner etc. or, knowing it has been so taken, driving it or allowing oneself to be carried in it). | Discretionary. | | |
| An offence under section 25 of the Theft Act 1968 (going equipped for stealing, etc.) committed with reference to the theft or taking of motor vehicles. | Discretionary. | | |

## Schedule 3 of the Road Traffic Offenders Act 1988

### SCHEDULE 3
### FIXED PENALTY OFFENCES

| (1) Provision creating offence | (2) General nature of offence |
|---|---|
| | *Offence under the Greater London Council (General Powers) Act 1974* |
| Section 15 of the Greater London Council (General Powers) Act 1974. | Parking vehicles on footways, verges, etc. |
| | *Offence under the Highways Act 1980* |
| Section 137 of the Highways Act 1980. | Obstructing a highway, but only where the offence is committed in respect of a vehicle. |
| | *Offences under the Road Traffic Regulation Act 1984* |
| RTRA section 5(1) | Using a vehicle in contravention of a traffic regulation order outside Greater London. |
| RTRA section 8(1) | Breach of traffic regulation order in Greater London. |
| RTRA section 11 | Breach of experimental traffic order. |
| RTRA section 13 | Breach of experimental traffic scheme regulations in Greater London. |
| RTRA section 16(1) | Using a vehicle in contravention of temporary prohibition or restriction of traffic in case of execution of works, etc. |
| RTRA section 17(4) | Wrongful use of special road. |
| RTRA section 18(3) | Using a vehicle in contravention of provision for one-way traffic on trunk road. |
| RTRA section 20(5) | Driving a vehicle in contravention of order prohibiting or restricting driving vehicles on certain classes of roads. |

| (1) Provision creating offence | (2) General nature of offence |
|---|---|
| | *Offences under the Road Traffic Regulations Act 1984 — continued* |
| RTRA section 25(5) | Breach of pedestrian crossing regulations, except an offence in respect of a moving motor vehicle other than a contravention of regulation 8 of the 'Zebra' Pedestrian Crossings Regulations 1971 or of regulations 16 or 17 of the 'Pelican' Crossings Regulations and General Directions 1987. [These regulations have been revoked and replaced by the Zebra, Pelican and Puffin Pedestrian Crossings Regulations and General Directions 1997 (**see para. 8.9**) but no specific amendment to sch. 3 has been made.] |
| RTRA section 29(3) | Using a vehicle in contravention of a street playground order. |
| RTRA section 35A(1) | Breach of an order regulating the use, etc., of a parking place provided by a local authority, but only where the offence is committed in relation to a parking place provided on a road. |
| RTRA section 47(1) | Breach of a provision of a parking place designation order and other offences committed in relation to a parking place designated by such an order, except any offence of failing to pay an excess charge within the meaning of section 46. |
| RTRA section 53(5) | Using vehicle in contravention of any provision of a parking place designation order having effect by virtue of section 53(1)(a) (inclusion of certain traffic regulation provisions). |
| RTRA section 53(6) | Breach of a provision of a parking place designation order having effect by virtue of section 53(1)(b) (use of any part of a road for parking without charge). |
| RTRA section 88(7) | Driving a motor vehicle in contravention of an order imposing a minimum speed limit under section 88(1)(b). |
| RTRA section 89(1) | Speeding offences under RTRA and other Acts. |
| | *Offences under the Road Traffic Act 1988* |
| RTA section 14 | Breach of regulations requiring wearing of seat belts. |
| RTA section 15(2) | Breach of restriction on carrying children in the front of vehicles. |
| RTA section 15(4) | Breach of restriction on carrying children in the rear of vehicles. |
| RTA section 16 | Breach of regulations relating to protective headgear for motor cycle drivers and passengers. |
| RTA section 19 | Parking a heavy commercial vehicle on verge or footway. |
| RTA section 22 | Leaving vehicle in dangerous position. |
| RTA section 23 | Unlawful carrying of passengers on motor cycles. |
| RTA section 34 | Driving motor vehicle elsewhere than on a road. |
| RTA section 35 | Failure to comply with traffic directions. |
| RTA section 36 | Failure to comply with traffic signs. |
| RTA section 40A | Using vehicle in dangerous condition etc. |
| RTA section 41A | Breach of requirement as to brakes, steering-gear or tyres. |
| RTA section 41B | Breach of requirement as to weight: goods and passenger vehicles. |
| RTA section 42 | Breach of other construction and use requirements. |
| RTA section 87(1) | Driving vehicle otherwise than in accordance with requisite licence. |
| RTA section 163 | Failure to stop vehicle on being so required by constable in uniform. |
| | *Offences under the Vehicle Excise and Registration Act 1994* |
| Section 33 of the Vehicle Excise and Registration Act 1994. | Using or keeping a vehicle on a public road without licence being exhibited in manner prescribed by regulations. |
| Section 42 of that Act. | Driving or keeping a vehicle without required registration mark. |
| Section 43 of that Act. | Driving or keeping a vehicle with registration mark obscured etc. |

# APPENDIX FOUR

# CPS DRIVING OFFENCES CHARGING STANDARD

## INDEX



## DRIVING OFFENCES CHARGING STANDARD
## AGREED BY THE POLICE AND CROWN PROSECUTION SERVICE

### 1 Charging Standard — Purpose

1.1 The purpose of joint charging standards is to make sure that the most appropriate charge is selected, in the light of the evidence which can be proved, at the earliest possible opportunity. This will help the police and Crown Prosecutors in preparing the case. Adoption of this joint standard should lead to a reduction in the number of times charges have to be amended which in turn should lead to an increase in efficiency and a reduction in avoidable extra work for the police and the Crown Prosecution Service.

1.2 This joint charging standard offers guidance to police officers who have responsibility for charging and to Crown Prosecutors on the most appropriate charge to be preferred in cases relating to driving offences. The guidance:

- **should not be used** in the determination of any **pre-charge** decision, such as the decision to arrest;
- **does not** override any guidance issued on the use of appropriate alternative forms of disposal **short of charge**, such as cautioning;
- **does not** override the principles set out in the Code for Crown Prosecutors;
- **does not** override the need for consideration to be given in every case as to whether a charge/prosecution is in the public interest;

- **does not** remove the need for each case to be considered on its individual merits or fetter the discretion of the police to charge and the CPS to prosecute the most appropriate offence depending on the particular facts of the case in question.

## 2 Introduction

2.1 The purpose of road traffic legislation is to promote road safety and to protect the public. The principal driving offences are contained in the Road Traffic Act 1988 ('RTA 1988'). This joint standard gives guidance about the charge which should be preferred if the criteria set out in the Code for Crown Prosecutors are met.

2.2 This standard covers the following offences:

- careless driving or inconsiderate driving — section 3 RTA 1988;
- dangerous driving — section 2 RTA 1988;
- causing death by careless driving when under the influence of drink or drugs — section 3A RTA 1988;
- causing death by dangerous driving — section 1 RTA 1988;
- manslaughter — contrary to common law;
- causing bodily harm by wanton or furious driving, etc. — section 35 of the Offences Against the Person Act 1861.

## 3 General Principles: Charging Practice

3.1 You should always have in mind the following general principles when selecting the appropriate charge(s):

(i) the charge(s) should accurately reflect the extent of the defendant's alleged involvement and responsibility thereby allowing the courts the discretion to sentence appropriately;
(ii) the choice of charges should ensure the clear and simple presentation of the case particularly where there is more than one defendant;
(iii) it is wrong to encourage a defendant to plead guilty to a few charges by selecting more charges than are necessary;
(iv) it is wrong to select a more serious charge which is not supported by the evidence in order to encourage a plea of guilty to a lesser allegation.

## 4 General comments about driving offences

4.1 The manner of the driving must be considered objectively. In practice, the difference between the two types of bad driving will depend on the degree to which the driving falls below the minimum acceptable standard. If the manner of the driving is **below** that which is expected, the appropriate charge will be careless driving; if the manner of the driving is **far below** that which is expected, the appropriate charge will be dangerous driving. There is no statutory guidance about what behaviour constitutes a manner of driving which is 'below' and 'far below' the required standard.

4.2 The purpose of this charging standard is to make sure that once a decision to prosecute has been taken, police officers and prosecutors select the most appropriate charge where there is a choice of two or more charges. The following factors are not relevant when deciding whether an act of driving is careless or dangerous:

- the injury or death of one or more persons involved in a road traffic accident, except where Parliament has made specific provision for the death to be reflected in the charge. Importantly, injury or death does not, by itself, turn an accident into careless driving or turn careless driving into dangerous driving;
- the age or experience of the driver;
- the commission of other driving offences at the same time (such as driving whilst disqualified or driving without a certificate of insurance or a driving licence);
- the fact that the defendant has previous convictions for road traffic offences;
- the disability of a driver caused by mental illness or by physical injury or illness, except where the disability adversely affected the manner of the driving.

4.3 There is no clear cut dividing line between acts of careless driving and acts of dangerous driving. True momentary inattention will not usually have very serious adverse effects and therefore does not usually warrant criminal proceedings. Something more than momentary inattention (which may have minimal or serious results) is generally careless driving. Substantial/gross/total inattention (which may have minimal or serious results) is generally dangerous driving, even though it may take place over a period of a few seconds. The factual examples set out in this standard are merely indicative of the sort of behaviour which may merit prosecution under either section 2 or section 3 RTA 1988.

4.4 It is important to put the facts of the case in context. Although the test is objective, the manner of the driving must be seen in the context of the circumstances in which the driving took place. Behaviour which may not be criminal in certain conditions may merit proceedings in other conditions, for example, a safe lane change in slow moving traffic may become unsafe on a motorway where speeds are faster, there is less time to react and the consequences of any accident are likely to be more serious. Similarly, behaviour which might merit proceedings under section 3 in certain conditions may merit a prosecution under section 2, for example, if there is poor visibility; increased volume of traffic; adverse weather conditions; or difficult geography, such as blind corners.

### Driving in emergency situations

4.5 When a member of the emergency services commits an offence while responding to an emergency call discretion should be used in deciding whether or not a prosecution is needed. Generally, a prosecution is unlikely to be appropriate in cases of genuine emergency unless the driving is dangerous or indicates a high degree of blameworthiness. For example, a prosecution of a driver who caused a minor accident while responding to an urgent, life threatening, emergency may not be appropriate; but a prosecution may be appropriate when a serious accident is caused by an over-enthusiastic driver responding to a less urgent emergency call in which life is not threatened. In each case it is necessary to weigh all the circumstances of the case, particularly the nature of the emergency known to, or reasonably perceived by, the driver and the nature of the driving.

4.6 There will be cases when persons who are not members of the emergency services drive in an emergency situation. Examples include doctors who receive an urgent call for assistance and a driver taking a sick child to hospital. As with members of the emergency services, all the circumstances of the case must be weighed, particularly the nature of the emergency known to, or reasonably perceived by, the driver and the nature of the driving.

### Driving and alcohol/drugs

4.7 The road traffic legislation treats the consumption of alcohol and drugs alike. The following principles apply to driving affected by the consumption of alcohol or drugs, though the case law, and the following paragraphs, focus on alcohol.

4.8 Assessing the relevance of the consumption of alcohol is a difficult area. The leading authority is *R* v *Woodward (Terence)* [1995] 1 WLR 375 (Court of Appeal). The following general principles come from that case:

- the mere fact that the driver has had drink is not of itself relevant to or admissible on the question of whether his driving is careless or dangerous;
- for such evidence to be admissible, it must tend to show that the amount of drink taken is such as would adversely affect a reasonable driver, or alternatively, that the accused was in fact adversely affected.

4.9 In practice, however, there will need to be some further evidence to show that the manner of the driving fell below or far below that which is to be expected in order to justify proceedings under section 3 or section 2 respectively.

## 5 Careless driving — section 3 RTA 1988

5.1 The offence of driving without due care and attention is committed when the driving falls below the standard expected of a reasonable, prudent and competent driver in all the circumstances of the case. It is a summary only offence carrying a level 4 fine (£2,500), discretionary disqualification for any period and/or until a driving test has been passed. The court must endorse the driver's licence with 3–9 penalty points unless there are special reasons not to do so.

5.2 The test of whether the standard of driving has fallen below the required standard is an objective one. It applies both when the manner of driving in question is deliberate and when the manner of driving occurs as a result of an error of judgement or simply as a result of incompetence or inexperience.

5.3 Section 38(7) RTA 1988 states that failure on the part of a person to observe a provision of the Highway Code shall not of itself render that person liable to criminal proceedings, but a failure, particularly a serious one, may constitute evidence of careless or dangerous driving.

5.4 In general, prosecution for careless driving will be appropriate when the manner of the driving demonstrates a serious miscalculation or a disregard for road safety, taking into account all the circumstances including road, traffic and/or weather conditions.

5.5 There will be rare occasions where an accident occurs and yet there is no evidence of any mechanical defect, illness of the driver or other explanation to account for why the accident happened. In these cases, a charge of careless driving may be appropriate. The prosecution can provide evidence to the court about the accident on the basis that in the absence of any explanation — such as the ones identified above — it is inevitable that the defendant must have been driving below the standard expected of a reasonable, prudent and competent driver, since otherwise the accident would not have happened.

5.6 The following are examples of driving which may support an allegation of careless driving:

1 acts of driving caused by more than momentary inattention and where the safety of road users is affected, such as:

- overtaking on the inside;
- driving inappropriately close to another vehicle;
- driving through a red light;
- emerging from a side road into the path of another vehicle;
- turning into a minor road and colliding with a pedestrian.

2 conduct which clearly caused the driver not to be in a position to respond in the event of an emergency on the road, for example:

- using a hand held mobile telephone while the vehicle is moving, especially when at speed;
- tuning a car radio;
- reading a newspaper/map;
- selecting and lighting a cigarette/cigar/pipe;
- talking to and looking at a passenger which causes the driver more than momentary inattention;
- leg and/or arm in plaster;
- fatigue/nodding off.

The above examples explain the driver's conduct rather than demonstrate a course of driving which necessarily falls below the objective standard of the driving itself. For example, they may explain why the driver veered across carriageways, passed through a red light or otherwise caused a danger to other road users. In these cases, it is necessary to go beyond the explanation for the driving and consider whether the particular facts of the case warrant a charge of careless or dangerous driving. The reason for the driver's behaviour is not relevant to the choice of charge: it is the acts of driving which determine whether the driver has fallen below (careless driving) or far below (dangerous driving) the standard required.

These examples are placed here because usually when this conduct occurs the appropriate charge will be section 3. But police officers and prosecutors must always consider the manner of the driving in the context of the other facts in the case to decide the most appropriate way forward.

5.7 In deciding whether a charge of careless driving is appropriate, you will want to consider whether the act of driving concerned was the result of either momentary inattention or an isolated misjudgment, or something more serious. A moment's inattention which causes the manner of the driving to fall below the objective standard required of the reasonable, prudent and competent driver need not, of itself, lead to a prosecution. It is acts caused by more than momentary inattention — especially where the manner of the driving adversely affects the safety of other road users — which will normally result in a charge of careless driving.

5.8 In cases where there has been an accident and the evidence suggests that more than one driver may have been at fault, it will be necessary to establish that there is independent evidence against each driver before charging any individual driver, or that the facts speak so strongly for themselves in relation to any individual driver that the only conclusion possible to draw is that he departed from what a reasonable, prudent and competent driver would have done in the circumstances.

5.9 The public interest in favour of a prosecution is proportionate to the degree of blameworthiness: the greater the blameworthiness, the greater the public interest in favour of prosecuting. In addition, the public interest will favour prosecuting in cases when the court may wish to make an order under section 36 of the Road Traffic Offenders Act 1988, disqualifying the driver until he passes a driving test; or where it appears that the court ought to notify the Secretary of State that the driver may be suffering from any relevant disability within the meaning of section 22 Road Traffic Offenders Act 1988.

5.10 However, the public interest does not call for a prosecution in every case where there is a realistic prospect of conviction for careless driving: prosecution for an act of slight carelessness is unlikely to have a deterrent effect; and it is not the function of the prosecution to conduct proceedings merely to settle questions of liability for the benefit of insurance companies.

5.11 The public interest will tend to be against a prosecution for careless driving where:

- the incident is of a type such as frequently occurs at parking places, roundabouts, junctions or in traffic queues, involving minimal carelessness such as momentary inattention or a minor error of judgement;
- only the person at fault suffered injury and damage, if any, was mainly restricted to the vehicle or property owned by that person.

5.12 In addition, there is often an overlap between careless driving and some other offences such as driving with excess alcohol, regulatory offences, offences of strict liability, or offences under the Road Vehicles (Construction and Use) Regulations 1986. The merits of many individual cases can be adequately met by charging the specific statutory or regulatory offence which Parliament made available, subject to paragraphs 5.13 and 5.14 below.

5.13 Sometimes, there will be evidence of a course of conduct which involves the commission of a number of different statutory or regulatory offences, or the commission of the same statutory or regulatory offence on a number of occasions which are very close in time with one another. For example, a driver may drive through a red traffic light, ignore a pelican crossing and fail to give way at a junction within what might reasonably be described as the same course of driving. Alternatively, a driver may drive through two or more sets of red traffic lights, one after the other, within what may reasonably be described as the same course of driving.

5.14 In these situations, it is not appropriate simply to charge a number of individual statutory or regulatory offences: the court needs to be made aware of the link between what might otherwise appear as isolated incidents, when in reality they form part of a more serious course of bad driving. This course of bad driving should be reflected in a more serious charge. Where this type of situation arises, the manner of the driving has, in reality, fallen far below that expected of a competent and careful driver because of the driver's systematic failure to pay heed to the relevant traffic directions. Accordingly, consideration should be given to prosecuting the driver under section 2 of the Act: see paragraph 7.

## 6 Driving without reasonable consideration — section 3 RTA 1988

6.1 The offence of driving without reasonable consideration is committed when a vehicle is driven on a road or other public place as a result of which other persons using the road or place are inconvenienced. It is a summary only offence carrying a level 4 fine (£2,500), discretionary disqualification for any period and/or until a driving test has been passed. The court must endorse the driver's licence with 3–9 penalty points unless there are special reasons not to do so.

6.2 The accused must be shown:

- to have fallen below the standard of a reasonable, prudent and competent driver in the circumstances of the case; **and**
- to have done so without reasonable consideration for others.

6.3 The difference between the two offences under section 3 is that in cases of careless driving the prosecution need not show that any other person was inconvenienced. In cases of inconsiderate driving, there must be evidence that some other user of the road or public place was inconvenienced.

6.4 An allegation of inconsiderate driving is appropriate when the driving amounts to a clear act of selfishness, impatience or aggressiveness. There must, however, also be some inconvenience to other road users, for example, forcing other drivers to move over and/or brake as a consequence. Examples of conduct appropriate for a charge of driving without reasonable consideration are:

- flashing of lights to force other drivers in front to give way;
- misuse of any lane to avoid queuing or gain some other advantage over other drivers;
- unnecessarily remaining in an overtaking lane;
- unnecessarily slow driving or braking without good cause;
- driving with undipped headlights which dazzle oncoming drivers;
- driving through a puddle causing pedestrians to be splashed.

6.5 A person who drives without reasonable consideration for other road users can be convicted of driving without due care and attention although the reverse does not apply.

## 7 Dangerous Driving — section 2 of the Act

7.1 A person drives dangerously when:

- the way he drives falls **far below** what would be expected of a competent and careful driver; **and**
- it would be obvious to a competent and careful driver that driving in that way would be dangerous.

7.2 Both parts of the definition must be satisfied for the driving to be 'dangerous' within the Act. Dangerous driving is an either way offence. In the magistrates' courts the maximum penalty is a level 5 fine (£5,000), and/or six months imprisonment; in the Crown Court, the maximum penalty is 2 years imprisonment and/or an unlimited fine. In both instances, the court must disqualify the driver from driving for at least one year and must endorse the driver's licence with 3–11 penalty points unless in either case there are special reasons not to do so.

7.3 The test of whether a driver has fallen far below the required standard is an objective one. It applies both when the manner of driving in question is deliberate and when the manner of driving occurs as a result of an error of judgement or simply as a result of incompetence or inexperience.

7.4 There is no statutory definition of what is meant by 'far below', but 'dangerous' must refer to danger either of injury to any person or of serious damage to property: s2A(3) of the Act. Additionally, s.2A(2) of the Act provides that a person is to be regarded as driving dangerously if it would be obvious to a competent and careful driver that driving the vehicle in its current state would be dangerous. When considering the 'state' of the vehicle, regard may be had to anything attached to or carried by the vehicle: section 2A(4) of the Act. Therefore, you must consider whether the vehicle should have been driven at all, as well as how it was driven.

7.5 The standard of driving must be objectively assessed. It is not necessary to consider what the driver thought about the possible consequences of his actions. What must be considered is whether or not a competent and careful driver would have observed, appreciated and guarded against obvious and material dangers.

7.6 In deciding whether a charge of dangerous driving is appropriate, you will want to consider whether the act of driving concerned was undertaken deliberately and/or repeatedly. Although the test of dangerousness is an objective one, deliberate or repeated disregard, for example, of traffic directions (be they 'stop' or 'give way' signs or traffic lights) may be evidence that the manner of the accused's driving has fallen far below the standard required, thereby making a charge of dangerous driving appropriate.

7.7 In addition, the following are examples of driving which may support an allegation of dangerous driving:

- racing or competitive driving;
- prolonged, persistent or deliberate bad driving;
- speed which is highly inappropriate for the prevailing road or traffic conditions;
- aggressive or intimidatory driving, such as sudden lane changes, cutting into a line of vehicles or driving much too close to the vehicle in front, especially when the purpose is to cause the other vehicle to pull to one side to allow the accused to overtake;
- disregard of traffic lights and other road signs, which, on an objective analysis, would appear to be deliberate;
- failure to pay proper attention, amounting to something significantly more than a momentary lapse;
- overtaking which could not have been carried out with safety;
- driving a vehicle with a load which presents a danger to other road users.

**8 Causing death by careless driving when under the influence of drink or drugs — section 3A RTA 1988**

8.1 This offence is committed when:

- the driving was without due care and attention or without reasonable consideration for other road users; **and**
- the driving has caused the death of another person; **and**
- the driver is either unfit through drink or drugs, or the alcohol concentration is over the prescribed limit, or there has been a failure to provide a specimen in pursuance of the RTA 1988.

8.2 It is an offence triable only on indictment and carries a maximum penalty of 10 years imprisonment and/or an unlimited fine and an obligatory disqualification for at least 2 years (3 years if there is a previous relevant conviction). The driver's licence must be endorsed with 3–11 penalty points.

8.3 The examples given in paragraph 5 of careless driving apply to this offence; in the context of section 3A, less serious examples of careless driving (which may not of themselves require a prosecution under section 3 alone) may also merit proceedings under section 3A.

8.4 The accused's driving must have been a cause of the death but need not be the sole one.

8.5 Proper procedures have to have been adopted in the requesting and/or obtaining of any sample of breath, blood or urine. In cases where the procedures are flawed, there is a risk that the evidence may be excluded. Where this is possible, careful consideration must be given to whether the remaining evidence will support an alternative allegation of causing death by careless driving while unfit to drive through drink/drugs, in which case, evidence other than that from an intoximeter machine can be relied upon to demonstrate the defendant's unfitness to drive.

8.6 It is not necessary to add a further charge relating to drink/driving when the defendant is charged with a section 3A offence, because a guilty verdict to the relevant drink/drive offence can be returned by the jury under the statutory provisions: see paragraph 14.

**9 Causing death by dangerous driving — section 1 RTA 1988**

9.1 This offence is committed when:

- the driving of the accused was a cause of the death of another person **and**
- the driving was dangerous within the meaning of section 2A of the Act (see paragraph 7.3 of this standard).

9.2 The offence is triable only on indictment and carries a maximum penalty of 10 years imprisonment and/or an unlimited fine with an obligatory disqualification for a minimum of 2 years. The driver's licence must be endorsed with 3–11 penalty points.

9.3 The accused's driving must have been a cause of the death but need not be the sole one.

9.4 The examples given in paragraph 7 of dangerous driving apply to this offence.

9.5 Where a section 1 offence can be proved and there is sufficient evidence of a section 4, 5 or 7 offence, the appropriate summary offence should be charged and adjourned sine die pending the outcome of the section 1 offence — these offences cannot be committed to the Crown Court under section 41(1) Criminal Justice Act 1988. If the defendant is convicted of the section 1 offence, the court will often make it clear that the sentence imposed reflects the element of drink/driving, in which case the summary offence should not subsequently be pursued. Where the defendant is acquitted of the section 1 offence (or is convicted but it is clear the court has not taken the element of drink/driving into account) prosecutors should consider re-activating the drink/drive offence.

**10 Relationship between section 1 and section 3A RTA 1988**

10.1 Offences under section 1 and section 3A carry the same maximum penalty, so the choice of charge will not inhibit the court's sentencing powers. The courts have made it clear that for sentencing purposes the two offences are to be regarded on an equal basis. (*Attorney General's Reference (No. 49 of 1994) R* v *Brown* [1995] Crim LR 437; *R* v *Locke* [1995] Crim LR 438.)

10.2 The court will sentence an offender in proportion to his criminality. The consumption of alcohol is an aggravating feature increasing the criminality of the offender and therefore the sentence passed. The consumption of alcohol is an aggravating feature within the definition of section 3A. The consumption of alcohol is not part of the definition of section 1 but may be treated as an aggravating feature in appropriate cases.

10.3 Where a section 1 offence can be proved, it should be charged. However, you may on occasions have to decide which is the more appropriate charge: section 1 or section 3A. This will almost always occur when the manner of the driving is on the borderline between careless and dangerous. The prosecution is likely to be put to election if the two offences are charged in the alternative. In borderline cases, section 3A should be chosen provided all the other elements of that offence can be proved. The prospects of a conviction will be greater and the court's sentencing power remains unaffected.

### 11 Manslaughter — contrary to common law

11.1 Manslaughter is committed when the driver, in breach of a duty of care, is criminally negligent and causes the death of the victim.

11.2 The offence is triable only on indictment and carries a maximum sentence of life imprisonment and/or an unlimited fine. The driver must be disqualified for at least two years and there is a compulsory re-test. The driver's licence must be endorsed with 3–11 penalty points.

11.3 The driver must be shown to have been in breach of a duty of care towards the person who died. The ordinary principles of the law of negligence apply to ascertain whether there is such a duty. There is a general duty of care on all persons not to do acts imperilling the lives of others. To show a breach of a duty of care will require proof that the driving:

- fell far below the minimum acceptable standard of driving; **and**
- involved a risk of death; **and**
- was so bad in all the circumstances as, in the opinion of the jury, to amount to a crime: *R* v *Adomako* [1994] 3 All ER 79.

11.4 The examples of driving which fall far below the minimum acceptable standard of driving set out in paragraph 7.7 apply here as well.

11.5 This charge will very rarely be appropriate in road traffic fatality cases because of the existence of the statutory offences.

11.6 Manslaughter should be considered when a vehicle has been used as an instrument of attack (but where the necessary intent for murder is absent) or to cause fright and death results.

11.7 Manslaughter should also be considered where the driving has occurred other than on a road or other public place, or when the vehicle driven was not mechanically propelled, and death has been caused. In these cases the statutory offences do not apply.

### 12 Causing bodily harm by wanton and furious driving — section 35 Offences Against the Person Act 1861

12.1 It is an offence for any person in charge of a vehicle:

- to cause or cause to be done bodily harm to any person; by
- wanton or furious driving, or other wilful misconduct, or by wilful neglect.

12.2 It is a offence triable only on indictment and carries a maximum penalty of a 2 years imprisonment and/or an unlimited fine.

12.3 This offence should be used rarely as it does not carry endorsement or disqualification. It should normally only be used on those occasions when it is not possible to prosecute for an offence under the road traffic legislation, for example:

- when the driving was not on a road or other public place;
- when the vehicle used is not a mechanically propelled vehicle within the RTA 1988;
- when the statutory notice of intended prosecution is a prerequisite to a prosecution and has not been given.

12.4 This offence is useful in cases when a victim suffers serious injury though there has been no direct contact between the victim and the vehicle. For example, when the driving caused the victim to take avoiding action and as a result of which sustained serious injury by, say, falling down a ditch.

12.5 When a vehicle has been deliberately used as a weapon and has caused injury, alternative charges of dangerous driving under s. 2 of the Act or s. 18 Offences Against the Person Act 1861 should be considered if all the elements of those offences can be proved.

13 **Road Traffic Fatality Cases: 'Nearest and Dearest'**

13.1 In addition to the public interest considerations set out in the Code for Crown Prosecutors, special considerations apply to cases when there is a family or other close personal relationship between the deceased and the accused driver. These are often referred to as 'nearest and dearest' cases. The considerations are unlikely to be relevant in any case where the evidence would support proceedings for manslaughter.

13.2 In each case, the particular circumstances and the nature of the relationship will have to be considered. The closer the relationship between the deceased and the accused driver, the more likely it will be that the guidance which follows will apply.

13.3 In cases of causing death by dangerous driving involving the death of a 'nearest and dearest', where there is evidence to suggest an aggravating feature which imperils other road users or that the accused is a continuing danger to other road users, the proper course will be to prosecute for dangerous driving (section 2). The focus of the case will then be imperilling of other road users.

13.4 Additionally, if the accused drove in such a way as to show serious disregard for the lives of the 'nearest and dearest' or other road users, notwithstanding that a 'nearest and dearest' has been killed, proceedings for causing death by dangerous driving should be considered.

13.5 However, in cases of causing death by dangerous driving involving the death of a 'nearest and dearest', where there is **no** evidence either of an aggravating feature imperilling other road users nor that the accused is a continuing danger to other road users, the proper course is not to prosecute.

13.6 In cases of causing death by careless driving while under the influence of drink etc. involving the death of a 'nearest and dearest', the proper course will be to prosecute for careless driving and the appropriate drink/driving offence.

13.7 In cases of careless driving which caused the death of a 'nearest and dearest' where there is evidence to suggest that the accused is a continuing danger to other road users, the proper course is to prosecute for careless driving (section 3).

13.8 However, in cases of careless driving which caused the death of a 'nearest and dearest' where there is **no** evidence that the accused is a continuing danger to other road users, the proper course is not to prosecute.

13.9 Evidence that an accused presents a continuing danger to other road users may be found in his/her previous convictions or medical condition. In such cases, the court may wish to make an order under section 36 of the Road Traffic Offenders Act 1988, disqualifying the driver until he passes a driving test; or when it appears that the court ought to notify the Secretary of State that the driver may be suffering from any relevant disability within the meaning of section 22 Road Traffic Offenders Act 1988.

13.10 If a person other than a 'nearest and dearest' is killed as a result of the dangerous driving, notwithstanding the fact that a near relative has also been killed. a charge for causing death by dangerous driving should normally follow. In order to present the case fully to the court a separate charge for the death of the close relative cannot, in these circumstances, be avoided.

## 14 Alternative Verdicts

14.1 In certain circumstances, it is possible for a jury to find the accused not guilty of the offence charged but guilty of some other alternative offence. The general provisions are contained in section 6(3) Criminal Law Act 1967 and are supplemented by other provisions which relate to specific offences.

14.2 Section 24 of the Road Traffic Offenders Act allows for the return of alternative verdicts where the allegations in the indictment amount to, or include, an allegation of an offence specified in the table set out in that section. The relevant statutory provisions are:

| Offence charged | Alternative verdicts |
|---|---|
| Section 1: death by dangerous driving | Section 2: dangerous driving<br>Section 3: careless, and inconsiderate, driving |
| Section 2: dangerous driving | Section 3: careless, and inconsiderate, driving |
| Section 3A: causing death by careless driving while under the influence of drink or drugs | Section 3: careless, and inconsiderate, driving and/or the relevant offence from:<br>Section 4(1): driving whilst unfit<br>Section 5(1)(a): driving with excess alcohol<br>Section 7(6): failing to provide a specimen |

14.3 Where the accused is charged with an offence under section 3A RTA 1988 he may not be convicted as an alternative with any offence of attempting to drive: section 24(2) Road Traffic Offenders Act 1988.

14.4 In the very rare cases when manslaughter is charged, it will normally be prudent to prefer an alternative charge for causing death by dangerous driving if the driving took place on a road or other public place. Further, when manslaughter is charged there should be no difficulty in also charging as an alternative a Section 3A offence if it is made out, although such a situation is most unlikely to arise.

14.5 It is essential however, that the charge which most suits the circumstances is always preferred. It will never be appropriate to charge a more serious offence in order to obtain a conviction (whether by plea or verdict) to a lesser offence.

# APPENDIX FIVE

# ROAD VEHICLES LIGHTING REGULATIONS 1989, REGULATION 27

TABLE

| (1)<br>Item No. | (2)<br>Type of lamp, hazard warning signal device or warning beacon | (3)<br>Manner of use prohibited |
|---|---|---|
| 1. | Headlamp | (a) Used so as to cause undue dazzle or discomfort to other persons using the road.<br>(b) Used so as to be lit when a vehicle is parked. |
| 2. | Front fog lamp | (a) Used so as to cause undue dazzle or discomfort to other persons using the road.<br>(b) Used so as to be lit at any time other than in conditions of seriously reduced visibility.<br>(c) Used so as to be lit when a vehicle is parked. |
| 3. | Rear fog lamp | (a) Used so as to cause undue dazzle or discomfort to the driver of a following vehicle.<br>(b) Used so as to be lit at any time other than in conditions of seriously reduced visibility.<br>(c) Save in the case of an emergency vehicle, used so as to be lit when a vehicle is parked. |
| 4. | Reversing lamp | Used so as to be lit except for the purpose of reversing the vehicle. |
| 5. | Hazard warning signal device | Used other than—<br>(i) to warn persons using the road of a temporary obstruction when the vehicle is at rest; or<br>(ii) on a motorway or unrestricted dual-carriageway, to warn following drivers of a need to slow down due to a temporary obstruction ahead; or<br>(iii) in the case of a bus, to summon assistance for the driver or any person acting as a conductor or inspector on the vehicle.<br>or |

TABLE

| (1)<br>Item No. | (2)<br>Type of lamp, hazard warning signal device or warning beacon | (3)<br>Manner of use prohibited |
|---|---|---|
| | | (iv) in the case of a bus to which prescribed signs are fitted as described in sub-paragraphs (a) and (b) of regulation 17A(1), when the vehicle is stationary and children under the age of 16 years are entering or leaving, or are about to enter or leave, or have just left the vehicle. |
| 6. | Warning beacon emitting blue light and special warning lamp | Used so as to be lit except—<br>(i) at the scene of an emergency; or<br>(ii) when it is necessary or desirable either to indicate to persons using the road the urgency of the purpose for which the vehicle is being used, or to warn persons of the presence of the vehicle or a hazard on the road. |
| 7. | Warning beacon emitting amber light | Used so as to be lit except—<br>(i) at the scene of an emergency;<br>(ii) when it is necessary or desirable to warn persons of the presence of the vehicle; and<br>(iii) in the case of a breakdown vehicle, while it is being used in connection with, and in the immediate vicinity of, an accident or breakdown, or while it is being used to draw a broken-down vehicle. |
| 8. | Warning beacon emitting green light | Used so as to be lit except whilst occupied by a medical practitioner registered by the General Medical Council (whether with full, provisional or limited registration) and used for the purposes of an emergency. |
| 9. | Warning beacon emitting yellow light | Used so as to be lit on a road. |
| 10. | Work lamp | (a) Used so as to cause undue dazzle or discomfort to the driver of any vehicle.<br>(b) Used so as to be lit except for the purpose of illuminating a working area, accident, breakdown or works in the vicinity of the vehicle. |
| 11. | Any other lamp | Used so as to cause undue dazzle or discomfort to other persons using the road. |

# APPENDIX SIX

# MOTOR VEHICLES (DRIVING LICENCES) REGULATIONS 1996, SCHEDULE 2 AND REGULATIONS 9 AND 17

## SCHEDULE 2

### CATEGORIES AND SUB-CATEGORIES OF VEHICLES FOR LICENSING PURPOSES

### PART I

| (1) Category or sub-category | (2) Classes of vehicle included | (3) Additional categories and sub-categories |
|---|---|---|
| A | Motor bicycles but excluding any motor vehicle in category K. | B1, K and P. |
| A1 | A sub-category of category A comprising learner motor bicycles. | P. |
| B | Any motor vehicle, other than a vehicle included in category A, F, K or P, having a maximum authorised mass not exceeding 3.5 tonnes and not more than 8 seats in addition to the driver's seat, including—<br>(i) a combination of such a vehicle and a trailer where the trailer has a maximum authorised mass not exceeding 750 kg, and<br>(ii) a combination of such a vehicle and a trailer where the maximum authorised mass of the combination does not exceed 3.5 tonnes and the maximum authorised mass of the trailer does not exceed the unladen weight of the tractor vehicle. | F, K and P. |
| B1 | A sub-category of category B comprising motor vehicles having three or four wheels and an unladen weight not exceeding 550 kilograms | K and P. |
| B1 (invalid carriages) | A sub-category of category B comprising motor vehicles which are invalid carriages. | |
| B + E | Combination of a motor vehicle and trailer where the tractor vehicle is in category B but the combination does not fall within that category. | |

PART I (continued)

| (1) Category or sub-category | (2) Classes of vehicle included | (3) Additional categories and sub-categories |
|---|---|---|
| C | Any motor vehicle having a maximum authorised mass exceeding 3.5 tonnes, other than a vehicle falling within category D, F, G or H, including such a vehicle drawing a trailer having a maximum authorised mass not exceeding 750 kilograms. | |
| C1 | A sub-category of category C comprising motor vehicles having a maximum authorised mass exceeding 3.5 tonnes but not exceeding 7.5 tonnes, including such a vehicle drawing a trailer having a maximum authorised mass not exceeding 750 kilograms. | |
| D | Any motor vehicle constructed or adapted for the carriage of passengers having more than 8 seats in addition to the driver's seat, including such a vehicle drawing a trailer having a maximum authorised mass not exceeding 750 kilograms. | |
| D1 | A sub-category of category D comprising motor vehicles having more than 8 but not more than 16 seats in addition to the driver's seat and including such a vehicle drawing a trailer with a maximum authorised mass not exceeding 750 kilograms. | |
| C + E | Combination of a motor vehicle and trailer where the tractor vehicle is in category C but the combination does not fall within that category. | B + E. |
| C1 + E | A sub-category of category C + E comprising any combination of a motor vehicle and trailer where—<br>(a) the tractor vehicle is in sub-category C1,<br>(b) the maximum authorised mass of the trailer exceeds 750 kilograms but not the unladen weight of the tractor vehicle, and<br>(c) the maximum authorised mass of the combination does not exceed 12 tonnes. | B + E |
| D + E | Combination of a motor vehicle and trailer where the tractor vehicle is in category D but the combination does not fall within that category. | B + E. |
| D1 + E | A sub-category of category D + E comprising any combination of a motor vehicle and trailer where—<br>(a) the tractor vehicle is in sub-category D1,<br>(b) the maximum authorised mass of the trailer exceeds 750 kilograms but not the unladen weight of the tractor vehicle,<br>(c) the maximum authorised mass of the combination does not exceed 12 tonnes, and<br>(d) the trailer is not used for the carriage of passengers. | B + E. |
| F | Agricultural or forestry tractor, but excluding any motor vehicle included in category H. | K. |
| G | Road roller. | |
| H | Track-laying vehicle steered by its tracks. | |
| K | Mowing machine or vehicle controlled by a pedestrian. | |
| P | Moped. | |

PART II

| (1) Category or sub-category | (2) Classes of vehicle included | (3) Additional categories and sub-categories |
|---|---|---|
| C1 + E (8.25 tonnes) | A sub-category of category C + E comprising any combination of a motor vehicle and trailer in sub-category C1 + E the maximum authorised mass of which does not exceed 8.25 tonnes. | |
| D1 (not for hire or reward) | A sub-category of category D comprising motor vehicles in sub-category D1 driven otherwise than for hire or reward. | |
| D1 + E (not for hire or reward) | A sub-category of category D + E comprising motor vehicles in sub-category D1 + E driven otherwise than for hire or reward. | |
| L | Motor vehicle propelled by electrical power. | |

**9. Eligibility to apply for provisional licence**

(1) Subject to the following provisions of this regulation, an applicant for a provisional licence authorising the driving of motor vehicles of a class included in a category or sub-category specified in column (1) of the table at the end of this regulation must hold a relevant full licence authorising the driving of motor vehicles of a class included in the category or sub-category specified in column (2) of the table in relation to the first category.

(2) Paragraph (1) shall not apply in the case of an applicant who is a full-time member of the armed forces of the Crown.

(3) For the purposes of paragraph (1), a licence authorising the driving only of vehicles in sub-categories D1 (not for hire or reward), D1 + E (not for hire or reward) and C1 + E (8.5 tonnes) shall not be treated as a licence authorising the driving of motor vehicles of a class included in sub-categories D1, D1 + E and C1 + E.

(4) In this regulation, 'relevant full licence' means a full licence granted under Part III of the Traffic Act, a full Northern Ireland licence, a full British external licence, a full British Forces licence, an exchangeable licence or a Community licence.

TABLE

| (1) Category or sub-category of licence applied for | (2) Category/sub-category of full licence required |
|---|---|
| B + E | B |
| C | B |
| C1 | B |
| D | B |
| D1 | B |
| C1 + E | C1 |
| C + E | C |
| D1 + E | D1 |
| D + E | D |
| G | B |
| H | B |

**17. Full licence not carrying provisional entitlement**

(1) . . .

(2) Subject to paragraphs (3) and (4), the holder of a full licence authorising the driving of motor vehicles of a class included in category or sub-category specified in column (1) of the table at the end of this regulation may drive motor vehicles of all classes included in a category or sub-category specified, in relation to that category or sub-category, in column (2) of the table as if he were authorised by a provisional licence to do so.

(3) In the case of a licence which authorises the driving only of—

(a) motor bicycles of a class included in sub-category A1, or

(b) standard motor bicycles,

section 98(2) shall not apply so as to authorise the driving of a large motor bicycle by a person under the age of 21.

(4) In the case of a provisional large goods vehicle driver's licence, this regulation shall apply as modified by regulation 51.

(5) . . .

(6) The holder of a Community licence to whom section 99A(5) of the Traffic Act applies and who is authorised to drive in Great Britain motor vehicles of a class included in a category or sub-category specified in column (1) of the Table at the end of this regulation may drive motor vehicles of all classes included in a category or sub-category specified, in relation to that category or sub-category, in column (2) of the Table as if he were authorised by a provisional licence to do so.

TABLE

| Full licence held | Provisional entitlement included |
|---|---|
| A1 | A, B, F and K |
| A | B and F |
| B1 | A, B and F |
| B | A, B + E, G and H |
| C | C1 + E, C + E |
| D1 | D1 + E |
| D | D1 + E, D + E |
| F | B and P |
| G | H |
| H | G |
| P | A, B, F and K |

APPENDIX SEVEN

# MOTOR VEHICLES (DRIVING LICENCES) REGULATIONS 1996, SCHEDULE 4

## SCHEDULE 4

## DISTINGUISHING MARKS TO BE DISPLAYED ON A MOTOR VEHICLE BEING DRIVEN UNDER A PROVISIONAL LICENCE

### PART 1

Diagram of distinguishing mark to be displayed on a motor vehicle in England, Wales or Scotland.

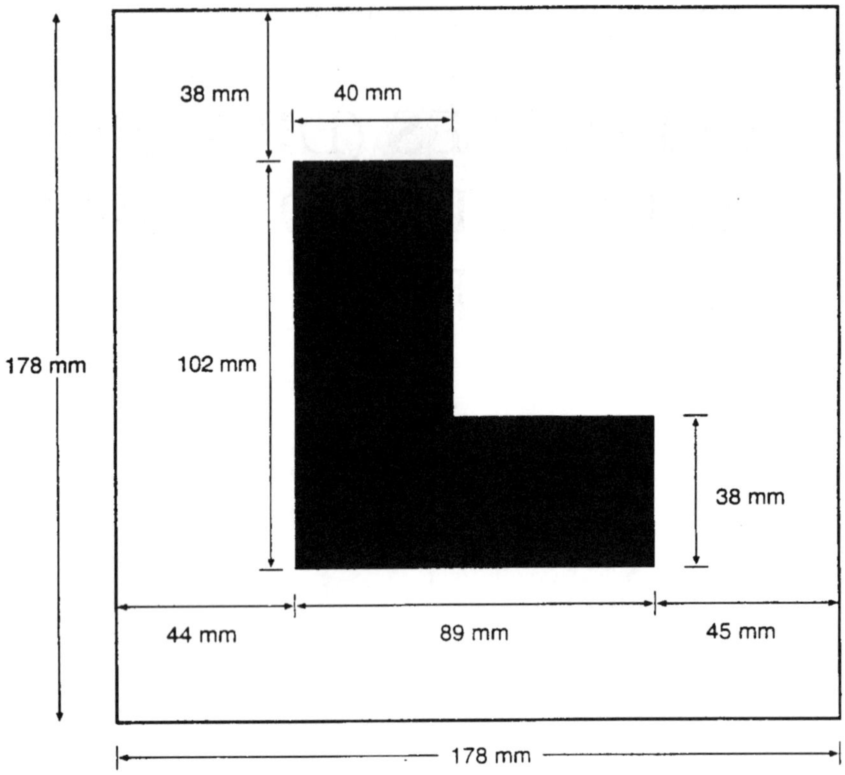


Red letter on white ground.
The corners of the ground can be rounded off.

PART 2

Diagram of optional distinguishing mark to be displayed on a motor vehicle in Wales if a mark in the form set out in Part 1 is not displayed.

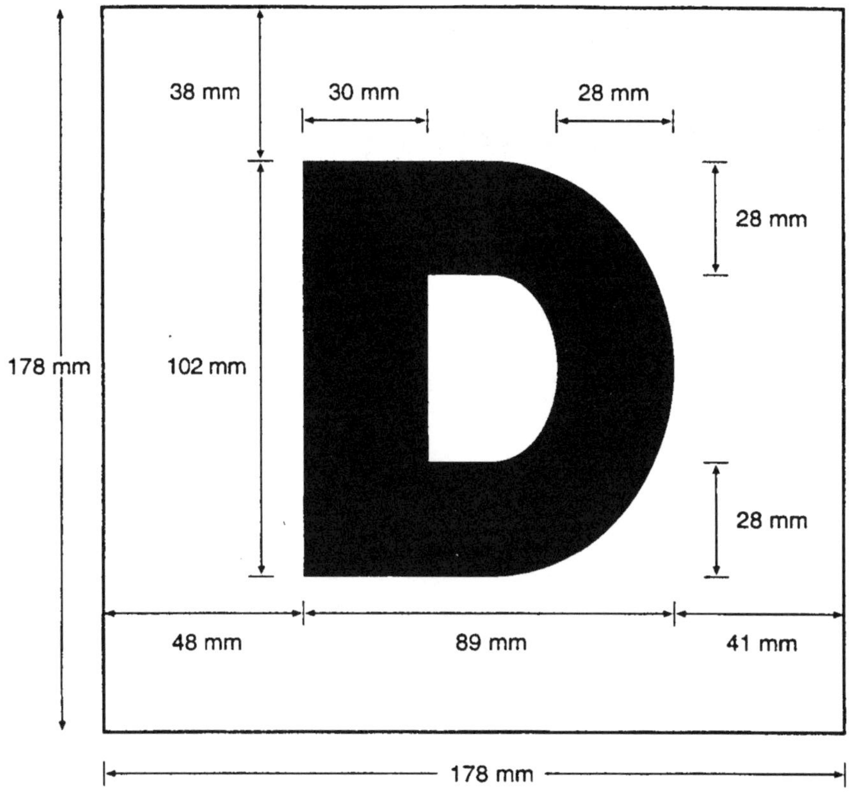


Red letter on white ground.
The corners of the ground can be rounded off.

APPENDIX EIGHT

# SCREENING BREATH TESTS

**Diagram 1 Screening Breath Test Following Accident (Subject to s. 9 Hospital Procedure)**

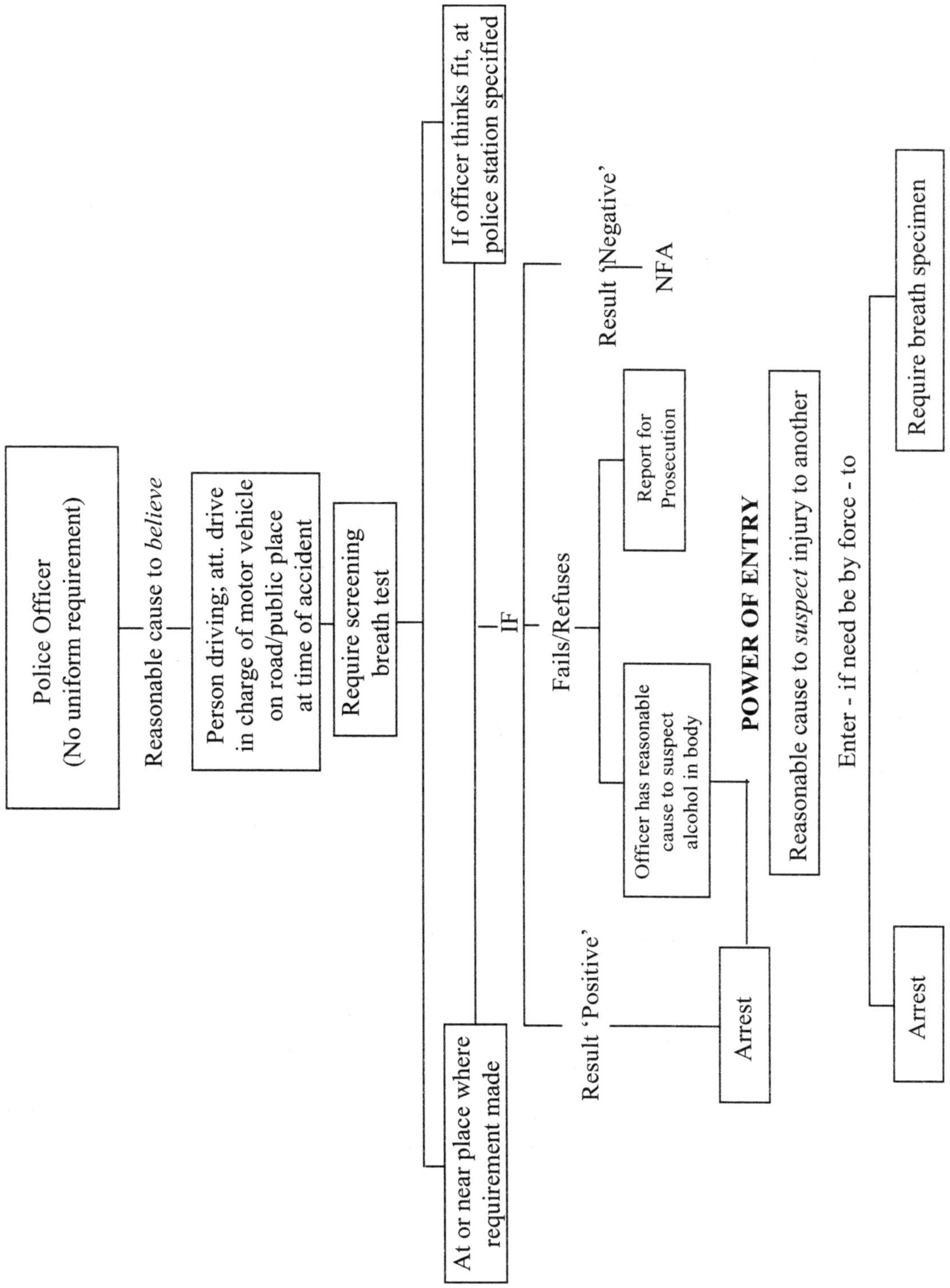

## Diagram 2 Screening Breath Tests1

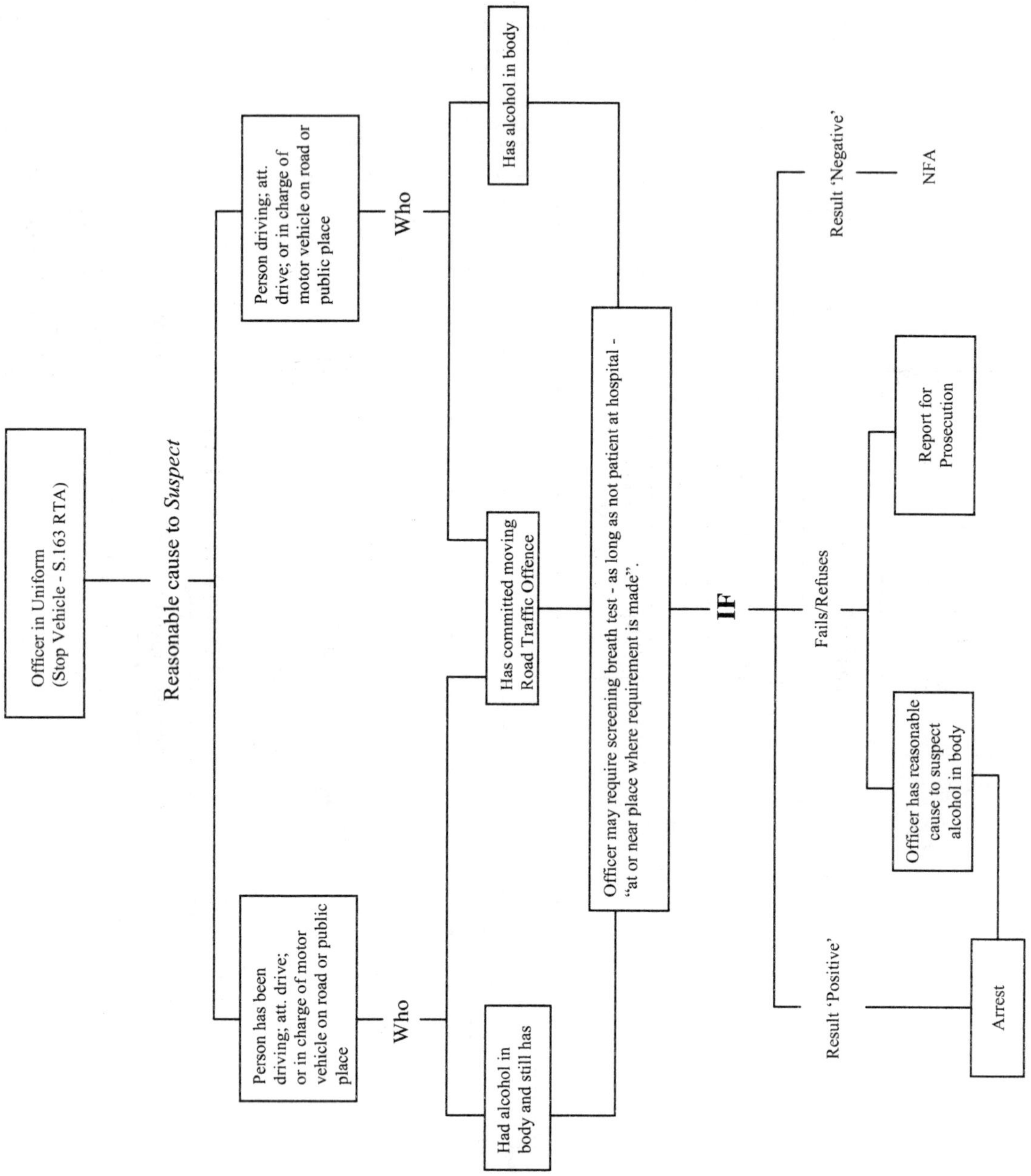
Officer in Uniform
(Stop Vehicle - S.163 RTA)
Reasonable cause to *Suspect*
Person has been driving; att. drive; or in charge of motor vehicle on road or public place
Person driving; att. drive; or in charge of motor vehicle on road or public place
Who
Who
Had alcohol in body and still has
Has committed moving Road Traffic Offence
Has alcohol in body
Officer may require screening breath test - as long as not patient at hospital - "at or near place where requirement is made".
IF
Result 'Positive'
Fails/Refuses
Result 'Negative'
NFA
Officer has reasonable cause to suspect alcohol in body
Report for Prosecution
Arrest

APPENDIX NINE

# FIXED PENALTY PROCEDURE

**Diagram 1 Fixed Penalty Procedure (Driver Not Present)**

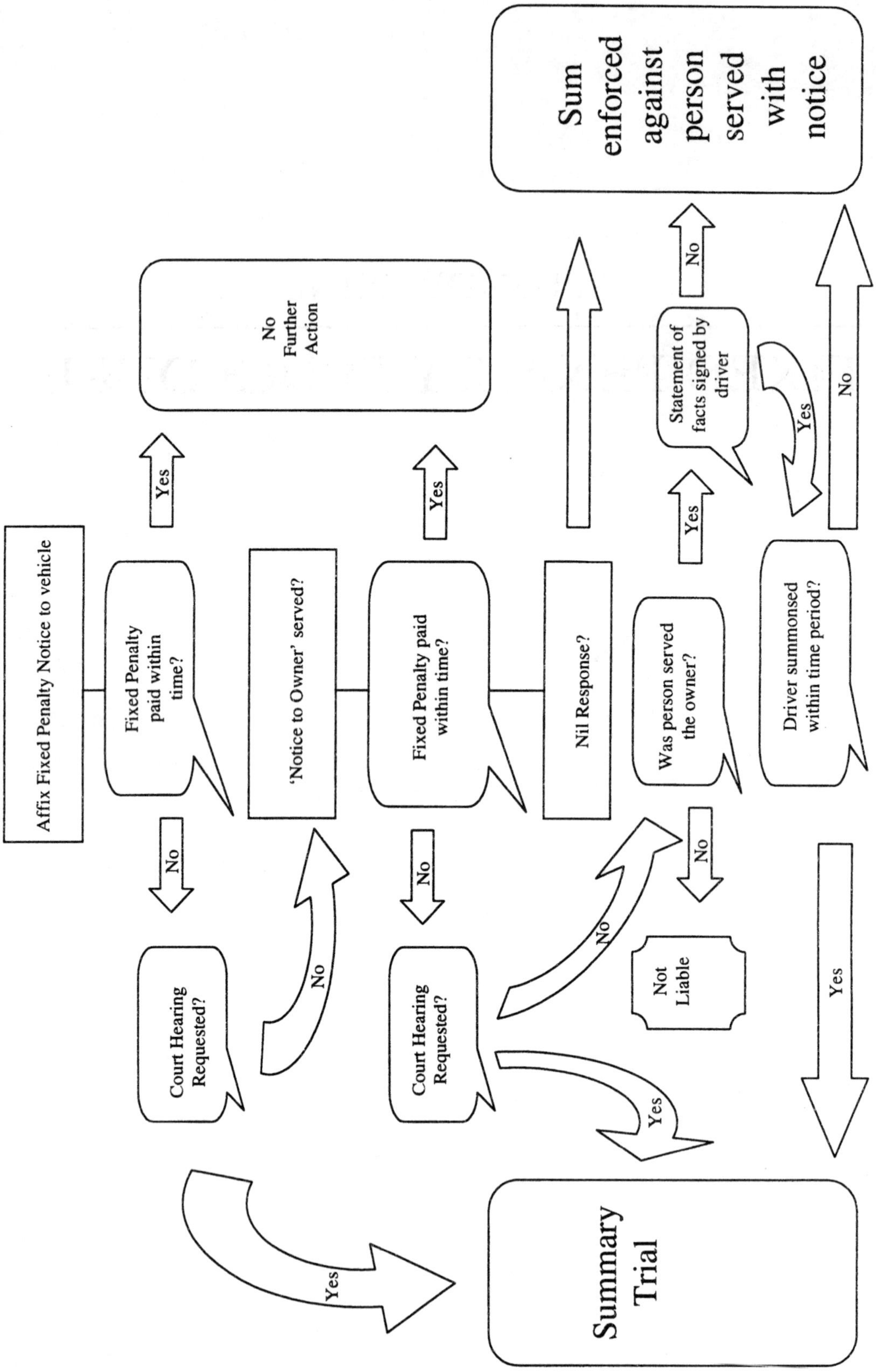

## Diagram 2 Fixed Penalty Procedure – Endorsable (Driver Present)

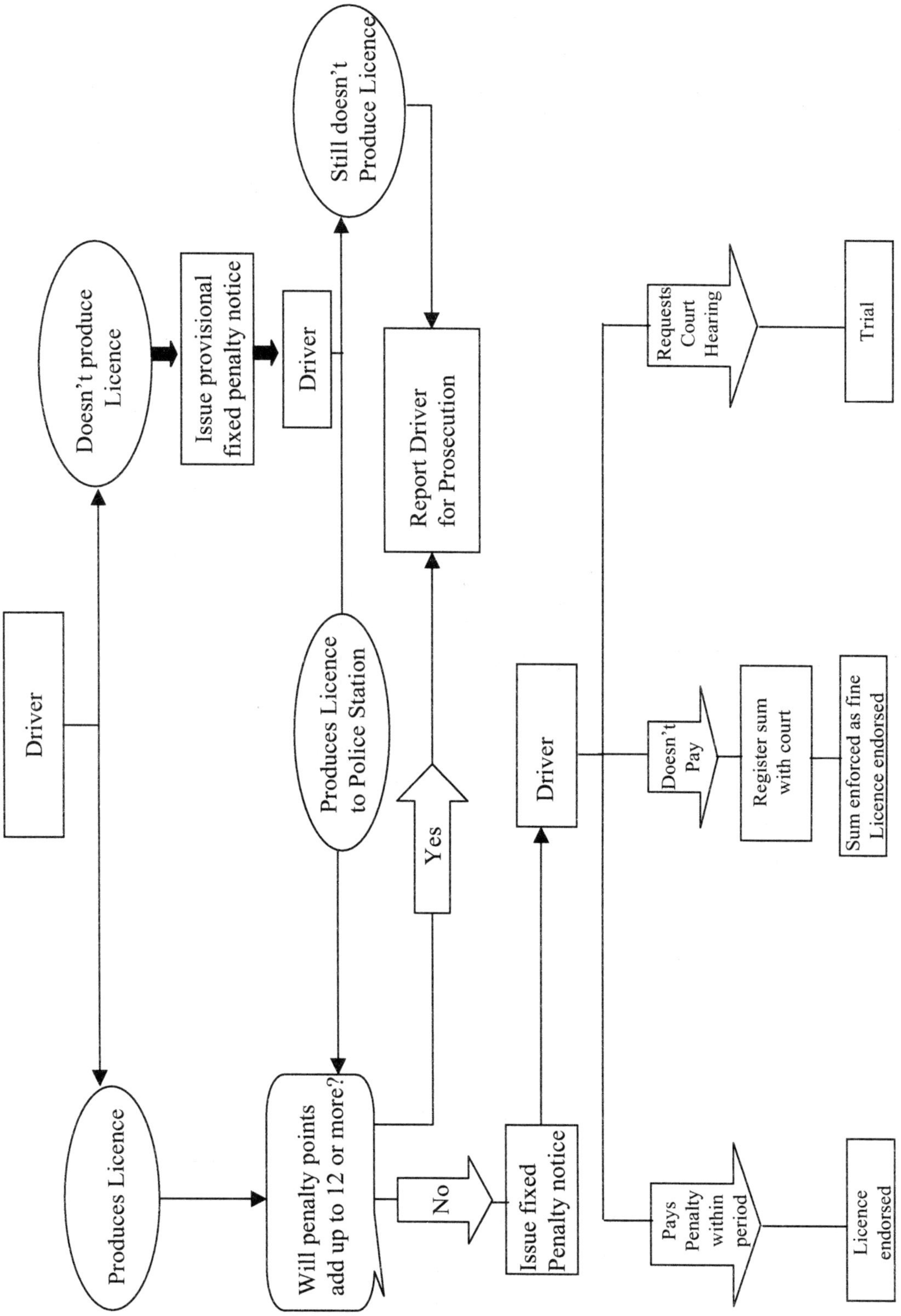

**Diagram 3 Fixed Penalty Procedure: Non-Endorseable (Driver Present)**

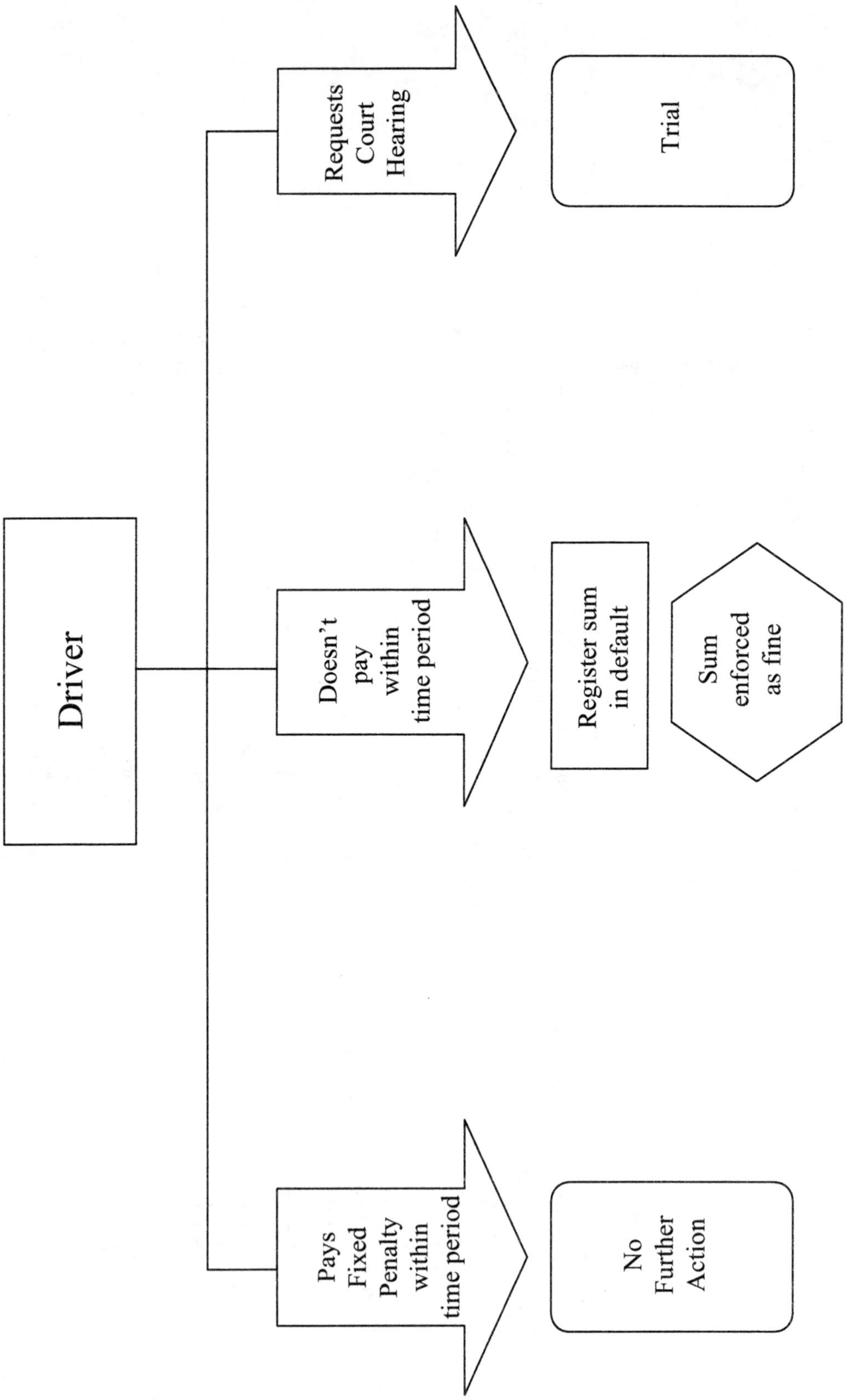

# APPENDIX TEN

# INFORMATION CODES

01 Eyesight correction
02 Hearing/communication aid
10 Modified transmission
15 Modified clutch
20 Modified braking systems
25 Modified accelerator systems
30 Combined braking and accelerator systems
35 Modified control layouts
40 Modified steering
42 Modified rearview mirror(s)
43 Modified driving seats
44 Modifications to motorcycles
45 Motorcycle only with sidecar
70 Exchange of licence
71 Duplicate of licence
78 Restricted to vehicles with automatic transmission
79 Restricted to vehicles in conformity with the specifications stated in brackets
101 Not for hire or reward
102 Drawbar trailers only
103 Subject to certificate of competence
105 Not more than 5.5m long
106 Restricted to vehicles with automatic transmission
107 Not more than 8250kg
108 Subject to minimum age requirements
110 Limited to invalid carriages
111 Limited to 16 passenger seats
113 Limited to 16 passenger seats except for automatics
114 With any special controls required for safe driving
115 Organ donor
118 Start date is for earliest entitlement
119 Weight limit does not apply
120 Complies with health standard for category D1

# APPENDIX ELEVEN

# ENDORSEMENT OFFENCE CODES

| Code | Accident Offences | Penalty Points |
|---|---|---|
| AC10 | Failing to stop after an accident | 5–10 |
| AC20 | Failing to give particulars or to report and accident within 24 hours | 5–10 |
| AC30 | Undefined accident offences | 4–9 |

| Code | Disqualified Driver | Penalty Points |
|---|---|---|
| BA10 | Driving while disqualified by order of court | 6 |
| BA30 | Attempting to drive while disqualified by order of court | 6 |

| Code | Careless Driving | Penalty Points |
|---|---|---|
| CD10 | Driving without due care and attention | 3–9 |
| CD20 | Driving without reasonable consideration for other road users | 3–9 |
| CD30 | Driving without due care and attention or without reasonable consideration for other road users | 3–9 |
| CD40 | Causing death through careless driving when unfit through drink | 3–11 |
| CD50 | Causing death by careless driving when unfit through drugs | 3–11 |
| CD60 | Causing death by careless driving with alcohol level above the limit | 3–11 |
| CD70 | Causing death by careless driving then failing to supply a specimen for analysis | 3–11 |

| Code | Construction and Use Offences | Penalty Points |
|---|---|---|
| CU10 | Using a vehicle with defective brakes | 3 |
| CU20 | Causing or likely to cause danger by reason of use of unsuitable vehicle or using a vehicle with parts or accessories (excluding brakes, steering or tyres) in a dangerous condition | 3 |
| CU30 | Using a vehicle with defective tyre(s) | 3 |
| CU40 | Using a vehicle with defective steering | 3 |
| CU50 | Causing or likely to cause danger by reason of load or passengers | 3 |

## ENDORSEMENT OFFENCE CODES

| Code | Reckless/Dangerous Driving | Penalty Points |
|---|---|---|
| DD40 | Dangerous driving | 3–11 |
| DD60 | Manslaughter or culpable homicide while driving a vehicle | 3–11 |
| DD80 | Causing death by dangerous driving | 3–11 |

| Code | Drink or Drugs | Penalty Points |
|---|---|---|
| DR10 | Driving or attempting to drive with alcohol level above limit | 3–11 |
| DR20 | Driving or attempting to drive while unfit through drink | 3–11 |
| DR30 | Driving or attempting to drive then failing to supply a specimen for analysis | 3–11 |
| DR40 | In charge of a vehicle when alcohol level above limit | 10 |
| DR50 | In charge of a vehicle while unfit through drink | 10 |
| DR60 | Failure to provide a specimen for analysis in circumstances other than driving or attempting to drive | 10 |
| DR70 | Failing to provide specimen for breath test | 4 |
| DR80 | Driving or attempting to drive when unfit through drugs | 3–11 |
| DR90 | In charge of a vehicle when unfit through drugs | 10 |

| Code | Insurance Offences | Penalty Points |
|---|---|---|
| IN10 | Using a vehicle uninsured against third party risks | 6–8 |

| Code | Licence Offences | Penalty Points |
|---|---|---|
| LC20 | Driving otherwise than in accordance with a licence | 3–6 |
| LC30 | Driving after making a false declaration about fitness when applying for a licence | 3–6 |
| LC40 | Driving a vehicle having failed to notify a disability | 3–6 |
| LC50 | Driving after a licence has been revoked or refused on medical grounds | 3–6 |

| Code | Miscellaneous Offences | Penalty Points |
|---|---|---|
| MS10 | Leaving a vehicle in a dangerous position | 3 |
| MS20 | Unlawful pillion riding | 3 |
| MS30 | Play street offences | 2 |
| MS40 | Driving with uncorrected defective eyesight or refusing to submit to a test | 3 |
| MS50 | Motor racing on the highway | 3–11 |
| MS60 | Offences not covered by other codes as appropriate | |
| MS70 | Driving with uncorrected defective eyesight | 3 |
| MS80 | Refusing to submit to an eyesight test | 3 |
| MS90 | Failure to give information as to identity of driver etc. | 3 |

## ENDORSEMENT OFFENCE CODES

| Code | Motorway Offences | Penalty Points |
|---|---|---|
| MW10 | Contravention of special roads Regulations (excluding speed limits) | 3 |

| Code | Pedestrian Crossings | Penalty Points |
|---|---|---|
| PC10 | Undefined contravention of Pedestrian Crossing Regulations | 3 |
| PC20 | Contravention of Pedestrian Crossing Regulations with moving vehicle | 3 |
| PC30 | Contravention of Pedestrian Crossing Regulations with stationary vehicle | 3 |

| Code | Speed Limits | Penalty Points |
|---|---|---|
| SP10 | Exceeding goods vehicle speed limits | 3–6 |
| SP20 | Exceeding speed limit for type of vehicle (excluding goods or passenger vehicles) | 3–6 |
| SP30 | Exceeding statutory speed limit on a public road | 3–6 |
| SP40 | Exceeding passenger vehicle speed limit | 3–6 |
| SP50 | Exceeding speed limit on a motorway | 3–6 |
| SP60 | Undefined speed limit offence | 3–6 |

| Code | Traffic Direction and Signs | Penalty Points |
|---|---|---|
| TS10 | Failing to comply with traffic light signals | 3 |
| TS20 | Failing to comply with double white lines | 3 |
| TS30 | Failing to comply with a 'stop' sign | 3 |
| TS40 | Failing to comply with direction of a constable/warden | 3 |
| TS50 | Failing to comply with a traffic sign (excluding 'stop' signs, traffic lights or double white lines) | 3 |
| TS60 | Failing to comply with a school crossing patrol sign | 3 |
| TS70 | Undefined failure to comply with a traffic direction sign | 3 |

| Code | Special Code | Penalty Points |
|---|---|---|
| TT99 | To signify a disqualification under 'totting up' procedure. If the total of penalty points reaches 12 or more within 3 years, the driver is liable to be disqualified | |

| Code | Theft or Unauthorised Taking | Points |
|---|---|---|
| UT50 | Aggravated taking of a vehicle | 3–11 |

# INDEX

# INDEX

# INDEX